WITH EVERY MISTAKE

GWYNNE DYER

WITH EVERY MISTAKE

 RANDOM HOUSE CANADA

www.randomhouse.ca

LIBRARY AND ARCHIVES CANADA CATALOGUING IN PUBLICATION

Dyer, Gwynne
   With every mistake / Gwynne Dyer.

ISBN 0-679-31402-4

   1. World politics—21st century. 2. Journalistic ethics.
3. Mass media—Influence. 4. Mass media criticism. I. Title.

D860.D94 2005   909.83   C2005-903767-9

Printed and bound in the United States of America

10 9 8 7 6 5 4 3 2 1

CONTENTS

I can remember telephone numbers that I haven't called in years. I can even remember all my children's names. But I generally cannot remember the topic, let alone the title, of the article I wrote twenty-four hours ago.

It's a defensive measure, an anti–brain-clutter device; I write at least a hundred of the things a year, and it has never caused me any anguish. Since I go through a laptop about every eighteen months, the old articles are not easily available for me to peruse even if I did want to revisit the scene of the crime. So it has been a new and rather humbling experience to make a selection of my newspaper pieces from 2001 to 2004—the first time I have done such a thing in thirty-two years of writing the column.

The main reason for doing so now is to try to understand why we all got things so badly wrong in the past few years. Not seeing the terrorist attacks of 9/11 coming was understandable enough because they did come rather out of the blue. But not foreseeing the scale of the American response, and not understanding the thinking that lay behind the neoconservatives' strategy, were major failures for which the Western media—we journalists, really—bear a heavy responsibility. As we watched, the world's greatest power was going rogue and the lies were growing bigger and more brazen than they had been in living memory, but we clung for far too long to the belief—the hope, maybe—that it was all just an aberration driven by the shock of 9/11.

I don't expect journalists to be wiser than other people, but we do have the time to think hard about what is actually going on in the world and the duty to tell the truth as we see it. Most other people don't have the time or the access to do this sort of investigation and interpretation, whereas that is actually our full-time job. The historians will only get at the same events far too late to make any difference, and everybody directly involved in them at the time will be spinning like mad for their particular interest, so who else is going to do the job of making sense of them for the public if journalists don't? We will disagree in our conclusions, of course, but at least we can agree on most of the facts and offer a range of coherent interpretations of those facts for the public to choose from. This privileged role imposes a corresponding obligation on journalists. At the risk of sounding idealistic, I would say that being truthful and, if necessary,

brave, are objective requirements of the journalist's trade—
but there was not nearly enough of those qualities on display
during the period under discussion.

Let's begin with the most shaming moment in the modern history of American journalism: it was at the annual dinner of the Radio and Television Correspondents' Association
in June 2003. The guest of honour was Vice-President Dick
Cheney and his closing remarks were about the journalists'
contribution to the US invasion of Iraq. "You did well," he
said. "You have my thanks." Some of the journalists presumably had the decency to squirm in their seats at that un-
solicited testimonial, but a great many of them weren't even
embarrassed. Which tells you that the American media, at
least, are in serious trouble.

There were some special reasons for that response. The
shock of the 9/11 attacks inevitably unleashed a tremendous
burst of raw nationalism in the United States, and there were
few Americans journalists who were willing to be openly
critical of their government's actions in the period that
followed. The attacks also came at the end of a decade when
there had been huge cutbacks in American coverage of
foreign news, and even 9/11 didn't really change that for
long. There are entire parts of the world that simply don't
exist as far as the American media—especially the broadcast
media—are concerned.

Two factors converged in the 1990s to dumb down and
demobilize the news-gathering operations of the American
electronic media. The end of the Cold War provided an
excuse to scale back sharply on foreign news, and the
takeover of the major networks by large corporations whose
principal interests lay elsewhere—ABC by Disney, NBC by
General Electric and CBS by Viacom—created a strong

incentive to do so. In the old scheme of things, television news had been treated as a loss leader to draw audiences for the network's profitable entertainment programming. Now news was expected to be a profit centre in its own right, and foreign news costs were about twice as much per broadcast minute as domestic news.

Add to all this the domination of American commercial radio by shock-jocks and right-wing ranters and the rise of Fox News, a thinly disguised political propaganda operation, and the utter failure of American broadcast news to challenge the Bush administration's spin on the "war on terror" becomes easier to understand. For more than 80 percent of Americans, radio and television are the principal sources of news, which explains most of what went wrong in the American media's coverage over the past four years. But American newspapers didn't exactly cover themselves with glory either. Several of them, including the *New York Times*, have had the decency to apologize to their readers for their uncritical acceptance of the administration's arguments in favour of invading Iraq and they have conducted internal inquiries into how they betrayed their own values. But there is one aspect of the problem that goes deeper than those inquiries can delve: even at the best of times, the American media are notably more deferential to authority than their counterparts in other English-speaking countries.

This attitude is a question of national culture: can you imagine the British or Australian or even Canadian media letting a national leader get away with a stunt like donning a flight-suit and landing on a carrier to announce the (allegedly) victorious end of a war? The United States is a deeply conservative, militaristic, church-going society, and even the boldest and most cynical of American journalists must work within the bounds of a national culture that views both its elected leaders and its armed forces with something near to reverence. In addition, the chill on critical comment that descended on the US media after 9/11 was still very much in force at the time of the invasion of Iraq in 2003, so maybe the American media's failure to do its job can be seen as a one-time aberration. But the truth is that the rest of us didn't do very well either.

Take, for example, the British press. The foreign-owned newspapers (Conrad "Lord" Black's *Daily Telegraph* and Rupert Murdoch's *Times* and *Sun*) did their duty by their North American–based masters and loyally supported Mr. Bush's war, whereas the British-owned papers mostly opposed the invasion of Iraq (*Daily Mirror*, *Daily Mail*, the *Independent* and the *Guardian*). But even the papers that opposed Britain's participation in the war did an absolutely awful job of analyzing the ludicrous claims about Iraqi "weapons of mass destruction" (WMD), which the Blair government used to sell the war to the British public.

Media Lens, a UK-based left-wing media-watch project, did a postwar survey of how often Scott Ritter, the former chief United Nations weapons inspector in Iraq, was mentioned in the prewar period in the *Independent* and the *Guardian*, the most vociferously antiwar of the British national dailies. Ritter had published a book in 2002 in which he asserted that the Iraqi regime had cooperated with his team in dismantling "90–95 percent" of its WMD by the time his mission was withdrawn in December 1998, leaving the country "fundamentally disarmed." Subsequent rearmament would have been impossible, Ritter said, and any chemical or biological weapons that Iraq still retained would long ago have turned into "harmless sludge." Ritter was almost constantly on the road in the year before the invasion, challenging the official assertions in Washington and London about Iraqi WMD. You would have expected him to be quoted almost daily in those papers' blanket coverage of the relentless march to war. In fact, he was scarcely mentioned at all: only a dozen brief references were made to him in the *Guardian* in 2002 and only eight (out of 5,648 articles on Iraq) in the *Independent* in 2003.

Neither of these papers has to apologize for its general coverage, but how can we account for this startling failure to use the most convincing testimony against the British government's fraudulent case for war? It is fairly easy to guess the answer. The British media may be less reverent of authority than their American counterparts, but for both, the starting point for most news coverage is what governments do and say, including their own. Most of the time official sources set the agenda and define what is legitimate news and the media play catch-up—and it is very hard, even in Britain, for the media to say that the government is simply flat-out lying. There was significantly less support for the war in Britain than in America, but it never seemed likely that Prime Minister Tony Blair, who had secretly promised President Bush to commit British troops to the invasion of Iraq as early as April 2002, would have to renege on his promise.

By contrast, Canada did manage to avoid being drawn into the American adventure in Iraq, but the Canadian media cannot claim much of the credit for that. With the exception of the *Toronto Star* (which does not circulate extensively outside the Toronto area), there was no news source that consistently and coherently criticized the American case for invading Iraq. *The Globe and Mail* and the CBC occasionally raised an eyebrow at some of the more outlandish assertions of US spokespersons, but by and large they treated the US government as a reliable source of information—while both the *National Post* and the CanWest chain, which virtually monopolizes English-language big-city dailies outside Toronto, acted as a full-time cheering section for the Bush administration. The Canadian government's decision to withhold both troops and diplomatic support for the US invasion of Iraq was driven by Ottawa's in-house analysis of American strategy and by an instinctive Liberal Party reluctance to get drawn into American military adventures. That abstentionist position clearly had the support of most Canadians, but they were acting mostly from habit; their own media didn't give them much to work with.

And what about me, a Canadian journalist based in Britain whose articles, due to the CanWest ban, appear in more American papers than Canadian and British ones put together? I am not proud of my own performance in the period 2001 to 2003. It was easy to figure out the terrorists' goals and strategies. They went on *ad nauseam* about their goals—and their strategies, while much less openly discussed, were absolutely standard terrorist fare. Where I did much less well was in understanding what was driving American strategy. In retrospect, what I wrote about the US strategy seems embarrassingly naive, and this has caused me to have some serious second thoughts about the process in which we are engaged as journalists. You will find some of those thoughts expressed in the running commentary that accompanies the articles included in this book, and I will return to this question at the end of the book.

———

I have another reason for publishing a collection of articles now, and that is that my column has been banned in most big-city Canadian papers for the past half-dozen years. The country has survived and so have I—most of what I earn from the column has always come from papers in other countries anyway. But for several decades the articles appeared regularly in most big-city Canadian dailies, and I'd like to think that former readers would be interested in what I have been writing recently. Canada now has the most highly concentrated newspaper ownership of any G8 country, and that seriously constrains the range of opinions and perspectives available to most Canadians.

My first intimation that there might be a problem looming for me personally came in 1997 when I got an e-mail from the *Jerusalem Post* thanking me for my many contributions in the past but explaining that, due to editorial considerations and budget constraints, etc., etc., my services would no longer be required. This was rather surprising, since they had used my stuff for many years and I knew they weren't broke. So I phoned Judy Montagu, who was then in charge of the opinion pages, to ask her what had really happened. "Oh," she said, "somebody called Conrad Black has bought the paper and his wife showed up to have a look. She was turning the pages and your column was in the paper that day, so she just said, 'What the hell is he doing there?' and you were gone. She's called Barbara Amiel. Do you know what she has against you?"

I didn't know then and I don't know for certain even now because I've never met the woman. I don't even know whether it was she or her husband or someone else who felt so strongly that readers must be protected from my views, but I suspect that it had to do mostly with what I write about Israel, a subject on which their views line up with those of the more extreme members of the Likud Party. It made perfectly good sense, therefore, that the first newspaper from which they had me expelled was the *Jerusalem Post*, for the debate about Israel's policies and strategy is far tougher and freer in Israel itself than it is in Canada, and the old *Post* welcomed a variety of opinions about Israel's policies and Middle Eastern events. Indeed, the people who worked on the *Post* at that time believed, probably correctly, that Black bought the paper mainly so that he could change it.

Change it he certainly did. It had previously been one of the liveliest venues for debate in the whole country, but under the Black regime it was turned into a house organ for the Likud Party and its hard-right policies. Indeed, Judy Montagu's post of opinion editor was abolished and the opinion pages were put on autopilot, filled each day with the work of the columnists deemed acceptable.

The phenomenon is not exactly unknown in journalism: rich proprietor buys small newspaper and his or her political prejudices are imposed on it. But although I don't usually pay much attention to these things, I did recall that Conrad Black had recently bought the Southam chain of papers in Canada. That could be a problem.

I was aware of Black as the Canadian proprietor of the *Daily Telegraph* in London, but it had been twenty years since I'd written anything for that paper. The Southam chain, on the other hand, then included all the big-city daily papers in English-speaking Canada outside Toronto and Winnipeg, and almost all of them ran my column. If Southam took the same tack as the *Jerusalem Post* had, then my future in Canadian newspapers was distinctly unpromising. And so it proved.

It didn't happen right away, but in late 1999 my column was dropped by all but one of the Southam papers in Ontario and also by the Montreal *Gazette*. None of them were allowed to contact me officially to explain what they were doing or why, but several editors sent me—from their home e-mail addresses—copies of the order they had received from Southam headquarters. Dated September 29, 1999, the memo had instructed them to stop using articles by "the likes of Gwynnen Dyer [*sic*]." Appended to it was a list of Southam papers, with ticks beside the names of the offending ones that ran my column—most of them.

And here's the striking thing. All the Ontario papers obeyed, except the Niagara Falls *Review* (whose editor later told me he had perfected the art of "flying beneath the radar," helped greatly by the fact that management rarely came that far out from Toronto). But west of Ontario and east of Montreal, almost all of the Southam-owned papers went right on running my columns as usual: the *Edmonton Journal*, the *Vancouver Sun*, the St. John's *Telegram*, the Victoria *Times Colonist*, the *Cape Breton Post*, the Regina *Leader-Post*—the lot. The radar simply didn't reach that far.

Whether it was Black or Amiel who had taken the initiative, or just some zealous underling trying to anticipate the bosses' wishes, there was no follow-through. Black was busy in Britain most of the time, angling for a baronetcy ("Lord Almost" was what they took to calling him in the British press), and the Hollinger management team seemed permanently distracted by the crushing financial burden that Black's launch of the *National Post* had imposed. In late

2000, I was openly having lunch with people from the editorial pages of Western Canadian newspapers that still blithely continued to run my columns.

Then Black sold. He had to sell, because he was so highly geared that the whole inverted pyramid of ownership he had built up might have crashed to the ground right then (rather than five years later) if he had not unloaded the former Southam chain and the *National Post*. Black's Canadian adventure was undertaken primarily for political and egotistical reasons, and when he had to choose between these and staying rich, there was no contest. But he must have taken some solace in the fact that he was selling his Canadian papers to Israel Asper, head of CanWest, who shared his convictions on many key political issues despite being formally a Liberal. Indeed, it's striking that when Black, by then even deeper in financial and legal trouble, sold the *Jerusalem Post* in 2004, he once again tried to ensure that CanWest ended up with a controlling interest in the paper.

In this latter case, Black's strategy may have failed, because the Israeli partner in the deal refused to hand over 51 percent of control to CanWest, as Black and the Asper family insist had been agreed. While that issue makes its way through the Israeli courts, the *Jerusalem Post* is busily reinventing itself as a real newspaper (and my column is starting to reappear in it). But the earlier Canadian sale stuck, and it quickly became clear that Israel Asper and Conrad Black were as one in their view of how Middle Eastern issues should be portrayed to the Canadian public. Moreover, the Asper family put much more effort into ensuring that its orders were obeyed and its views faithfully reproduced in its papers than the arrogant and rather inattentive regime of Conrad Black had done.

On the public front, this policy was most evident in the centrally produced editorials on subjects close to the Asper family's heart, which all CanWest papers were now obliged to run. In the particular case of my column, this strategy was manifested in a new drive to expel it from the papers outside central Canada—the ones that had simply ignored the poorly enforced edicts of Black's crew.

In early 2001 the management at CanWest began to work their way systematically through the recalcitrant papers that were still running my column. It was done almost entirely by phone call—this is not the sort of action that a good management team will put on paper—but they made it clear to their editors that either my column went, or they did. That was when the column disappeared from all the Western Canadian papers owned by CanWest, and from all the papers in the Atlantic Provinces. Even the St. John's *Telegram* was not exempt, although the publisher there, Miller Ayre, fought a particularly long rearguard battle to keep the column in his paper because I was the hometown boy.

In fact, the *Telegram* went on paying me for the column for several months after they had obeyed orders and had stopped running my articles (I didn't know this at the time), while Miller Ayre fought CanWest management on the issue. Gordon Fisher, group editor for CanWest, eventually gave Ayre permission to go above his head, but simultaneously warned him that it wouldn't make a bit of difference—the decision was cast in stone. Ayre wisely decided that there was no point in pushing the issue any further. "How are you going to win what boils down to a religious argument with Izzy Asper?" he said to me in an interview in 2005—and he gave in.

By mid-2001, the pre-Black total of about fifty Canadian papers running my column decreased to only eighteen. But the tide actually began to turn in the following year, 2002, when CanWest's unlimited commitment to the *National Post* as the standard-bearer of neoconservative politics in Canada began to put a serious strain on its finances.

In midsummer 2002 CanWest sold all its papers in the Atlantic Provinces to the newly created Transcontinental chain. In a matter of months my column reappeared in all eight papers that had previously been running it in Nova Scotia, Prince Edward Island and Newfoundland. (The three New Brunswick papers never passed into Black–Asper ownership and had never dropped it.) Then in early 2003 CanWest also sold off its small-city Ontario papers to the Osprey chain and suddenly the column began to appear again in about twenty Ontario cities, from Pembroke to Chatham and from Welland to Timmins. When Israel Asper died in late 2004, there was a flurry of discussions with former Southam papers in big cities in central and western Canada that were interested in running my column if the CanWest son and heir turned out to be less ideological in his interpretation of the publisher's role. But these discussions quickly came to naught.

CanWest has not yet relinquished its hold on the big-city dailies in Canada. Economics may yet triumph over ideology in this area as well, but it could be a long time before it does: these papers are cash cows and would only be put on the block if the entire CanWest empire were in deep trouble. So, for readers in Montreal, Ottawa, Windsor, Edmonton or Victoria, it's this book or nothing, as far as my columns are concerned, for the foreseeable future.

What are we to make of all this? A sufficiently lofty view would see it as a storm in a teacup: a mid-sized country has most of its print media captured by ideologues for a decade. I confess that I take it more personally, but I don't plan to waste any time being a martyr. There's all the rest of the world to play with, and the column already has more readers in the Indian subcontinent than it has in North America. Conrad Black no longer has any significant presence in the Canadian media, and the Aspers will probably have to bail out of the newspaper business eventually because they treat their papers too much as political tools and not enough as businesses. In the meantime they are a nuisance, but they will not change the character of the country, and in due course they'll be gone.

So will we all, of course, and the issues that seem so important to us today will mostly not even feature in the history that our great-grandchildren learn. We should not take ourselves too seriously, but we should at least strive to understand what is going on and get more of our decisions right. With every mistake, we must surely be learning . . .

CHAPTER ONE

A LONG WAY IN A SHORT TIME

The world really has changed since September 11, 2001, though the changes turned out not to have very much to do with a "war on terror." Compare the first article below, written on the day of 9/11 when everybody was still struggling to figure out who had carried out the attacks and why, with the following article, written in 2004. It's not just that more time has passed and more things have happened. There is a huge shift of perspective and a complete redefinition of the nature of the problem — and I keep wondering if I could have arrived there much faster.

The knee-jerk anti-Americans suspected the worst from the beginning, of course, but even stopped clocks are right twice a day. The neoconservative project was little known before 9/11, and even those who did read their stuff didn't take it very seriously. (Without 9/11, we might never have had to take it seriously.) Besides, we were all busy at first trying to figure out what the terrorists were up to.

WHAT NEXT?
September 11, 2001

The initial response of the US government to the immensely destructive terrorist attacks in New York and Washington has been remarkably responsible. No rush to judgment, as in the hasty and mistaken attribution of the Oklahoma City bomb to "Middle Eastern" terrorists; just an assurance that when they identify who committed these crimes, they and those who harbour them will be punished severely. But what if a week passes and they still haven't identified them?

It's not likely that the perpetrators left no clues: the sheer scale of the operation must have left some evidence of who they were. For example, it's clear that no commercial airline pilot would fly his aircraft, laden with passengers, into a building full of people: even the threat of death has no effect when the consequence of obeying the person who threatens you is also your death, plus the deaths of those whose lives you are responsible for.

So the terrorists had their own pilots at the control of those aircraft when they struck the Pentagon and the twin towers of the World Trade Center—and to train four people willing to commit suicide up to the point where they could fly commercial airliners cannot have occurred in some isolated terrorist camp. Granted, they may not have been able to take off and land, but they could at least keep them in the air and steer them into the buildings, which means they must have had access at least to simulators, if not actual aircraft.

In the long run, therefore, there will almost certainly be clues pointing in the direction of those who planned the attacks. But there is absolutely no guarantee that this evidence will come to light in a week, and that is a big problem for the US government. What happens if a week passes, and they still don't have enough evidence to carry out retaliation on a scale that satisfies the understandable anger of the American public?

You can win a couple of days while the media crucify those responsible for airport security, and they will richly deserve their fate. One successful hijacking you might forgive — even the best system breaks down occasionally if human beings are running it — but four within the same hour, in three different airports? There is going to be a lynching in the media, and for once the media will be right.

The government can probably win another couple of days while the media go after the "failures" in the intelligence services that gave Washington no advance warning of these attacks. That will be less justifiable, for the intelligence game almost never deals in certainties. It deals with hints that may be true, buried amidst a deluge of other bits of information that look equally plausible but are actually false or irrelevant. Once you know what has happened, you can go back into the data and see the bits that pointed in the right direction, but hindsight is always 20–20. Foresight is a lot harder.

Nevertheless, there will be another media lynching for the intelligence services, and that will also win the Bush administration a couple of days. But no more. If it hasn't got hard evidence of who planned and carried out the attacks by next weekend, say, the pressure to act on whatever indications it does have, however soft, will become well nigh irresistible. Bush practically has to bomb somebody by next Monday.

And the harshest truth is this: that's probably what the terrorists want.

One of the stock phrases in situations like this is "mindless terrorism," but of course it's not mindless at all. The people who showed such determination and organizational skill in planning these attacks clearly had some specific goal in mind, and that was almost certainly the goal of goading the US government into some ill-considered response that would hurt its own interests.

Nobody yet knows who the terrorists are, but if the Bush administration does have to act on inadequate information, the odds are very high that its chosen target will be some group in the Arab, or at least the Muslim, world. That is where most of its leading suspects live. And whether the terrorists are themselves Muslim or not, that is where a massive US attack will do the most harm to American's own long-term interests.

You don't think the people who planned this extremely complex operation could have such subtle motives? Of course they can. They aren't lunatics. They are chess players, long-range planners, people whose strategies need to be taken as seriously as their tactics.

Not too bad for a first response, perhaps, except that the Bush administration didn't actually bomb anybody for almost three weeks. But how innocent it all seems now.

SAUCE FOR THE GANDER

September 8, 2004

It didn't get much media play, but did you notice what the Russian chief of staff, General Yuri Baluyevsky, said after the horrors at Middle School Number One in Beslan? He said that in future Russia will be prepared to carry out preemptive strikes against terrorist bases anywhere in the world. One man who would not have been surprised to hear it is Kofi Annan.

Kofi Annan is only the secretary-general of the United Nations, so the big powers don't have to listen to him, but he is a clever man, and his job is to watch over the peace of the world. National leaders may care about that too, but they also have a hundred other priorities; world peace is his primary and almost his sole responsibility. And this is what the Ghanaian-born diplomat said at the UN's General Assembly meeting last September, just six months after the United States, Britain and Australia invaded Iraq:

"Until now it has been understood that when states decide to use force to deal with broader threats to international peace and security, they need the unique legitimacy provided by the United Nations. Now, some say this understanding is no longer tenable, since an armed attack with weapons of mass destruction could be launched at any time, without warning, or by a clandestine group. Rather than wait for this to happen, they argue, states have the obligation to use force preemptively, even on the territory of other states.

"This logic represents a fundamental challenge to the principles on which world peace and stability have rested for the last fifty-eight years."

Many people saw Kofi Annan as an American pawn when he was elected secretary-general, and he certainly was the US choice for the job, but what he was actually saying in that speech, in thinly disguised diplomatic code, was that the new US doctrine of preemptive war against potentially threatening groups and countries is illegal and a danger to world peace. He hasn't been a very popular man in official Washington since then, but he is absolutely right, and General Yuri Baluyevsky is all the evidence he needs.

Most Americans were not alarmed when President George W. Bush wrote in the introduction to the National Security Strategy statement of 2002, "America will act against emerging threats before they are fully formed. We will not hesitate to act alone, if necessary . . ." After all, Americans are good people, and surely others would understand that America's intentions were good even if it occasionally acted outside the law.

That confidence may be slightly dented in the United States after the Bush administration did act on that doctrine in invading Iraq, only to find that there was no "emerging threat" there to American security: no weapons of mass destruction, and no evidence of any links between Saddam Hussein's regime and the Islamist terrorists who staged 9/11 and other atrocities. But it is only slightly dented.

Vice-President Dick Cheney still gets cheers when he trots out the line about the United States not needing a "permission slip" from the UN to attack countries it suspects of evil intentions towards America. The problem that is practically invisible from inside the United States is that other countries then don't need "permission slips" to invade their neighbours, either. They can just announce that they have uncovered a grave threat to their security in some other country—they don't actually have to prove it, any more than the United States did—and then they are free to invade it. What's sauce for the goose is sauce for the gander.

Russia was the natural next candidate to break out of the constraints of international law and embrace unilateralism. It had already been sneaking up on it, with highly illegal operations like the car-bomb assassination of former Chechen leader Zelimkhan Yanderbiyev in Qatar earlier this year by Russian intelligence agents (two of whom were caught and have been sentenced to life in prison). But that was just the learner slopes. Now General Baluyevsky has proclaimed a doctrine that claims the same right to use force on other people's territory as part of the "war on terror" that the Bush administration claimed two years ago.

This is the doctrine under which Mr. Bush invaded Iraq, although there were no terrorists there at the time; which country will the Russians invade on the same pretext? They probably haven't even chosen one yet: part of the reason Baluyevsky announced this doctrine now was simply to look tough and distract attention from Moscow's failure to prevent the terrorist attacks. But the doctrine will still be there when the current outrage has subsided, to be used as and when Moscow wants.

Russia, unlike the United States, is not strong enough militarily to invade countries halfway around the world from it, but all the countries of Central Asia and the Caucasus that used to be ruled by Moscow will certainly see themselves as potential targets. Eastern European countries won't be feeling too happy about it either. And of course, other big countries like China and India are quite likely to follow where the US and Russia have blazed the trail.

Which is why Kofi Annan is looking so worn and worried these days. He has every right to be.

CHAPTER TWO

JUST WALKING DOWN THE ROAD, MINDING MY OWN BUSINESS . . . 2001, PRE-9/11

Column writing is ideal for intellectual butterflies because you only need enough of an idea to keep going for about 875 words. The year 2001 was productive for these sorts of ideas, and there were also enough long-running problems to revisit and update that finding a topic was never a problem. We did not need the obsessions of post-9/11 to keep our minds occupied.

In fact, the picture that emerges of the world that we have lost is a rather attractive one. Several parts of the world were in trouble, of course—there always are a few—but what you see here is a nascent global civilization that is getting most things right most of the time and learning a lot with every year that passes. I'd really like to have that world again, and I deeply resent the manipulative cynics and brutal fools who are trying to drag us back to a perpetual 1957 instead.

Almost all of these 2001 columns were written before 9/11. The last, about Harrison, was written afterwards, but before I realized how stupid things were going to get.

AFGHANISTAN AND THE GOD OF THE LITTLE THINGS
February 3, 2001

God's preferences on dietary matters are well known: no pork for Jews or Muslims, no beef for Hindus and no saturated fats or refined sugar for the Western upper-middle class. But this is the first time he has taken such a strong line on haircuts.

True, it is the sort of haircut that would offend any deity of taste: a Leonardo DiCaprio–style haircut, with the gorgeous locks flopping boyishly over the forehead. It's called a "Titanic" in Kabul, and over the past week the Taliban government of Afghanistan has arrested twenty-two barbers for giving it to their clients.

It's hard enough to earn a crust of bread in Kabul nowadays anyway, what with twenty years of war and no modern economy apart from the drug trade. The barbers were already being tempted into crime by customers sneaking in asking to have their beards trimmed, even though the trimming of beards is also banned by the Taliban. And now comes the Leonardo DiCaprio haircut.

This really annoys the Taliban because it means the proud owners of the haircuts must have seen a video of *Titanic* to get the idea. (The Taliban regime has banned all films, television and even music as contrary to their particularly rigorous interpretation of religion, and it has even hanged a couple of TVs in symbolic public executions.) So the guilty barbers are in deep trouble, and so are their clients.

The Taliban government (the name means "students" and especially students of religion) truly does believe that God dislikes the DiCaprio haircut. He must be pretty busy looking after 100 billion galaxies with an average of 100 billion stars each and only He knows how many intelligent species with immortal souls of one sort or another—but He still has time to worry about men's hairstyles in Kabul.

No need to flog it to death: there are some very petty-minded people in charge of Afghanistan at the moment. The indignities that they inflict on barbers and their customers are nothing compared to what they have done to their female fellow-citizens, who have been driven from almost all employment outside the home, denied any chance of a higher education and subjected to even more minute regulation of every aspect of their dress and behaviour. But why is the Taliban so concerned about petty things?

It's not because they are Afghans, or because they are Muslims either. Every country and every religion has some people who get permanently lost in their obsession with rituals and minor details of dress, appearance and etiquette. It's just that in Afghanistan, they happen to be running the place.

In every major religion, there is a kind of schizophrenia between the Big Ideas and the Little Things. The big philosophical ideas like reverence for life are not identical from one religion to another, but they do bear a strong family resemblance. Whereas the Little Things are very specific and local, and they almost always came first.

11

Depending on your own religious beliefs or lack of them, you may see the similarities among the philosophies as evidence of the divine will at work in the world, or as evidence for the similarity of all human beings. But there is almost always a revelation involved, a moment in history when these universal ideas and values were communicated to the believers. Whereas the Little Things hail back to the long tribal past. Christmas is not a Christian feast—it is the old pagan midwinter festival redefined. The veiling of women, now seen by many Muslims as an Islamic tradition, was commonplace among the upper classes of ancient Greece, Rome and Byzantium, though rare among the Arabs until they conquered the Byzantines. Circumcision and other forms of ritual physical mutilation are even older.

Fasting, offering up sacrifices, saying special formulas, making special gestures and scarring yourself in special ways—all these Little Things come from the time before the revelations. From a time, in fact, when religion was humanity's only plausible means of influencing how the world worked. If we get all the rituals just right, then the gods will make the sun come back, or make it rain or whatever it is we need right now.

The Little Things are tolerated even after the big revelations because ordinary people get comfort from them. In general, the less educated the person, the bigger the part that the Little Things play in his practice of religion. Being desperate can push you in that direction too. And there are few places more ignorant or more desperate than rural Afghanistan.

This is a country where millions have died in twenty years of war, where two-thirds of Kabul has been destroyed and famine stalks the countryside, where nothing makes sense any more. In the face of such a senseless disaster, the Taliban is a village-based phenomenon whose militants are trying to win back God's favour by imposing a mixture of conservative Islamic values and Pathan tribal customs on the country.

One of the slogans written up outside the Ministry for the Prevention of Vice and the Promotion of Virtue in Kabul reads: "Throw reason to the dogs. It stinks of corruption." The Taliban is trying to rescue the country by magic, and there's no point in arguing with them about haircuts or women's rights or anything else. Everyone will just have to wait until things calm down.

A RUSSIAN RENAISSANCE?

April 9, 2001

Forty years ago today (April 12), Yuri Gagarin became the first human being to go into space. Last month, the decrepit space station Mir plunged back into the atmosphere, incinerating among other things the photograph of a youthful, happy Gagarin (he died in a plane crash in 1968) that hung on its wall for the past fifteen years.

The symbolism was obvious—but is it Russia that has fallen, never to rise again, or only the old Soviet Union?

Many older Russians are nostalgic for the lost Soviet past, when their country was feared around the planet and there was always another sausage. For the pensioners who populate the regular pro-Communist demonstrations, Gagarin has become a symbol for all that used to be right in the country, and is now wrong.

But security is not the only value any Russian aspires to. There have been huge protests in the past week in both

Moscow and St. Petersburg in which many thousands of people, most of them young, came to the defence of the four hundred journalists of the NTV television network. NTV, which broadcasts all over Russia, is as truthful, brave and independent as the best media anywhere in the world, and the journalists believe it is under attack by the government.

They are probably right. NTV's major shareholder, the giant natural gas company Gazprom, carried out a board-room coup last week and then fired the network's top managers. Gazprom insists that it only wants to sort out the network's finances, but there are suspicions that it really wants to stop the network's annoying habit of criticizing the government.

"We are witnessing the final stage of the state monopolization of the media in Russia," said Pavel Gutionov, head of the Union of Russian Journalists that organized the Moscow demonstration. That, too, may be true: President Vladimir Putin's shameful route to power (he was essentially given the job by ex-president Boris Yeltsin, in return for a Nixon-style amnesty for past wrongdoings) makes him ultra-sensitive to criticism.

Gazprom is a state-owned company, and most people assume that its goal is to make NTV subservient to Putin. This suspicion is strengthened by the relentless harassment of NTV founder Vladimir Gusinsky (now under arrest in Spain awaiting extradition on fraud charges), and the twenty-seven police raids over the past two years on the headquarters of Media-Most, NTV's holding company.

So there you are: Russians cannot change their spots. Soviet tyranny is only being replaced by a different type of dictatorship. Well, no, actually.

The capitalist Russia of today is a brutal society, akin to

the United States of the 1880s, where money gives the orders, the police and the courts do what they are told, and the weakest go to the wall. But this is not 1880, and today's Russia is full of brave, well-educated people who know that they deserve better.

That golden-haloed Soviet Union of the 1960s, when Gagarin soared into space and everybody respected the Russians, was a better place than thirty years before. The prison-camp population had fallen from 20 million in the late '40s to only a few million by the '60s, and the state had stopped the mass murder of politically suspect "elements." There was even economic security for those who kept their heads down and their mouths shut.

But it was still a terrible place. Even when I first visited it in the early '80s, it remained a society of petty bullies and brazen liars flaunting their little bits of power — easy enough to bear if you were visiting for a month, but perpetual misery and insult if you had to live there. The Soviet Union, down to the day it died, treated its citizens like backward children.

The new Russia ain't great. The transition to a market economy was run by cynical apparatchiks who privatized the old state industries into their own pockets, and cost the country at least a decade of economic growth. The government is still in the hands of people who grew up under the old system. It is ugly, it is poor, and it is about as democratic as Chicago in the '30s.

I'll settle for that. This country was the model for George Orwell's 1984 only half a century ago. Now the big controversy is about whether NTV, a better television network than any of the Big Three in the United States, can retain its editorial freedom. I hope it does, but I still won't despair if it doesn't.

Russia is a democracy. It is a shoddy democracy, where the last presidential election was even more questionable than that in the United States. Money doesn't just talk there — it yells. But that is already so much better than what went before that even Yuri Gagarin might like it. And it probably will get better, simply because most of its citizens want it to.

You begin to pick up the tone of the time, at least as I interpreted it: not a golden age, but a time when political change had slowed down and people seemed to be behaving more or less sensibly in most places. There were still problems out there on the horizon, as there always are, but nothing, apart from environmental issues, that threatened to do major long-term damage to our increasingly secure and comfortable lives. We even had time to start unravelling some of the old issues that had dogged us for generations.

OF GENOCIDES, MASSACRES AND TRAGEDIES
May 6, 2001

Eighty-six years late, the Armenian massacres of 1915 are at last forcing themselves onto the international agenda. For a long time it was a private quarrel, with most Turks in deep denial about it while Armenians passionately claimed that they were the victims of the twentieth-century's first genocide. But now the whole world is getting drawn in.

By last year, the European Commission, France, Belgium, Sweden and Italy had all formally acknowledged that there had been an Armenian genocide. The US House of Representatives was about to vote on a similar resolution until the Clinton administration persuaded the bill's sponsor to withdraw it because it would severely damage US interests in Turkey. Meanwhile, a $50 million "Armenian Holocaust" museum is under construction in Washington.

The Turkish government fights back hard: when the French parliament unanimously adopted a declaration last January "recognizing the Armenian genocide of 1915," Ankara promptly cancelled defence production deals with France worth $349 million. By now, however, the momentum of the Armenian campaign for recognition is unstoppable: France did not even blink.

Yet what actually happened eighty-six years ago is still open to dispute. There was certainly a great massacre of Armenians in the eastern part of what is now Turkey in 1915, early in the First World War. Even the most conservative estimates put the Armenian death toll of that year at six hundred thousand, though most Armenians prefer the figure of 1.5 million.

The Turkish authorities don't deny that many Armenians living in the Ottoman (Turkish) Empire were killed in 1915, but they claim that the deaths were triggered by an Armenian uprising in which there were massacres of both Turks and Armenians in the then-intermingled communities of eastern Anatolia. They are being highly economical with the truth here—and yet they do have a point. The killing in 1915 was so great that the word *holocaust* might well apply, but it was not the premeditated, industrialized genocide that befell the European Jews under Hitler.

It is a fact that some Armenians in eastern Anatolia conspired with the Russians to launch an uprising behind the Turkish lines in 1915 to coincide with a Russian offensive into the area. The Russian archives document it fully. Other Armenians, farther south, were plotting with the British in Egypt to start a rebellion to coincide with a planned British landing on Turkey's south coast. The British archives document it fully. But then the British switched the landing far to the west, to the Dardanelles, for a direct attack on Istanbul—and it would appear that they failed to get news of the change of plan through to their Armenian allies in southern Anatolia in time.

So there were scattered, ineffective Armenian uprisings, and then the "Young Turk" army officers who ran the Turkish Empire (many of them barely out of their twenties) panicked. The Russians were flooding into eastern Anatolia, the British were about to break through to Istanbul, and they had stupidly led their country into a war that would destroy it—quite literally, for their enemies had already agreed to carve it up into colonies after victory.

So they ordered all Armenians to be "deported" from the threatened regions of eastern Anatolia all the way south to Syria (knowing full well that many would be killed or die of hunger and exposure). As the Armenian death toll soared, they did nothing to rescind their orders. Many probably welcomed it, for by now they were in an apocalyptic frame of mind. But they hadn't planned it, and they did pay for it: most of the surviving Young Turk leaders were killed by Armenian assassins in the years just after the war.

There are only seventy thousand Armenians living in Turkey today, and the country has much to be ashamed of. But Israeli Foreign Minister Shimon Peres was not just toadying to his Turkish allies when he said in an interview in April, "Nothing similar to the Holocaust occurred. It is a tragedy what the Armenians went through, but not a genocide."

The problem is the word. Nowadays the survivors of any mass killing see *genocide* as the only word adequate to describe their ordeal, but every use of the word evokes the premeditated extermination program of the Nazis' "Final Solution." Common sense says that while all mass murder is terrible, there was a real distinction between the Nazis and the Young Turks, but the descendants of the Armenian victims won't settle for less.

And though the Turkish government still tries to keep the past buried by bluster and threats, there is a new spirit of honesty abroad in the country as a whole. As a Turkish historian, Dr. Taner Akçam, said during a remarkable debate televised nationwide in Turkey in March, "If you can't bring yourself to describe it as genocide, call it a massacre. But it was a crime against humanity. . . . Ask forgiveness from the Armenian people."

On the same day, in the newspaper *Milliyet*, Yavuz Baydar wrote: "[T]hese men [the Young Turk leaders] are our Pol Pots, Berias and Stalins, and the sooner we call these crimes to account, the better our chances of redeeming ourselves from this scourge of being accused of genocide." Much too late, and with great reluctance, the Turks are starting to come to terms with their past.

LABOUR'S LONG GAME: BEATING THE THATCHERITE STRATEGY
May 31, 2001

The Labour campaign poster for the final week of the British general election shows Opposition Leader William Hague (who is bald) wearing Margaret Thatcher's inimitable hair-do, with the caption "Be Afraid. Be Very Afraid." But who could be afraid of Little Willy?

Margaret Thatcher devised the electoral strategy that showed conservative leaders all over the West how to win and keep power, but on her own home turf it's not working anymore. Or at least her successor as leader of the Conservative Party, William Hague, is not making it work.

He follows the script faithfully. He purveys the same anti-European Union rhetoric, warning that the next Labour government will abandon the pound and join the common European currency (though Labour has actually promised a separate referendum on that).

Knowing that almost no nonwhite Britons back the Conservatives anyway, he begs in code for the anti-immigrant vote by accusing Labour of being too soft on asylum-seekers. Above all, he pursues the core Thatcher electoral strategy of trying to build an alliance of the rich and the middle class against the poor. But somehow, the magic is gone.

Only one opinion poll was published in Britain last week, because Prime Minister Tony Blair's re-election is such a foregone conclusion that most media organizations don't want to waste their money on further polling. That poll showed that Labour's lead has widened to a stunning 19 points (47 percent for Labour and only 28 percent for the Conservatives).

If nothing changes before the vote on June 7, Blair will have a majority of 267 seats in the new parliament—nearly one hundred more than in Labour's 1997 victory that ended almost two decades of Conservative rule. Something has gone wrong with the old Thatcher strategy.

This is of interest not only to the British, for the same strategy was adopted by other right-wing parties throughout the English-speaking world in the '80s and early '90s. It's how Brian Mulroney's Conservatives ended sixteen years of Liberal government in Canada, and how the Republicans under Reagan and Bush the Elder held power for twelve years in the United States. It depended on one key insight: that the poor no longer count politically.

They used to matter a lot. When 30, 40 or 50 percent of the citizens of the industrial democracies lived in poverty, they could not be ignored. The liberal democracies would not have survived if their major political parties, both left and right, had not shaped their policies to lift this huge mass of citizens out of misery.

Conservative governments under Churchill, Macmillan and Heath in Britain in the '50s, '60s and '70s did little to cut back the welfare state. The contemporary Republican administrations under Eisenhower, Nixon and Ford in the US were equally careful not to attack the poor directly.

But as time passed and economies grew, the poor dwindled to as little as 20 percent of the population. That laid the groundwork for the Thatcher revolution. Margaret Thatcher's brilliance lay in realizing that when only a fifth of the voters are poor, you can stop worrying about them (especially since relatively few of them vote).

Instead, you can win an election simply by getting the votes of a majority of the better-off. And you win their votes by promising to cut their taxes—which you do mainly by cutting government services to the poor. "There is no such thing as 'society,'" as Thatcher once said.

However, the strategy means you have to go on cutting taxes to continue to win elections, no matter what the budget numbers are. "Read my lips. No new taxes," as George Bush the First once said. Since a lot of government spending can't be cut quickly or easily, however, the only solution is to let the deficits grow—until eventually they sabotage growth in the real economy, and the prosperous start to hurt too.

At this point a new coalition of voters emerges: disillusioned fiscal conservatives who once believed in the magic, that significant part of the middle class who never felt comfortable about screwing the poor, and of course the poor themselves. These voters turn out to be a majority—and so in the '90s George Bush lost to Bill Clinton, and the Conservatives in Canada were routed by Jean Chrétien's Liberals, and Tony Blair won by a landslide in Britain.

All these governments, though left of their predecessors politically, turned out to be more responsible fiscally. They had to be, because their political support base demanded it. They all spent their first years in office rebuilding the national finances and getting the debt under control. Only then (and only very cautiously) could they start to repair the damage done to the social safety net and reward the poorer part of their electorate.

But it is a patient and a durable coalition. In the US, Bill Clinton never really got much past dealing with the deficit in eight years of office, and yet a narrow majority of American voters still voted for the Democrats in 2000 (though Al Gore lost the presidency through the vagaries of the Electoral College).

In Canada, Jean Chrétien strolled back into a third term last year, though he too has hardly begun to repair the services that the poor depended on. And in Britain, Tony Blair will waltz back into office with the promise that this term he'll really start to spend money on mending the fabric of what used to be called the welfare state. Not that he'd ever be caught calling it that.

Then we hit the summer. Politics pretty much packed up for the season, and there was time to consider other things.

THE PRICE OF THE "NEW-WORLD BLITZKRIEG"
June 14, 2001

"The survivors are scraps," says evolutionary biologist Dr. John Alroy about the large mammal species that remained in North America after the wave of extinctions that followed the arrival of the first humans less than fourteen thousand years ago. And there is no longer any question about why all the rest—mammoths, mastodons, giant sloths, camels, horses, giant armadillos, and deer the size of moose—died out. In his article in this month's *Science*, Alroy puts the blame firmly on human beings.

Paul Martin of the University of Arizona first raised this "New-World Blitzkrieg" theory back in 1967. It has always been puzzling how many more big animal species there are in Africa, Europe and Asia, where humans and their immediate ancestors have lived for hundreds of thousands of years, than in the Americas and Australia, where they arrived all of a sudden and relatively recently. Martin suggested that it was because the Indians and the Australian Aborigines killed them off—and he unleashed a firestorm of protest.

The angriest protesters were the North American Indians themselves, who felt they were being robbed of their last shred of cultural dignity. They had lost their land, their future, and in many cases even their language to the European invaders. About their only consolation was their belief that they had some special spiritual status as the stewards of the land—that they were people with a special gift for living in harmony with nature.

Now the damn Europeans were saying that it was their ancestors who killed off thirty-two of the forty-one large plant-eating species that lived in North America fifteen thousand years ago (plus, indirectly, several large carnivores that used to live off of them). It was just too hurtful to be borne, so they rejected the evidence—and so did many nonnative scientists who were unhappy about this vision of Man the Exterminator.

It particularly didn't fit the majority society's five-hundred-year-old image of native Americans as simpler, wiser, more virtuous societies. From Rousseau on down, the idealized Noble Savage has been a major icon in Western culture (however much real-life Indians were abused), and the transformation of this old image into its modern version, the Ecological Indian, occurred in precisely the decade when Martin brought up his blitzkrieg hypothesis.

So the theory was roundly condemned, and a generation of academics tried to refute it with implausible theories about how climate change or disease or some other non-human cause triggered these extinctions. The "controversy" ran on for decades.

Never mind that human numbers soared in the Americas at the very time when this alleged climate change was wiping out the other big animals. Never mind that we *know* that it was human beings that did in most of the larger animals on mid-ocean islands, such as New Zealand and Mauritius, that have been settled by people only in the past thousand years or so. Martin's hypothesis was simply politically unacceptable.

For Indians, who have appropriated European myths about their special relationship with nature as a new source of self-respect (a process documented in Shepard Krech III's fine 1999 book *The Ecological Indian*), it was simply unbearable. The position of almost all Indians and most white environmentalists was summed up by Lakota writer Vine Deloria Jr.: "The Indian lived with his land. The white destroyed his land. He destroyed the planet Earth."

And now, into this orgy of Indian self-righteousness and white guilt steps Dr. John Alroy to point out that the emperor has no clothes. He will doubtless regret it.

The extermination of most large land-animal species within a few thousand years of the arrival of the first human beings in North America, says Alroy, was inevitable. He offers a simple computer simulation based on how early human beings hunted and travelled, and where the animals lived and how they reproduced. No matter how you adjust the variables to make the people worse hunters or the animals more prolific breeders, most of them die out.

A companion article in the same issue of *Science* documents a similar episode of mass extinction in Australia forty-six thousand years ago that seems to have human causes. People in these new environments not only found animals that did not fear them very easy to hunt, but they also set huge fires to open up the landscape and destroyed the animals' habitats. They were seriously into overkill, but as Dr. Alroy says, it was "an ecological catastrophe that was too gradual to be perceived by the people who unleashed it."

Never mind the sententious moralizing that normally ensues at this stage of the discussion. The more important point is made most clearly in Jared Diamond's brilliant book *Guns, Germs and Steel*. It is that ecological destruction is its own punishment.

The newly arrived hunters in the Americas and Australia were no more efficient or less intelligent than their ancestors in Eurasia. They were just up against species that had not co-evolved with human beings, like those of the Old World, and so had no inherited fear of people. So they quickly killed most of the larger species off—thereby eliminating precisely the animals that might later have enabled them to build civilizations able to rival those of Eurasia.

The irony is brutal. Early civilizations in Eurasia depended on domesticated animals, but the New World blitzkrieg exterminated all the leading candidates for domestication in the Americas and Australia long before the local people started down the road to civilization.

When they did start down it, in places like Mexico, the central Andes and even the Ohio Valley, they moved far more slowly because they had almost no domesticated animals: horses, camels, mastodons, wild pigs and the like were all gone long ago. And so the New World civilizations were eventually overwhelmed by Europeans whose civilizations grew faster, thanks to horses, cows, sheep, pigs and goats.

Nobody understood what was happening. Nobody was to blame. And if you want a parable for our own times, make it up yourself.

I have to apologize for this one. It's really about Rupert Murdoch, who is one of the most destructive influences on the planet, but I couldn't resist getting a little slap in at Conrad Black as well. It just seems mean now. But I will stand by everything I said in the George Harrison piece that follows this one, even if it would take a much longer argument these days to get anybody to agree with me.

MURDOCH'S OBSESSION
September 7, 2001

It hardly seems worth what he went through to get it. After eight years of crawling over broken glass in penance for one careless remark, News Corp owner Rupert Murdoch is finally about to get permission to broadcast TV by satellite to parts of southern Guangdong province, the corner of China that is already most exposed to the relatively uncensored media of Hong Kong. It contains perhaps 3 percent of the Chinese population.

That's still a significant number of people: about as many as a fair-sized country such as Spain. But the Chinese target audience are far less affluent than Spaniards, so why has Rupert Murdoch been eating dog waste with a smile for almost a decade to achieve this breakthrough? Partly because he and his partner in the venture, AOL Time Warner chief Jerry Levin, believe that this is an entering wedge that will in time give them access to the entire Chinese market. But partly also because he is an obsessive with a tincture of megalomania.

This is traditional among media barons, from monsters of the founding generation like William Randolph Hearst and Lord Northcliffe down to more housebroken contemporary figures like Murdoch and his Canadian-born colleague Conrad Black ("Lord Almost"), whose obsession with getting a British peerage has turned him into a laughingstock. At least Murdoch's obsession is vaguely connected with his business—but it is, nevertheless, a strange fixation.

Breaking into the Chinese media market has become the Australian-born entrepreneur's obsession. He is as fascinated by the sheer size of the Chinese population (now 1.3 billion) as those nineteenth-century Western merchants who dreamed of controlling the market in "oil for the lamps of China."

If only he could get direct broadcast rights to China, Murdoch dreamed, the advertising revenues would flow in endlessly, he'd be the richest media magnate who ever lived, and he'd be able . . . well, he'd be able to afford three or even four lunches a day, if he wanted them. A less than magnificent ambition, perhaps, but at least a big enough goal to keep the boredom at bay for a few years—and back in 1993 it did look like it would be only a few years.

Eight years ago Murdoch bought a majority shareholding in Hong Kong–based Star TV and began broadcasting directly to China by satellite. It seemed only a matter of time until enough Chinese had satellite dishes to turn it into a paying concern—but then he put his foot in it. Speaking to a Western audience in September 1993 (and forgetting that local events do actually get reported elsewhere), he made the fatal remark that direct TV broadcasts from satellites were "an unambiguous threat to totalitarian regimes everywhere."

Not only did it strike the right note for a Western business audience—here is a dedicated capitalist busily spreading freedom—but it also contained some truth. It was not, however, what a man trying to do a deal with a totalitarian regime for direct broadcast by satellite should be saying in public.

The Chinese government was very cross, and it punished Murdoch severely. One month later it banned private satellite dishes throughout China. At this point Murdoch should have walked away from the project, but his obsession wouldn't let him. Instead, he embarked on one of the most impressive feats of protracted grovelling that has been seen since Iago.

Trying to win back China's favour, he dropped the BBC World News feed from his Star TV in 1994, replacing it with something much blander. The following year he sponsored Deng Ron, the late Chinese leader Deng Xiaoping's daughter, on a US book tour to promote her biography of her father. In 1998 his HarperCollins publishing subsidiary dropped plans to publish the memoirs of Chris Patten, the last British governor of Hong Kong, who had greatly annoyed Beijing with his attempts to inject some democracy into the political system there before leaving.

Then two years ago he made his most important move, dumping his wife of thirty years for Wendi Deng, a young Chinese woman less than half his age, with excellent connections in China. By now the Beijing regime was softening, and he helped the process along with ingratiating remarks like his dismissal of the Tibetan leader, the Dalai Lama, as "a very political old monk shuffling around in Gucci shoes." China, the new Murdoch line goes, is run by very sweet people who are just misunderstood.

So now Murdoch has his deal, after a fashion. He gets to broadcast *The Simpsons* and *Friends* to a tiny corner of China—"We have agreed that they can broadcast in parts of Guangdong, but not all the province. There are limits," said Beijing's spokeswoman—and in return AOL Time Warner will carry China's English-language CCTV-9 on its North American cable network. You wonder who is more deluded.

CCTV-9 is slick enough, in its way, but it's not going to change many Americans' view of the Chinese regime (nor should it, for the view is essentially correct: the regime is a corrupt dictatorship). Star TV is not going to start a revolution in Guangdong, or even change viewing habits much. The reason these people are doing deals is because deals are all they know how to do.

Yet Murdoch was right, basically, in the remark that caused all the trouble. The media in general (not just satellite TV broadcasts) are a mortal threat to totalitarian regimes. We used to believe otherwise, but surely that has been the underlying lesson of the past fifteen years of upheaval in the world. Mass media, however brutally censored or cynically commercialized, are a democratizing phenomenon.

THE AGE OF INNOCENCE
November 30, 2001

Nobody under the age of thirty would write the kind of drivel that has been filling newspapers in the English-speaking world since the death of George Harrison. Take the *Globe and Mail* of Toronto, where I was when he died: "Central to [Beatlemania] was the profound sense of cheeky, benign optimism, long distant from the cynical, frightened age in which we now live. . . . [But people] were not shocked yesterday in the way they were by John Lennon's murder in 1980, a defining moment in the erosion of the age of innocence."

Look at the choice of words: "cheeky, benign optimism"; "erosion of the age of innocence"; "cynical, frightened age in which we now live." I very much doubt that George Harrison would ever have talked like that: it is simply a projection of the anonymous leader-writer's perspective on the trajectory of his or her own life, now probably some forty or fifty winters long, from optimism to cynicism. That is not history; it's just the aging process.

Let us conduct a little exercise in historical comparisons. Let's take the fifteen years from 1962, when the Beatles first made the British top twenty, to 1977, when Harrison's divorce from Pattie Boyd marked the definitive loss of his own innocence (Boyd ran away with Harrison's old friend, guitar hero Eric Clapton, who had written the rock anthem "Layla" about her), and compare that period with the past fifteen years. What was better in the world then, and what was worse?

The Beatles' first hit, "Love Me Do," entered the British charts in October 1962, which was the month of the Cuban missile crisis. I was a very young naval officer at the time, and I don't recall much optimism or innocence. My parents' generation had finished fighting the worst war in history less than twenty years ago, and here I was about to be killed in a global nuclear war before I even turned twenty myself.

After that came the assassination of President Kennedy in 1963, the US takeover of the Vietnam War in 1964–66, the Six-Day War in the Middle East in 1967 (accompanied by another trip to the brink of nuclear war), the Soviet invasion of Czechoslovakia in 1968, followed by, over the next few years, the genocide in Biafra, the India–Pakistan war and the slaughter in Bangladesh, millions killed by the Red Guards in China, the destruction of the Allende government in Chile, My Lai, Watergate, the 1973 Middle East War, the fall of Saigon, the betrayal of East Timor, and "Year Zero" in Cambodia. No wonder we were all singing happy tunes.

Now compare the period 1986 to 2001. It opened with the world's first successful nonviolent revolution against a dictator, in the Philippines, and an unprecedented internal thaw (*glasnost* and *perestroika*) in the former Soviet Union. The trickle of democratization rapidly turned into a flood, with copycat revolutions sweeping first across Asia, then jumping to Europe in 1989, reaching Moscow itself by 1991. Apartheid went under in South Africa without a fight, and even today the phenomenon of nonviolent democratic revolution continues to transform countries as different as Indonesia and Yugoslavia.

In 1986, at least two-thirds of the world's people lived under tyrannies. Now, at least two-thirds live in more or less democratic countries. Many of the newer democracies are poor and their governments corrupt, but it is nevertheless an epochal change for the better. The threat of a global nuclear holocaust has simply vanished, and those in the military-industrial complexes of the planet who once made their livings by loudly worrying about (and quietly preparing for) the deaths of hundreds of millions are reduced to talking up the marginal threats from terrorists and "rogue states."

(You dare to call the attacks on the United States on September 11 "marginal"? Yes, of course, if the standard of comparison is a major war. The losses at the World Trade Center were comparable to one average night's bombing casualties in the Second World War.)

From the Gulf War through the Bosnia and Kosovo episodes down to the current campaign in Afghanistan, there is at least the semblance of a legal framework for the wars through some form of UN backing, and at least partial justification for the military action in terms of the defence of international law or of human rights. (Of course, the Law of Mixed Motives always applies.)

We certainly have not taken up residence in paradise, but compared to the '60s and '70s, *this* is the age of innocence.

It was still true when I wrote it, even after 9/11. It is less true now.

CHAPTER THREE

THEN SUDDENLY . . .
SEPTEMBER 11–DECEMBER 31, 2001

Like everyone, I wrote about the terrorists and the US response to the exclusion of almost everything else in the first months after 9/11. They could have discovered a cure for cancer in October 2001 and it would have been reported in one paragraph on page 10. Like everybody else, I was working my way through the evidence as it emerged, trying to figure out motives and strategies.

The terrorists' motives were easy to understand—they had already been in business for a long time, after all—and their strategy was absolutely bog-standard. Getting US military strategy right was harder than usual, because the Pentagon turned out to be a good deal more imaginative than I had expected. It only took the US one month to strike back, and the way it did it minimized both American and Afghan casualties. In military terms, it was an elegant operation, although it left lots of political problems stored up for the future.

But as to the administration's political strategy, I didn't have a clue. I thought it was all about fighting terrorism.

"AMERICA'S NEW WAR": STRATEGIES
September 19, 2001

There are only two questions that matter as the world waits for the United States to strike back at the terrorists who planned the attacks in New York and Washington on September 11. The first is: what did the terrorists want the US to do in response? The terrorists must have known that there would be an American response to such a huge and dramatic atrocity; they presumably calculated what it might be—and then they went ahead in the hope of getting Washington to do just that.

The other question is whether the United States will fall into their trap.

What the terrorists wanted, it seems clear, was massive and indiscriminate US retaliation against one or more Muslim countries of the Middle East, with huge civilian casualties. This is what the Clinton administration did on a smaller scale after the terrorist bombings of US embassies in East Africa in 1998, dropping showers of cruise missiles on suspected terrorist sites in Sudan and Afghanistan that rearranged much scenery and killed many civilians but few terrorists.

So if a liberal softie like Clinton did that when a couple of hundred people, mostly Africans, were killed, what would a right-wing president like George W. Bush do when Muslim fundamentalist terrorists kill thousands of American citizens in their own cities? The planners of the operation would have predicted that Bush would bomb the daylights out of every Muslim country he remotely suspected of harbouring terrorists, killing huge numbers of innocent Muslim civilians.

And why would the terrorists wish such attacks upon their co-religionists? Because their aim is to trigger a cataclysmic war between the West (which they see as their enemy and main oppressor) and the entire Muslim world. Osama bin Laden's followers have always had this goal. As bin Laden said of his first really successful operation, a truck bomb that killed nineteen Americans in Saudi Arabia in 1996, it was "the beginning of the war between the Muslims and the United States."

Bin Laden believes that if the US can be driven to use excessive force in retaliation for his attacks, it will so outrage the world's 1.3 billion Muslims that they will rise up, overthrow their shamefully collaborationist governments and launch the final victorious jihad against those who have inflicted such pain and humiliation on the Muslims of the Middle East. The fundamentalist fanatics imagine that the Muslims would win this war (with God's help), and restore the world to its proper balance—one in which Muslims, and particularly Arabs, are prosperous, proud and on top.

Even if America did fall into their trap, it wouldn't come out the way the terrorists hope. There might be great uproar in some Muslim countries, but almost all their governments would survive. If you doubt that, recall the very similar (and equally false) predictions of anti-Western uprisings throughout the Muslim world before the counterattack that drove the Iraqis out of Kuwait in the Gulf War ten years ago.

Most Muslims understand that the terrorists of al-Qaeda and associated groups are no more benevolent and no more democratic than Saddam Hussein was. Some even recall that the last two times NATO used military force, in Bosnia and in Kosovo, it was to protect innocent Muslims from murderous Christians. The world is a great deal more complicated than the terrorists think, and their fellow Muslims are a good deal more sophisticated.

Nevertheless, an indiscriminate US military response could cause not only great harm to the innocent but also great instability in sensitive countries like Egypt, Saudi Arabia and Pakistan. So what will the US response actually be?

Even after Bush's speech to the joint houses of Congress on Thursday night, it is far from clear what the actual sequence of military events will be, but all the language being used by the US administration suggests that it is acutely sensitive to this danger. So do its actions, from the successful pressure on the Israeli government to stop its daily bashing of the Palestinians to the very serious attempt that is underway to build a broad antiterrorist coalition incorporating as many Muslim and Arab states as possible. It worked in the Gulf War, and if the US goes slowly and carefully enough it could work again.

All this suggests that there will *not* be early air strikes on Afghanistan, for they would hinder the courtship of potential coalition members merely for the sake of letting off steam. The current manoeuvring of US forces in the Persian Gulf and the dispatch of additional combat aircraft to the region is more likely just an attempt to frighten the Taliban government of Afghanistan into handing over bin Laden and the other terrorists on its soil.

But it was also clear, after Bush had finished speaking to Congress, that in the longer run there will probably be a real war, with ground troops and all, because the list of demands he made of the Taliban, including American access to the terrorists' camps, stands zero chance of being met. That real war, however, is probably months away.

In the meantime, everybody in the Bush administration is working hard to dampen down public expectations of early action, let alone early success in the "war on terrorism." It is still highly questionable whether the potential rewards of getting some or all of the terrorists based in Afghanistan are worth the very serious risks of upheavals elsewhere in the Muslim world that would accompany an invasion, but at least the strategy of the operation is being handled quite intelligently.

The attack on Afghanistan wasn't months away—it was barely three weeks away. They were playing their cards very close to the chest in Washington, and you can hardly blame them for trying to mislead us: they were planning a war, after all.

Al Gore would have had to fight that war too, if he had won the presidency the previous year and 9/11 had happened on his watch, but I suspect he would not have done it as well. Credit where credit is due.

QUESTIONS AND ANSWERS
September 26, 2001

More than two weeks since the terrorist attacks in New York and Washington, and still not a shot fired in retaliation by American forces anywhere in the world. No immediate prospect of retaliation, either: "I think that it can't be stressed enough that everyone who's waiting for military action . . . needs to re-think this thing," said US Deputy Secretary of Defense Paul Wolfowitz last Wednesday. So at least we know that the United States is not going to walk blindly into the trap the terrorists set for it.

Instead, Washington is playing a much longer and more cautious strategy, building a worldwide coalition against terrorism. Meanwhile it carefully avoids any action that might alienate Muslim opinion from this coalition, for it badly wants the Muslim countries in. But the final goal is probably still a full-scale invasion of Afghanistan, apparently the terrorists' major base. And that means a war.

Some time will elapse before this invasion is ready, but what will happen when it comes? Amidst all the unknowns, there are some questions that we can answer with a fair degree of confidence.

COULD THIS TRIGGER A WORLD WAR? No, because the whole structure of rival great-power alliances that led to world wars dissolved a decade ago. All the world's big industrialized countries and all its nuclear weapons powers, including Russia, China, India and Pakistan, will be on the same side in the coming clash.

WILL NUCLEAR WEAPONS BE USED? No. See above.

WILL THERE BE MORE TERRORIST ATTACKS? Quite possibly, for it's unlikely that the terrorists used up all their "sleepers" in one go. If they don't get sent into action now, the next point where they might is the date that American forces attack Afghanistan. And they would be very unlikely to use commercial aircraft again: their style would be to look for another surprise approach.

WOULD THEY USE CHEMICAL OR BIOLOGICAL WEAPONS? The planners of the attack on the World Trade Center towers would use any weapon that came to hand, but there is no evidence that they have such weapons.

WILL THE US AND ITS ALLIES BRING BACK THE DRAFT? No, because invading Afghanistan wouldn't require extra manpower. The combat phase of the operation would probably be over before people recruited now could emerge as trained soldiers—ten to twelve months—and no government wants to inflame public opinion by raising the question of conscription anyway. In today's world, it is a dead issue.

HAVE THEY GOT THE RIGHT TARGET? The US government insists that Osama bin Laden and his lieutenants are the right targets, though it has produced nothing in public that would stand up in a court of law. It is probably being honest in its judgment, but that doesn't mean its information is complete. We may never know the full details of who planned and financed the terrorist attacks, but bin Laden very probably was involved.

WOULD INVADING AFGHANISTAN STOP TERRORISM? Of course not. Fighting terrorism is like fighting crime: you may bring the statistics down, but you never eliminate it. But attacking Afghanistan might punish some of those involved in the recent attacks on the US, and it would certainly make a lot of Americans feel better.

Does this all make sense? As much sense as you can reasonably ask for in a world full of human beings. Emotions drive, and rationality tries to moderate. Sometimes it succeeds.

US air strikes against Afghanistan began on October 7, 2001.

PLAN A OR PLAN B
October 8, 2001

Two days of air strikes by now, and we still don't know whether it's going to be Plan A or Plan B. In fact, we may not know for some time, because the Pentagon isn't going to tell us and the beginning of Plan B would look just like Plan A. But there is reason to fear the worst.

Plan A is the traditional low-risk "strategy lite" approach of bombing raids and brief incursions into Afghanistan. This will keep US casualties down to a minimum, but it would also kill lots of innocent Afghans with bombs and missiles. It certainly wouldn't destroy the organization that planned last month's attacks on American cities, and it might not even get Osama bin Laden himself. Against an organization as professional and as dispersed as al-Qaeda, it is a futile and even a frivolous tactic.

It is, however, what US administrations habitually did in response to terrorist attacks on US targets overseas in the late '80s and '90s, when the public was totally allergic to American military casualties. Occasionally it even worked, as in the 1988 air raids that scared Libya's Colonel Gadafy into being a good boy.

More often, as in the shower of cruise missiles on Afghanistan and Sudan that followed the 1998 attacks on

US embassies in East Africa, it merely annoyed America's allies and amused its enemies. But it was all that the United States *could* do at the time, even though many American planners and commanders realized that it was mere tokenism.

There is now another option, however, for US public opinion seems more tolerant of the prospect of US military casualties in the wake of the thousands of American civilian dead last month. Hence, Plan B: if Americans will now support a truly serious military response even if it costs a considerable number of American soldiers' lives, then why not take advantage of that fact and do the job right?

That would involve invading Afghanistan, overthrowing the Taliban regime, imposing a relatively sane and respectable government of nonfanatical Afghans in its place, and then deluging the country with food and aid so that the new regime survives. With a friendly government in Kabul and good local intelligence, the US could then track down and dismantle the whole bin Laden organization in Afghanistan—provided, of course, that it didn't get bogged down in a long guerilla war against the remnants of the Taliban instead.

An invasion would get the job done, if it succeeded, whereas nothing else really will. Nevertheless, the risks of an actual ground war still feel so big (especially given the dismal history of previous invasions of Afghanistan) that most American military planners continue to favour a more limited option: some glorified version of good old Plan A.

It is the political side of the house, as usual, that is tempted by the more extreme option. The politicians will be blamed by the public if the operation doesn't actually destroy bin Laden's organization, whereas it is the generals who will carry the can if an invasion of Afghanistan turns into a new Vietnam. But beyond merely selfish motives, who is right—and who will win?

The right answer, in terms of capturing or killing bin Laden, destroying his organization and satisfying the American public, is undoubtedly Plan B: invasion. If those are the results you want, then these are the actions you must take, at whatever cost. And the cost would not necessarily be too great, since Afghanistan has never been a difficult country to invade.

It is much harder to hold, as both the British and the Soviets learned to their cost, but with the right policies there need not be a long guerilla resistance. The Taliban is very unpopular with most Afghans, and this time there would be no outside powers supplying and subsidizing a guerilla resistance movement. Put in the equivalent of a mini-Marshall Plan to rebuild a country that has been shattered by twenty-two years of war, and you could even have a success story on your hands.

But this is unlikely to happen, because the instinct of the US military will always be to minimize the risks to its own interests. The compromise that is leading the pack in Washington, therefore, is to overthrow the Taliban, but without involving American ground troops in any large way. Just hire the thugs of the Northern Alliance, the losing side in the civil war that was almost over, and give them enough money and guns to do the job for you.

They would then kill, rape and rob their way back into power, with the assistance of US air power used in the customary lavish way. Thousands of innocent Afghans would be killed and Muslim opinion elsewhere would be outraged, but the new regime, once it got power, would collaborate (after a fashion) in the US search for bin Laden and company.

It would be a classic imperial solution: get foreigners to do the dying for you, and accept a rather muddy outcome in terms of results. But it would also be the wrong thing to do.

"Even women can fight through computers and airplanes," said Mullah Muhammad Omar, the Taliban leader, last Thursday. "If [the Americans] are men, let them come to the Afghan battlefield to see who the Afghans are." And though the mullah's sentiments are not even remotely correct politically, his advice is good. If the United States is serious about this, then it should do it the hard way.

It didn't, of course.

THE WORST THAT COULD HAPPEN
October 21, 2001

As the Rent-a-Threat analysts expound their ever more ingenious scenarios for new kinds of terrorist attacks on prime-time television, it seems fitting to ask: what is the worst that can happen?

It certainly isn't "bio-terror." We have had weeks of saturation publicity about "anthrax attacks" throughout the United States (the vast majority of which are actually talcum powder, baking soda and cocaine attacks). To date, only one person has died, but most of the other 275 million Americans, if you believe the media accounts, have turned into panic-prone wimps.

Perhaps it's because their knowledge of statistics is inferior to that of the average New Guinea highlander, so the infinitesimal risk of being infected by anthrax frightens them more than the far greater dangers posed by their neighbour's driving and their neighbour's handgun. Even Canadians (who have not had a single anthrax case) have taken to running out of buildings at the drop of a hat in what one Canadian journalist scathingly called "panic envy."

Things would get a lot more interesting if terrorists had access to some really dangerous disease such as smallpox, which can spread from person to person and would encounter no resistance whatever in most of the present population. But no terrorists would be wasting their time with anthrax if they had smallpox, so that is probably not a danger in the present situation. Even if it were, prompt quarantine measures by an already alert medical establishment would probably confine the loss of lives to some thousands or tens of thousands.

That would be quite a lot of people, but no more than the toll in a single big air raid in the latter years of the Second World War. Today's people are not really more timorous than those of fifty years ago, but they have fallen victim to media hype. Having become targets, North American journalists have also become the chief panic-mongers.

So if "bio-terrorism" is not the worst that can happen, what is? Nuclear terrorism, maybe?

The time for stealing nuclear weapons is past, thanks largely to the decade-long effort (subsidized by the US Congress) to track down and render safe every nuclear weapon that belonged to the former Soviet Union. Terrorists of the ilk of al-Qaeda cannot make nuclear weapons on their own, lacking the specialized scientific personnel and the sophisticated equipment that would be needed. The most they could manage, given access to lots of fissile material, is a subnuclear explosion that scatters radioactive material over an area with a radius of one kilometre or so—the so-called dirty bomb.

Even that is very unlikely, but imagine for a moment that terrorists did get their hands on a real nuclear weapon, smuggled it into a major Western city, and set it off. (Go on, pour your money down the Ballistic Missile Defence rathole. None of your real enemies care.) It would be a calamity that would dwarf the attacks of September 11, or indeed anything else that has happened to the citizens of an industrialized country in the past half-century. But it would not be the end of the world.

Such an attack could kill hundreds of thousands of people, maybe even half a million. But it would happen once, in one place, and then it would be over. If it were to happen in the United States, it would be a loss equivalent to four or five months' population growth—and life would go on much as usual for everybody else.

Making these calculations and comparisons may seem a bit cold-blooded or even ghoulish, but there is a reason for it. The point is that the very worst attack that terrorists could plausibly make would cause no more casualties than any single month of the Second World War. And it would not cost as many lives as the opening five minutes of the Third World War.

A sense of proportion is always useful in times like these. Imagine what it would be like if the current military operations in the Persian Gulf region were taking place just a dozen years ago, when the world was still divided into two rival blocs bristling with nuclear weapons. With American aircraft bombing within earshot of the former Soviet Union's border, we would probably already be deep into a situation as bad as the Cuban missile crisis of 1962. One false step and hundreds of millions could die.

We have emerged from a long period of deadly peril, when the great powers were perpetually ready to go to war

45

with one another and blow half the world up. We now live in a period so safe that the worst threat is mere terrorism, and it is practically impossible to imagine a scenario in which the great powers could drift back into that kind of confrontation. Yet very few people seem to understand how great the change has been, or how lucky we are.

In fact, if historical ingratitude were a crime, the entire chattering classes of the West would be serving life sentences at hard labour.

By mid-November 2001 it was clear that the US had achieved a virtually flawless military success in Afghanistan (though the political arrangements left much to be desired). The obvious next step was to shift from a military to a civilian-led antiterrorist operation, since the only military task—smashing up the terrorist training camps and overthrowing the only government on the planet that supported al-Qaeda—was just about accomplished. Terrorists are civilians, living for the most part among other civilians, and the appropriate tools for dealing with them are normally police work, intelligence-gathering and all the other techniques that are used in the "war on crime." Armoured brigades and military offensives are irrelevant.

But there were already signs that this was not at all what the Bush administration had in mind, and that further wars were being contemplated in Washington. That made no sense in terms of a "war on terror," and I confess that I had no clear idea at the time of the agenda that had really taken over in the White House. If I had been more diligent in my research and not so busy with the play-by-play reporting of television journalism, I would have been able to figure a lot of it out just by reading the last two or three years of postings on the

Project for a New American Century's *website; but as it was,
I just felt a growing sense of unease. So I began emitting the
kind of warnings that you would offer to a well-intentioned
friend who was going wrong. We all could have done a good
deal better.*

TIME TO STOP

November 14, 2001

Four out of five: Mazar-i-Sharif, Herat, Kabul and Jalalabad.
All but one of Afghanistan's major cities have been lost by the
Taliban and captured by the Northern Alliance in less than a
week, and the last, Kandahar, is likely to fall at any time.
Neither Washington nor anyone else expected so sudden a
collapse. So the burning question at the Pentagon, in the
National Security Council, in all the decision-making centres of the United States and the other members of its antiterrorist coalition, is what to do next. The answer is to stop.

Stop the bombing, above all. It has achieved a lot by
breaking up the Taliban's fixed defences and demoralizing
its troops, but it can do little more for you now that they are
pulling back into the hills and reverting to guerilla warfare.
Ramadan arrives this weekend, and there is far more to be
gained in goodwill by stopping the bombing, both in
Afghanistan and in the rest of the Muslim world, than there
is militarily by continuing to bomb.

Yes, we know that bombing pauses have a dreadful reputation among the US military after the way they were used in
Vietnam, but that really was different. There, you were
facing an entire people in arms, and trying to persuade them
to abandon the military victory they were gradually winning

47

on the ground by punishing them from the air. Every once in a while you'd stop to see if they were hurting enough yet. Ridiculous.

In Afghanistan, by starkest contrast, you have *won* on the ground—or at least your local allies have—and the Afghan people are not your enemies. Even among the Pashtuns who are the Taliban's ethnic base, most people will be ready to abandon them as losers now—provided that you don't plaster every hilltop in their territory with bombs and convince them that you are yet another foreign invader who must be resisted.

Ask yourself: do you really intend to send American and other foreign troops up and down every hill in the Pashtun-populated parts of Afghanistan, taking casualties every step of the way, in a vast campaign to "pacify" the south, wipe out the Taliban, and hunt down Osama bin Laden? Of course not.

Do you think that the Northern Alliance troops, with scarcely a Pashtun among them, are going to volunteer to do that job for you, or that they *could* do it without turning every Pashtun in the country against you? Of course not.

Well, then, what is the point in just bombing the rural areas of southern Afghanistan? You will kill lots of innocent civilians and drive the rest back into the embrace of the Taliban without accomplishing a single useful thing. Surely the objective now must be to create a competent and broadly based Afghan government as fast as possible, and let it do the final work of tracking down the Taliban diehards and "foreign guests" who linger in the hills.

Creating that government is admittedly going to be trickier now, given the sheer scale of the victory that the Northern Alliance has won with your help. They are bound to want the lion's share in the new government, even though the various minority ethnic groups they represent probably only account for half of Afghanistan's population. To stop them from achieving that aim, you need to get lots of your own troops into Afghanistan's cities. Now.

Do it under the pretext of delivering aid—and *do* deluge the country with aid: God knows it needs it. But make sure your troops go in as formed units, with impressive amounts of military equipment. They don't have to fight the Taliban, but they do need to overawe Northern Alliance commanders who are tempted to set up little local empires in the good old Afghan style.

You won't have to fight your way in now. Provided you do it in the next few days, before Northern Alliance control hardens into some form of local administration in the captured cities, you won't meet overt resistance. Make sure to include lots of non-US coalition troops, not just from the usual suspects like Britain, France, Canada and Germany but also from as many Muslim countries as possible. (The Turks are probably ready to move right now, and are thoroughly professional soldiers.)

And remember that the point of the operation is not to mop up the Taliban. It is to create a competent, ethnically balanced, and potentially popular Afghan government, give it enough resources (that's spelled M-O-N-E-Y) to win that popular support and start building a real Afghan army—and then leave it to that new Afghan government to finish off the Taliban and hunt down Osama bin Laden.

If you get some intelligence about bin Laden's whereabouts in the meantime, by all means send your special forces after him, but don't count on it. Your main problem now is to stop him from slipping across that mostly uninhabited fourteen-hundred-kilometre border into Pakistan.

But if he stays in Afghanistan, he'll be easy enough for the new government to find once the flow of defections from the Taliban begins to grow. And it will grow, especially if the new army pays three or four times as well as the existing tribal militias.

As for the US and other Western troops, they should stay just long enough to stabilize the situation and persuade the Northern Alliance that it must share power with other groups. (Money can do wonders here, too.) Then they should be replaced with a robust, UN-backed force made up entirely of Muslim troops that stays until the new government is securely on its feet—and make sure that none of those troops come from Afghanistan's immediate neighbours, all of which have been backing rival sides in the civil war for the past decade.

Do all this, and you might walk away from Afghanistan with a success on your hands. But remember that you have been very, very lucky, and don't get overconfident. Above all, don't let anybody talk you into attacking Iraq.

A SLIGHT CASE OF HUBRIS
December 12, 2001

"Get them by the balls, and their hearts and minds will follow," went the Vietnam-era adage of the professional US military. But the United States, despite the enormous firepower that gave it so many military victories, ultimately lost the Vietnam War.

With the Taliban regime destroyed and the al-Qaeda organization deprived of its bases in Afghanistan, the hawks in the Bush administration are in full charge. Last weekend,

American military officers were in Somalia meeting with warlords from the Rahanwein Resistance Army to discuss a joint attack on that country's fledgling government, and Undersecretary of State for Near Eastern Affairs Ryan Crocker was in Kurdish-controlled northern Iraq laying the groundwork for an assault on Saddam Hussein's regime.

The next phase of the "war on terrorism" may be no further away than the traditional New Year's hangover, and the voices of doubt and dissent in Washington have almost all been stilled. "Bombing works" is the cry, and casualty-free victories are coming to be taken for granted in the United States, and almost anything seems possible. The ancient Greeks called this state of mind "hubris"—and expected nemesis to follow.

Elsewhere, the sense is that the United States is overextending itself, and alarm among its closest allies is growing. On December 11, for example, Britain's chief of defence staff, Admiral Sir Michael Boyce, warned that the emotionally satisfying fireworks in Afghanistan had hardly affected the real level of the terrorist threat. Al-Qaeda, he said, remains "a fielded, resourced, dedicated and essentially autonomous terrorist force, quite capable of atrocity on a comparable scale" to the attacks on New York and Washington on September 11.

The whole Afghan sideshow will have only a marginal impact on the ability of those cells to act. Indeed, the long-term effect of such extended bombing campaigns could be to expand the recruiting base for al-Qaeda and like-minded organizations, both in the Muslim world and the diaspora.

As Admiral Boyce put it, the risk is that handing over Western security policy to a "high-tech twenty-first-century posse" will radicalize the entire Muslim world, and produce a global confrontation far more serious than the dramatic but strictly limited threats posed by occasional terrorist strikes. Indeed, a failure to wage a campaign for "hearts and minds" (he actually said those deeply unfashionable words) will probably make the terrorist threat worse too.

Admiral Boyce was not just saying the first thing that came into his head. Such speeches are vetted at cabinet level, and the anxieties Boyce expressed are those that all of America's friends and allies feel as Washington, encouraged by the easy Afghan victory, plunges on to new campaigns. But nobody in the White House is listening.

Three months ago, as the United States was busy rounding up support for its new war on terrorism, there was a brief pause in the Bush administration's relentless war against any treaties that might constrain American power in any way, but the unilateralist drive has now resumed with full force.

The Anti-Ballistic Missile Treaty is being cancelled with six months' notice, and the US will push ahead with Bush's beloved Ballistic Missile Defence despite near-universal misgivings among friends and allies. Washington recently blocked moves to tighten the convention aimed at prohibiting the development of biological weapons. The US has forced European countries to put their plans for a joint NATO–Russia council on hold for at least six months: the Bush administration doesn't want its old allies and its new one to get too cozy. Even when it does make a commitment—as with Bush's recent verbal agreement with Russian President Vladimir Putin on cutting missile numbers—it doesn't want to commit the deal to writing.

This combination of technological hubris and ideological triumphalism is leading the Bush administration into dangerous waters. The United States is a big, rich, powerful and technologically innovative country, but it is still only 4 percent of the world's population. In the sixty years since the Pearl Harbor attack pulled it into the Second World War and made it a full-time player in global politics, it has always played the alliance game because successive administrations all understood that even American power could be overstretched.

If the lesson now has to be re-learned, we are all in for a rough time.

CHAPTER FOUR

THE MUSLIMS: MALEVOLENT, MYSTERIOUS AND PROBABLY CRAZY

I dislike the religion of Islam just as much as I do Christianity and Judaism. I realize that I am myself embedded in a culture whose roots are in the Abrahamic religions, and most of my friends have grown up in one or another of these religions, but I don't believe their theologies and I detest the weird things that the more virulent forms of religious belief do to people's heads. So it has been very odd to find myself defending Islam all the time.

After 9/11, all the old Western fears and prejudices about Islam re-emerged in full force, accompanied by some new and thoroughly paranoid fantasies. It was not just unfair to

Muslims; it was a huge impediment to clear thinking about the situation.

HUNTINGTON'S FOLLY (AND BIN LADEN'S)

October 9, 2001

> "The nations of infidels have all united against the Muslims.
> . . . This is a new battle, a great battle, similar to the great
> battles of Islam like the conquest of Jerusalem. . . . [The
> Americans] come out to fight Islam in the name of fighting
> terrorism. These events have split the world into two camps:
> the camp of belief and the camp of nonbelief . . ."
>
> —*Osama bin Laden, early October 2001*

Bin Laden's videotaped message to the Muslim world, pre-taped for release after the first US strikes against Afghanistan, should give Samuel Huntington a warm glow of satisfaction, for it was he who predicted in his best-selling book in the mid-'90s that Islam and the West would become global adversaries in a "clash of civilizations." Bin Laden also contends that this clash will define the next phase of world history, and he is doing his best to hurry it along.

Huntington's book was especially popular among the Washington-based professionals who had built lucrative careers on fighting the Soviet threat and by the early '90s were desperately in need of a new threat to replace it. Just substitute bearded fanatics for godless commissars, and carry on making money.

In Islamic fundamentalist circles, on the other hand, they had no need of Huntington. They already believed that contemporary history is a morality play in which the oppressed and despised peoples of the Muslim world are destined to unite, wage a final battle against "Western civilization" and overthrow its domination throughout the world.

This is the worldview that bin Laden pushes relentlessly every time he finds a camera to address, and there are plenty of Muslims, especially in the Arab world, who already believe it. The current crisis will give this definition of the world a big boost in both of the "civilizations" in question, but it remains, nevertheless, pure parochial nonsense. There is no clash of civilizations, only a clash between traditionalists and modernizers within each culture, religion and civilization. All bin Laden's real enemies are Muslims.

The battle between reformers and conservatives has been underway in the West for more than five hundred years, long before it began in other parts of the planet. This lets the defenders of the old ways everywhere else portray their opponents within their own society as mere pawns of Western influence—and some of the defenders are pretty extreme in their rejection of the modern. As a pro-Taliban youth in an Afghan refugee camp in Pakistan put it recently, staking his claim to the moral high ground: "The Americans love Coca-Cola, but we love death."

It's a striking statement, but there's nothing particularly Islamic about it. A Japanese kamikaze pilot in 1945 could have said it with equal sincerity. Every major culture on the planet is at some stage or other of working its way through the same series of changes, and occasionally some country or even some entire "civilization" may spin out for a while and go slightly mad.

This is *not* happening to "the Muslims" as a whole, some 1.3 billion people of wildly diverse languages, histories and traditions who live in approximately fifty different countries in three continents. It is not even happening to the Arabs, who account for only one-fourth of the world's Muslims. It is conceivable (though not likely) that a couple of Arab states might face revolutionary takeovers by Islamic fundamentalists if the current crisis lasts too long or involves too many innocent Muslims' deaths, but you still don't get a clash of civilizations out of that.

There is something profoundly amiss in the Arab world, to be sure. Out of eighteen genuinely Arab countries, not one is a fully democratic country. Most do not even make a decent pretense of it. From Algeria to Egypt to Iraq to Yemen, the political culture is one of repression and torture, violence and lies—and in most Arab countries living standards are falling as population soars. (Even Saudi Arabia's per capita GNP has been halved in the past twenty years.)

But this is an Arab problem, not a Muslim one. The vast majority of the world's Muslims live in Asia, not in the Middle East, and countries such as Indonesia and Bangladesh, while they certainly have their problems, have not been long-term failures at either democracy or development. They will not be joining in Osama bin Laden's jihad against the West—nor, for that matter, will many Arab countries.

There are large and genuine global trends at work today: democratization, globalization of the economy, equality for women. The "global village" that Marshall McLuhan predicted to much puzzlement forty years ago is a reality, thanks to the new media technologies, and we can and do see everybody all the time.

But these trends, although they cause much puzzlement and frustration, do not show any signs of leading towards a titanic clash of civilizations. Instead, we are all muddling through the mess, far too busy coping with the deluge of change in our own lives to fall into the grand historical patterns foreseen for us by men like Huntington and bin Laden.

Such optimism almost always conceals certain doubts about whether people will actually live up to your expectations for them, and by the next spring I was starting to have reservations.

EUROPE: ISLAMOPHOBIA, NOT ANTI-SEMITISM
June 4, 2002

"The most stupid religion is Islam," said best-selling French novelist Michel Houellebecq. In his latest novel *Plateforme* he has the narrator say, "Each time that I hear that a Palestinian terrorist, or a Palestinian child, or a pregnant Palestinian woman has been shot in the Gaza Strip, I shiver with enthusiasm at the thought that there is one less Muslim."

Houellebecq is a cynical poseur who would say anything to gain attention, but the problem is that many Europeans give him the attention he craves rather than shunning him. Yet, what are we all being urged to worry about (especially by American political commentators)? Not about rampant Islamophobia in Europe, but rather about the alleged upsurge of anti-Semitism in the continent.

The anti-Semitism scare was unleashed by National Front leader Jean-Marie Le Pen's surprise success in pushing the Socialist candidate into third place in the first round of the French presidential elections in April. But Le Pen is not a new Hitler; he is just an opportunistic political thug whose dismissive remarks about the Holocaust ("a detail of history") have never been forgotten or forgiven by the majority of French voters.

In the run-off round of voting in May, 82 percent of French voters held their noses and supported President Jacques Chirac despite his obvious corruption, rather than vote for the racist rabble-rouser Le Pen. As for the 18 percent who did back Le Pen, far more would have been motivated by their hatred and fear of "immigrants" (i.e., Muslims) than of Jews.

The reality is that the recent and unprecedented entry of far-right political parties into governing coalitions in a number of European countries is directly connected with rising popular resentment of "immigrants," and that the majority of those immigrants almost everywhere are Muslims. Look at the recent inclusion of far-right parties in the Danish, Norwegian and Portuguese governments: not an anti-Semitic word or hint in any of their campaigns.

Look at the remarkable success of assassinated politician Pim Fortuyn's party in last month's Dutch election: he won his popularity by calling for an end to immigration and referring to Islam as "a backward religion," but he never uttered a single word that suggested he harboured anti-Semitic views. Even Italy's Prime Minister Silvio Berlusconi, a right-wing populist who freely airs his anti-Muslim views, would never dream of saying anything anti-Semitic in public.

There are occasional anti-Semitic outrages in Europe — desecration of Jewish graveyards, daubing swastikas on synagogues and the like — because in a continent of 700 million people there are bound to be some malevolent fools. The recent increase in these incidents is probably due to the fact that some Muslims resident in Europe have picked up the anti-Semitic ideas that once flourished in the continent, but are alien to traditional Islamic cultures. But there is no new wave of anti-Semitism in western Europe, and it is no worse in eastern Europe than it was ten years ago.

In all of Europe, however, there is a rapidly rising tide of Islamophobia: politicians capitalizing on popular dislike of Muslim immigrants, and even outright vilification of Islam. It is no worse than the routine public vilification of infidels and their satanic creeds by Islamic extremists that goes unrebuked in many of the world's Muslim countries, but that is no excuse for Europeans to behave the same way. Why is it happening?

Part of the reason is the sheer number of Muslim immigrants. Whether they're Turks in Germany, Algerians and Moroccans in France, or Bangladeshis and Pakistanis in Britain, Muslims occupy the same dominant position in immigration flows to western Europe that Latin Americans do to the United States, so they become the targets for anti-immigrant hostility in general. Coming mostly from poor, rural areas of their old countries, they also trend to end up at the bottom of the socioeconomic heap in their new ones, and poor people make easy victims.

There is also an ancestral memory in western European cultures of a time when the Muslims of the Middle East were a powerful and terrifying enemy. None of this old history has much real relevance today, but it is still there for unscrupulous politicians and attention-seeking journalists to exploit. So we have, for example, the case of Oriana Fallaci, formerly a well-known war correspondent and always a relentless self-promoter, who at the age of 72 has found a new hobby horse to ride.

Last December she published a book called *Anger and Pride* in which she denounced Europeans who sympathize with the Palestinian cause as anti-Semites "who would sell their own mothers to a harem in order to see Jews once again in the gas chambers." Her pro-Israeli stance, however, is only a pretext for an attack on Muslims: "vile creatures who urinate in baptistries" and "multiply like rats."

The book is in its fifth printing in Italy and has also become a best-seller in Spain. It is published in France this week and stands to do even better than Houellebecq's filth.

AL-JAZEERA AND ARAB DEMOCRACY

January 10, 2003

Given that well over two-thirds of the countries on the planet are now democracies, how come none of the eighteen Arabic-speaking countries is genuinely democratic? There are a number of sham democracies, such as Egypt, where the elections are always rigged, a couple of halfway democracies, such as Jordan, where the king still has the last word, and one brave experiment in tiny Qatar, but that's it.

Part of the reason for the Arab failure to achieve democracy is the curse of oil, which has led foreigners to meddle nonstop in the Arab world. Certainly, the half-century of confrontation with Israel, marked by repeated Arab defeats, also played a role. But rather than trying to answer the question, maybe we should note instead that the situation is probably about to change, because at last there is uncensored news available in Arabic.

Once information starts to flow freely, it's hard to stop democracy. Consider former East Germany, whose Communist rulers were unable to block West German television broadcasts. Seventy percent of the East German population could pick up uncensored news in their own language with only a twisted coat hanger for an antenna—and the television told them all the things their rulers didn't want them to know.

In particular, it showed them the nonviolent democratic revolutions in Asian countries in the late 1980s, especially the one where Chinese students tried to overthrow their own Communist regime in the spring of 1989. "We could do that," the East Germans said to themselves, and six months later they began their own nonviolent revolution, starting the avalanche that swept away all the Communist regimes of Europe with hardly a shot fired.

The Arab world has never had that kind of access to uncensored news and free debate—at least, not until five years ago, when al-Jazeera went on the air. It's only a single television channel, but it broadcasts by satellite twenty-four hours a day, and can be picked up by anybody with a dish almost anywhere in the Arab world.

Al-Jazeera has six hundred journalists operating in all the Arab capitals (except those where they have been expelled), plus London, Paris, New York and Washington, and it has single-handedly transformed the nature of political debate everywhere in the Arab world. It has interviewed Israeli cabinet ministers live. It has broadcast tapes sent to it by Osama bin Laden. It has allowed Saudi Arabian dissidents to criticize the monarchy. It has even given air time to critics of the government of Qatar, where it is based.

This may seem like no big thing. After all, it's only one channel, and you have to be rich enough to own a dish to get it. But that is to misunderstand the nature of the media environment. When a major outlet starts to tell the truth, even if only one Arab in ten sees it (al-Jazeera claims a regular audience of 35 million), the word gets around very fast.

Al-Jazeera grew out of a failed attempt by the British Broadcasting Corporation to create an Arabic-language TV service. It was a joint venture with a Saudi company that tried to censor a documentary hostile to the Saudi regime, so the BBC pulled out—leaving behind talented team of Arab TV journalists who had got a whiff of editorial freedom. So they went to Sheikh Hamad bin Khalifa al-Thani, the British-educated ruler of the small Gulf state of Qatar, and pitched the idea of al-Jazeera to him.

They picked the right man. Only recently come to power, he was starting to introduce democracy in his own tiny sheikhdom, and was so attracted by the idea of providing uncensored news to the whole Arab world that he agreed to bankroll the channel to the tune of $150 million over five years. It still isn't making a profit—partly because a lot of local companies, and some multinational ones too, have been instructed not to advertise on al-Jazeera—but in five years it has transformed the political environment in the Middle East.

"I think that if al-Jazeera had been there fifteen years ago, there would have been no September 11," said marketing director Ali Mohammad Kamal three months ago. If it is still in business fifteen years from now, there will be a lot fewer dictatorships and absolute monarchies in the Arab world.

By now there are several other Arabic-language TV networks broadcasting across the Arab world, and you don't need to be able to afford your own personal dish to watch them. Practically every corner café in the Arab world has a dish and a TV set, and everybody gets to watch. Not all the new channels are as fair and impartial as al-Jazeera, but they are making the idea of free political debate real for a generation

*of Arabs who have never experienced it and creating a new
kind of pan-Arab consciousness. Of course, we in the West
watch different media.*

ALL THE NEWS THAT FITS THE STEREOTYPE
August 17, 2003

Sitting in Cairo in a flat borrowed from a friend. Turn on the
TV and catch the news on BBC World: six stories in fifteen
minutes. Iraqi guerillas blow up a couple of pipelines.
European hostages released by Muslim guerillas in Mali.
Nigerian peacekeeping troops in Liberia. Rioting between
Muslim sects in Pakistan. Iceland resumes whaling. Islamist
terrorists arrested in Indonesia. End of world news.

Four out of six: that's how many of the stories were about
Muslims who do violent things. That would make sense if
two-thirds of the world's people were Muslims, and most of
them were violent. Since only one-fifth of the world's people
are Muslims, and many of them don't even spank their children, it calls for an explanation. Especially because the
international news is like this most of the time.

BBC World is not particularly bad. In fact, from
Minneapolis to Moscow to Manila it is the preferred source
of TV news for people with an interest in the world, knowledge of English and access to cable. It is serious about delivering "balanced" news to a multinational audience, and yet
it is doing an absolutely terrible job. Why?

The BBC is not American, so it's not following the White
House's agenda. It is not pandering to the paranoid belief,
quite widespread in the United States since September 11,
2001, that Islam is a more violent and dangerous religion

than, say, Christianity. Its selection of stories is genuinely driven by what it thinks will be of interest to its audience of a hundred nationalities on five continents, a great many of whom are Muslims. And yet its selection of international stories comes out not very different from Fox News.

The bias in favour of "violent Muslim" stories is less obvious on domestic news channels where the foreign items are buried under a far larger number of domestic stories, but it is the same. Wherever you are in the world (apart from the Muslim parts of the world, of course), try keeping track yourself for a few nights. You'll find that at least half the foreign stories are about violence committed by or against Muslims.

Consider the four "Muslim" stories among the six BBC World ones I listed at the top of this article. The Iraq story is legitimate: when the world's greatest power is sinking into a political and military quagmire, it is going to get coverage. But why Muslim hostage-takers in Mali rather than politically motivated kidnappers in Colombia? Why sectarian clashes between Muslims in Pakistan rather than intercaste violence among Hindus in India?

The story of suspected terrorists arrested for the Marriott Hotel bombing in Jakarta is of legitimate interest, but there's a lot less follow-up when suspected Basque terrorists are arrested in Spain, or when a resurgent Sendero Luminoso blows something up in Peru. The BBC is not anti-Muslim, but it is responding to a definition of international news that makes "violent Muslims" more newsworthy than violent people in other places.

It is largely a Western definition, following an agenda set mainly by the dominant US media. It is rooted in Western perspectives on the long-running Arab–Israeli conflict, and has been vastly strengthened by the Islamist terrorist attack on the United States two years ago. It is also a huge, steaming heap of horse feathers.

I'm not preaching pious nonsense about Islam being a "religion of peace": the only peaceful religions are dead religions. And I'm not denying that the Muslim world has a big historical chip on its shoulder: having run one of the most powerful and respected civilizations on the planet for the first thousand years after they burst out of Arabia and conquered large chunks of Europe, Asia and Africa, Muslims have spent the past three centuries being overrun, colonized and humiliated by the West. But the image of Muslims that the rest of the world gets through international news coverage is deeply misleading.

For the past month I have been wandering around the Middle East with eight other members of my extended family. For some, it was their first time in the region; others of us have lived here or visited often enough to be able to lead everybody astray. And we gave less thought to our personal safety—and much less to petty theft—than we would have done on a comparable trip across America, or even through Europe.

I won't go on about how kind and friendly most of the people we met were, because most people are like that everywhere. I would point out that every single person I discussed current events with was against the American invasion in Iraq but I nevertheless encountered no personal hostility although I am easily mistaken for an American. (Would an Arab doing a similar trip around America have the same experience?)

If Iraq gets completely out of hand, the patience and tolerance that still prevail at street level in the Muslim Middle East will be severely eroded, and even Asian

Muslim countries may end up taking sides against the US and Britain. But for the moment, Samuel Huntington's nightmare vision of a coming "clash of civilizations" is still a long way off, and the most striking thing is the sheer ordinariness of daily life in the Muslim world. Don't be misled by television.

But if neither your audience nor your commentators know any history, then you can lie to them to your heart's content, even in countries with free media.

WHAT'S WRONG WITH THE ARAB WORLD?
July 19, 2004

It was just a random statistic, but a telling one: only three hundred books were translated into Arabic last year. That is about one foreign title per million Arabs. For comparison's sake, Greece translated fifteen hundred foreign-language books, or about one hundred and fifty titles per million Greeks. Why is the Arab world so far behind, not only in this but in practically all the arts and sciences?

The first-order answer is poverty and lack of education: almost half of Arabic-speaking women are illiterate. But the Arab world used to be the most literate part of the planet: what went wrong? Tyranny and economic failure, obviously. But why is tyranny such a problem in the Arab world? That brings us to the nub of the matter.

In a speech in November 2003, US President George W. Bush revisited his familiar refrain about how the West now had to remake the Arab world in its own image in order to stop the terrorism: "Sixty years of Western nations excusing and accommodating the lack of freedom in the Middle East did nothing to make us safe . . . because in the long run, stability cannot be purchased at the expense of liberty"—as if the Arab world had wilfully chosen to be ruled by these corrupt and incompetent tyrannies.

But the West didn't just "excuse and accommodate" these regimes. It created them, in order to protect its own interests—and it spent the latter half of the twentieth century keeping them in power for the same reason.

It was Britain that carved the kingdom of Jordan out of the old Ottoman province of Syria after the First World War and put the Hashemite ruling family on the throne that it still occupies. France similarly carved Lebanon out of Syria in order to create a loyal Christian-majority state that controlled most of the Syrian coastline—and when time and a higher Muslim birth rate eventually led to a revolt against the Maronite Christian stranglehold on power in Lebanon in 1958, US troops were sent in to restore it. The Lebanese civil war of 1975–90, tangled though it was, was basically a continuation of that struggle.

Britain also imposed a Hashemite monarchy on Iraq after 1918, and it deliberately perpetuated the political monopoly of the Sunni minority that it had inherited from Turkish rule. As Gertrude Bell, an archaeologist and political adviser in the British administration in Baghdad, put it: "I don't for a moment doubt that the final authority must be in the hands of the Sunnis, in spite of their numerical inferiority, otherwise you'll have a mujtahid-run, theocratic state, which is the very devil." When the Iraqi monarchy was finally overthrown in 1958 and the Baath Party won the struggle that followed, the CIA gave the Iraqi Baathists the names of all the senior members of the Iraqi Communist Party (then the main political vehicle of the Shias) so they could be liquidated.

It was Britain that turned the traditional sheikhdoms in the Gulf into separate little sovereign states and absolute monarchies, carving Kuwait out of Iraq in the process. (Saudi Arabia, however, was a joint Anglo–US project.) The British Foreign Office welcomed the Egyptian generals' overthrow of King Farouk and the destruction of the country's old nationalist political parties, failing to foresee that Gamal Abdul Nasser would eventually take over the Suez Canal. When he did, the British conspired with France and Israel to attack Egypt in a failed attempt to overthrow him.

Once Nasser died and was succeeded by generals more willing to play along with the West—Anwar Sadat and now Hosni Mubarak—Egypt became Washington's favourite Arab state: to help these thinly disguised dictators hang on to power, Egypt has ranked among the top three recipients of US foreign aid almost every year for the past quarter-century. And so it goes.

Britain welcomed the coup by Colonel Gadafy in Libya in 1969, mistakenly seeing him as a malleable young man who could serve the West's purposes. The United States and France both supported the old dictator Bourbuiga in Tunisia, and they still back his successor Ben Ali today.

They always backed the Moroccan monarchy no matter how repressive it became, and they both gave unquestioning support to the Algerian generals who cancelled the elections of 1991. Nor did they ever waver in their support through the savage insurgency unleashed by the suppression of the elections that killed an estimated one hundred and twenty thousand Algerians over the next ten years.

Excuse and accommodate? The West *created* the modern Middle East, from its rotten regimes down to its ridiculous borders, and it did so with contemptuous disregard for the wishes of the local people. It is indeed a problem that most Arab governments are corrupt autocracies that breed hatred and despair in their own people, which then fuels terrorism against the West, but it was the West that created the problem—and invading Iraq won't solve it.

If the US really wants to foster Arab democracy, it might try making all that aid to Egypt conditional on prompt democratic reforms. But I wouldn't hold my breath.

CHAPTER FIVE

MEANWHILE, IN ANOTHER PART OF THE FOREST . . .

The "terrorist threat" is just a very big tempest in a teapot, and if nothing else were at stake we could just wait for it to blow over. The problem is that it is a huge distraction from the genuinely urgent agenda on global climate change — and if the US government is exploiting the panic about terrorism to pursue traditional great-power goals, as many other governments are coming to suspect, then the international cooperation that is needed to deal with global warming may be in very short supply.

To make matters worse, the Bush administration has been actively trying to sabotage the one existing international *agreement that addresses the issue of climate change, the Kyoto Accord. Despair is always a temptation — but people can also get things right.*

THE END OF "THE SMOKE"
November 30, 2002

This week is the fiftieth anniversary of the last of London's great fogs, a pea-souper that killed more than four thousand people. Visibility dropped to about half a metre and some died just by falling into the Thames and drowning, but most died of lung problems. For five days, the concentration of sulphur in the air exceeded 1,600 parts per billion. Theatres and cinemas closed because audiences could not see the stage, and undertakers ran out of coffins.

Everybody knew the cause of London's fogs. Practically every house and business was heated by coal fires, and almost all electricity was generated by coal-fired power stations. Whenever cold, still air settled on the city in wintertime, the smoke from all those fires was trapped, and the result was a "London fog."

In 1952, the problem was made worse by the fact that Britain, impoverished by the Second World War, was exporting its best coal and burning sulphur-laden "dirty" coal at home; however, the fogs went back a long time. London was already called "The Smoke" two centuries ago, even before it passed the million mark and became the world's biggest city. Sherlock Holmes's London was famous for its pea-soup fogs, and it went on getting worse.

In that fatal December fifty years ago, London had 8 million people—and around 3 million open coal fires.

It was an illustration of what environmentalists call the "frog in the pot" phenomenon. Drop a frog into a pot of boiling water, and he will promptly hop out again. Put him into cold water and bring it to the boil slowly, and he'll sit there until he dies. Londoners had grown used to the fogs, and didn't realize they were killing people because the victims weren't clutching their throats and falling over in the streets. Most of those who died were very young, very old, or people with serious respiratory problems, and they mostly died in bed. So nobody did anything about it.

That's how most environmental problems work: they creep up on you gradually, and rarely give you a clear wake-up call. Add short-term self-interest, which makes many people resist changes no matter how harmful the established way is, and you can see why most environmentalists live on the ragged edge of despair.

"The human brain evidently evolved to commit itself emotionally only to a small piece of geography, a limited band of kinsmen, and two or three generations into the future," wrote Edward O. Wilson in his latest book *The Future of Life*. "To look neither far ahead nor far afield is elemental in a Darwinian sense. . . . For hundreds of millennia those who worked for short-term gain within a small circle of relatives and friends lived longer and left more offspring—even when their collective striving caused their chiefdoms and empires to crumble around them." Hard-wired short-sightedness: it's enough to make you cut your throat.

But hang on a minute. They *did* do something about the killer fogs: 1952 was the last one. The British government invented an entirely fictitious flu epidemic in the winter of

1952–53 to account for the surge in deaths, but the disaster was just too big to hide. In 1956 Parliament passed the *Clean Air Act*, the world's first serious attempt to control air pollution. From that date, only smokeless coal (charcoal, basically) could be burned in Britain's big cities—and by the mid-sixties, London fogs were a thing of the past.

Today's London has twice as many hours of sunshine per year as it did in 1952, and coal fires are practically extinct. London houses today are centrally heated by gas or electricity and air pollution comes mainly from cars: Britain has gone from 4 million vehicles registered in 1952 to 28 million today. We will never run out of problems—but that doesn't mean that we should despair.

Human beings do learn from other people's experience in other places and times. We can even respond to purely statistical evidence of danger. Nobody has ever seen the "ozone hole," for example, but for the past fifteen years the whole world has been trying to close it.

The hole went on growing until 2000, partly because the 1987 Montreal Protocol only required developing countries to halve their use of CFCs by 2005 (with a targeted 85 percent cut by 2007), but mainly because of the huge overhang of old refrigerators and air-conditioners in the developed world. "We knew they were out there and we knew they were leaking," says Dr. Paul Fraser, chief atmospheric research scientist with Australia's Commonwealth Scientific and Industrial Research Organization. But Fraser now predicts that the ozone hole will start shrinking in 2005. With luck, it will have closed entirely by 2050.

"I think this shows global protocols work," said Fraser—and he is quite right. From the moratorium on cod-fishing (almost ten years old in Newfoundland, and probably soon to extend to the whole European Union) to the Kyoto treaty on climate change, decisions tend to get made late, after the problem is already huge, because human beings focus on the nearby and the short-term. But they do get made, in the end.

Enough people understand the need for a template for future global cooperation on environmental issues that even an inadequate document like the Kyoto treaty has already been ratified by ninety countries. We are not fully rational all the time, but we are not frogs either.

WHAT THEY DON'T MENTION ABOUT CLIMATE CHANGE
August 14, 2003

On several days last week, it was hotter in London than in Cairo. France has just declared a national emergency because of the extreme heat. But the winemakers of Germany are ecstatic about this year's vintage, and Asian manufacturers of compact air-conditioning systems are having a boom year for European sales.

That's how most people see climate change: a gradual warming-up that will hurt some people and benefit others. So no rush, no panic, and don't take any measures that might hurt economic growth.

But anyone who has been paying attention to the evidence coming out of the Greenland ice cores for the past twenty years should know that the real threat is not gradual warming. It is that the warming will trigger an abrupt and rapid cooling of the global climate, with catastrophic consequences for existing human populations. And the Europeans would be hit first and worst, for the mechanism that would cause this shift is the disappearance of the Gulf Stream.

People talk about the "last ice age" as if it were over, but it's not. The current cycle of global glaciation began about three million years ago, when the land that is now Panama rose above sea level, closing the old ocean channel between North and South America and forcing a major reorganization of ocean currents. Since then, ice sheets have covered about 30 percent of the land surface of the planet most of the time, although this has been regularly interrupted by major melt-offs called "interglacials" when the ice coverage drops to about 10 percent.

During the past million years these warm, wet episodes have come along approximately every one hundred thousand years. The present interglacial began about fifteen thousand years ago, and nobody knows for sure how long it will last. We do know, however, that the previous interglacial began about 130,000 BC and lasted for thirteen thousand years—so we could already be in overtime on this one.

The good news is that we don't automatically slide back into maximum glaciation. What happened in 113,000 BC was that the global climate flipped into a cool, dry, windy phase that was much less pleasant than our current balmy conditions: the average temperature was at least 5 degrees C lower than the present, and there were massive droughts all over the place. It took a further push—probably massive volcanic eruptions in Indonesia around 70,000 BC—to start the ice sheets growing again.

The bad news is that even the "cool, dry, windy" phase of the global climate would wreck human civilization. The whole enterprise of civilization that has allowed the human population to grow from perhaps 10 million to over 6,000 million has occurred within the warm, wet climatic bubble of the past ten thousand years. At least half the lands that now support agriculture would revert to tundra or semi-desert if we flipped back to the cool, dry and windy climate, and billions would die in the chaos of war and starvation that would follow.

Now for the worse news. When the flip happens, it isn't gradual at all. The Greenland ice cores, a quarter-million-year record of annual snowfall that also tells us about average temperature, precipitation and even wind speed, contain an alarming message. When the climate mode shifts, global temperatures crash in ten years or less—and stay down for centuries or millennia. And the very worst news is that the sudden flip into cool-and-dry is caused by gradual global *warming*.

The key to the whole cycle seems to be the Gulf Stream, which normally delivers huge amounts of warmth to the northern North Atlantic and western Europe (which would otherwise have the climate of Labrador). But ocean currents are basically conveyor belts for moving salt around the world's oceans. The salty, warm water of the Gulf Stream, made even more saline by evaporation on its long journey north, normally cools, becomes denser and sinks to the bottom when it reaches the Greenland–Iceland–Norway gap. There it dumps its load of excess salt and begins flowing back south underneath the northbound surface current—but if it fails to sink, then the whole conveyor belt shuts down.

What would stop the salty water from sinking? Dilution by too much fresh water on the surface, coming either from increased rainfall over the North Atlantic or from glacial melting and sudden outflows of fresh water from the Greenland fjords, would do the trick. What might cause

these events? A rise in temperature in the polar regions—
and while average global temperature has only risen less
than one degree in the past century, the rise in the Arctic
region has been several times greater.

The evidence in the Greenland ice cores is absolutely
clear: the abrupt, high-speed flips in global climate known
as Dansgaard-Oeschger events have happened dozens of
times. Maybe if we have a couple of more centuries of warm-
and-wet conditions, we will learn enough about the fine
detail of global climate to postpone the next flip indefinitely.
But if it goes over the edge now, it's a calamity for everybody.

The Europeans, whose agriculture could no longer feed
even a tenth of their current population, would be hit hardest of all, though nobody would get away with less than a
50 percent loss. So why didn't this prospect get more media
attention during the recent unprecedented heat wave in
Europe? Maybe all the science journalists were on vacation.

*Amid all the doom and gloom about what's happening to the
natural world, it's important to note that some trends in the
human world are actually quite hopeful. It would be a good
idea, for example, if people used less fossil fuel.*

A BLESSING IN DISGUISE
August 22, 2004

Sometime this week or next, oil is likely to reach fifty dollars
a barrel for the first time ever. The price is up by a third
since the end of June, and US prices have set record peaks
in all but one of the past fifteen trading sessions. This is a
Good Thing.

This isn't an "oil shock" like 1980, when the price of oil spiked at the equivalent in today's money of eighty dollars a barrel after the Iranian revolution and then slid back down after a year or so. It is a "demand shock," which is a much more enduring change. Thanks mainly to the rapid economic growth of China and India, there is now a market for every barrel of oil that the producers can pump.

Ever since 2000, the Organization of Petroleum-Exporting Countries has tried to keep the price of oil in the twenty-two to twenty-eight-dollar range, cutting production if it fell below that band and increasing output if it climbed above it, but the price of oil may never actually fall back that far again. That is a Good Thing, because global warming is coming on faster and harder than even the pessimists feared.

In a system as complex as climate, all sorts of things change in unpredictable ways when you raise the total amount of heat in the system, and the worst changes are those that set up feedback mechanisms. Some of the changes we are observing now are very worrisome.

It was assumed, for example, that the rise in global temperature would be partly cancelled out by a higher rate of evaporation from the oceans that produced more cloud cover. Instead, the higher temperatures seem to be burning the clouds off. And recent research suggests that the higher level of carbon dioxide in the atmosphere is stimulating the bacteria that live in peat bogs and greatly increasing the speed with which they dissolve the peat. The peat is almost pure carbon, and when it dissolves it turns into — carbon dioxide.

If that turns out to be a runaway feedback loop, we are in serious trouble, because the peat bogs of the northern hemisphere contain the equivalent of seventy years' worth of

global industrial emissions of carbon dioxide. New calculations suggest that we may be facing a global temperature rise
over the next century, not of 5.8 degrees C, which would be
bad enough, but of as much as 10 to 12 degrees C.

That would be calamitous, but key players in the world of
politics and most of the business world (apart from the insurance industry) remain in denial. The Kyoto Accord is a good
template for the global regulation of greenhouse gases, but
the actual cuts in carbon dioxide production that it envis-
ages do not begin to address the problem. The only short-
term hope of slowing the rise in temperature is a steep drop
in the use of oil and gas—and the only thing that is going to
make that happen is a steep rise in price.

It has happened before. Alternative energy sources take a
long time to build, but energy conservation works relatively
quickly: the big oil-price rises of the 1970s caused the industrialized countries to bring in energy conservation measures
that cut global oil consumption drastically. Twenty-five
years of profligacy in energy use since then means that there
is once again huge scope for rapid gains from conservation.
It will only happen, however, if the oil price goes up and
stays up.

*At the time of writing (June 2005) the oil price was sixty-one
dollars per barrel. Good. But you did notice that by 2004
there was a new twist to the global-warming-followed-by-
global-cooling scenario: the possibility that temperatures
could rise so fast that we would break out of the "ice age"
pattern entirely and tumble into runaway global warming.
We still don't fully understand the climate system, but we are
putting extraordinary stresses on it, and it is clearly starting to
shift under the pressure. We wouldn't like either of the extreme*

outcomes that now seem possible—"cool, dry, windy" Earth or Hothouse Earth—and we can't really afford to wait until we understand it fully before we cut back on greenhouse gas emissions. That might well be too late.

KYOTO COMES INTO EFFECT
February 6, 2005

That sound you don't hear in the street outside is the crowds who aren't cheering to celebrate the entry into effect of the Kyoto Protocol on February 16. Thirteen years after the Climate Change Convention was agreed upon at the Earth Summit in 1992, and eight years after each country's targets for cuts in greenhouse-gas emissions were defined in a marathon haggling session at Kyoto, they are finally starting to do something about global warming. No wonder the euphoria has worn off a bit.

Despite the best efforts of the Bush administration to sabotage the treaty entirely by persuading other countries not to ratify, they almost all did. Only four of the original thirty-four developed countries at the talks—the US, its faithful sidekick Australia, and Monaco and Liechtenstein— have refused to take part. Russia's assent was vital, however, since its own emissions are second only to those of the United States.

Why did Russian President Vladimir Putin decide to ratify the Kyoto Protocol on climate change only six months after his top adviser, Andrei Illarionov, called it a "death treaty"? One reason is that the European Union offered him visa-free travel between Russia and the twenty-five-country bloc plus EU support for Russia's membership in the World Trade Organization. The other reason is that Russians aren't stupid.

Only a few months ago, Russia and the EU looked light-years apart on global warming. Andrei Illarionov, speaking in St. Petersburg in April, outdid even the Bush administration, warning that the restraints put on carbon dioxide emissions by the Kyoto Accord would stifle the Russian economy like "an international gulag or Auschwitz."

Illarionov seemed to be in a different world from senior EU officials such as Sir David King, the British government's chief scientific adviser, who said in July, "We are moving from a warm period into the first hot period that man has ever experienced since he walked on the planet." Carbon dioxide concentrations in the atmosphere over the past several million years have varied from 200 parts per million (ppm) at the depth of the ice ages to 270 ppm during the warming periods between them; but we have now reached 379 ppm—and that figure is going up by 2 ppm per year.

If the current trend continues, Professor King predicted, by the end of this century the earth will be entirely ice-free for the first time since 55 million years ago, when "Antarctica was the best place for mammals to live, and the rest of the world would not sustain human life." The positions of Russia and the EU seemed utterly irreconcilable—and then, last October, Russia suddenly ratified Kyoto.

The Bush administration was deceiving itself if it thought that Russia was really opposed to Kyoto. Russian scientists understand the urgent need to slow climate change as well as their counterparts elsewhere, and Russia has closed down so many old high-emission industrial plants since 1990 that it will have less difficulty in meeting the Kyoto limits than almost any other country. Traders on the new London carbon exchange, where the price of CO_2 jumped 20 percent to over eleven dollars per tonne in October on news of Moscow's ratification, estimate that Russia will earn around $10 billion a year by selling the unused part of its carbon quota to countries that cannot meet their own quotas.

The only reason that Moscow delayed ratification was that the Bush administration had given it what amounted to a veto on the treaty. It used that to extort major concessions from the European Union on various other issues, and then it signed. The treaty is now in effect. What difference will it make?

The Kyoto limits are certainly not going to stop global warming in the short term. All the greenhouse gases that will cause the next thirty years of damage have already left the chimneys and the tailpipes and are moving up through the atmosphere.

That's worrisome, because the climate conference at the United Kingdom Meteorological Office in Exeter heard last week that the West Antarctic Ice Shelf, previously seen as stable, is probably starting to melt, which would ultimately raise sea levels worldwide by three metres. And a study by the Met Office's Hadley Centre for Climate Prediction (just published in *Nature*), showed that the impact of manmade greenhouse gases on climate may be twice as great as we previously thought.

It was the Met Office's study that really rattled everybody. It concluded that if manmade greenhouse gas emissions just doubled the amount of carbon dioxide in the atmosphere from the 260 ppm of the preindustrial era to 520 ppm—and we've covered more than a third of that distance already—the resulting global temperature rise could go beyond anything the planet has experienced since the time of the dinosaurs. The upper limit of likely outcomes is not 6 degrees C hotter, as previously thought; it's 11 degrees C.

"If we go back to the Cretaceous, which is a hundred million years ago," Professor Bob Spicer of the Open University told the *Independent*, "the best estimate of the global mean temperature was about 6 degrees C higher than present. So 11 degrees C is quite substantial, and if this is right we would be going into a realm that we really don't have much evidence for even in the rocks."

Measured against such potentially catastrophic consequences, the modest controls on greenhouse emissions ordained by the Kyoto Protocol—a few percentage points less than the 1990 level, for most countries—seem like a total waste of time. The cuts are shallow and will not even be enforced until 2008 to 2012. The world's leading producer of greenhouse gases, the United States, has opted out. And developing countries, including the rapidly industrializing Asian giants China and India, don't even have to stop increasing their emissions.

And yet it is worthwhile. It is the first legally binding international treaty on the environment, with a system of auditing greenhouse-gas emissions for each country and financial penalties for those that do not meet their targets. Getting countries to surrender their national sovereignty over domestic industrial policy in this way was so unprecedented—but so vital to dealing with a global problem like climate change—that the equally painful question of deeper cuts was left until the next round. In an ideal world it would all have been done at once, but governments only have so much political capital to spend.

Now, however, the principle is established, and the next round of talks, to set the post-2012 targets and rules, will have to agree on much deeper cuts in emissions than this time. Moreover, the developing countries, which were exempted from the first-round controls because the existing problem was caused almost entirely by the old industrialized countries, will have to accept emission control targets too. It's cumbersome, because human politics is inherently cumbersome, but it is heading in the right direction.

If the measures we take today can stop global warming by 2050, say, with a temperature rise of only two degrees, global warming will still be a very big problem, but it probably won't be an utter catastrophe. That is what Kyoto is about, so get out there and start cheering.*

At the Buenos Aires meeting of February 2005, which was meant to discuss the agenda for the 2008 conference that will negotiate new, lower limits on emissions for the industrial countries and finally impose emission limits on the developing countries, the United States delegation did everything possible to block the process, and no agenda proposals were actually considered. But at least the other countries managed to preserve the principle that there will be an agenda, and that it will be discussed beforehand.

---

* I have amalgamated two articles, one of which appeared on Russia's ratification of the treaty on October 2004 and the other when the Kyoto treaty entered into effect in January 2005, to produce this single longer piece.

CHAPTER SIX

AXIS OF EVIL: THE SUBJECT HAS CHANGED
JANUARY–DECEMBER 2002

Hindsight can fool you: most of us have forgotten that we really thought for a little while that the military phase of the "war on terror" had ended with the conquest of Afghanistan. After all, there was no other military target in a war against terrorism because no other government was actively giving shelter and support to the al-Qaeda network. There would be a long second phase to the struggle, perhaps lasting for many years, but it would be mainly intelligence-gathering and police operations, backed up by diplomatic pressures and maybe the occasional special forces action.

Then President Bush announced in his State of the Union

message on January 29, 2002, *that he had discovered the "axis of evil." This was when the Bush administration switched from a war against terrorism to a quite different and deeply worrisome agenda, and by now it's clear that this was when the neoconservatives took control of American strategy. At the time, however, it came as a complete surprise.*

I was sitting in a CBC *studio, all wired up to comment on Bush's speech as soon as he had finished. My mind was racing to make sense of this ugly development when Bush finished speaking. Luckily, I was let off the hook. Bush had neglected to thank Canada for sending troops to Afghanistan in his speech, although he thanked the Mexicans, the Tongans and all sorts of other people who hadn't sent troops, so in the best Canadian fashion we spent a quarter-hour fretting about that instead.*

JUST WHEN YOU THOUGHT IT WAS SAFE . . .
January 30, 2002

It's gone to his head, I'm afraid. If we're lucky, George W. Bush will turn out to be just another cynical politician who is glad to be able to change the subject in the midst of a recession, but it really sounds as if he likes being a war leader. To a politician, an 80 percent approval rating is a dangerously addictive drug.

President Bush's State of the Union speech on January 29 pushed all the right buttons in an American population that is still feeling frightened and beleaguered, but it also sounded downright naive. Here is a man with practically no real military experience, and little more in dealing with the wiles of the professional military, who takes intelligence briefings at face value. He even believes in an "axis of evil."

Let's start with that remarkable notion: that Iran, Iraq and North Korea—total population 125 million, average annual per capita income under five thousand dollars—are linked in a terrorist conspiracy to bring the world to its knees.

All of these countries have sponsored terrorist acts in the past, but nothing whatever has changed in their behaviour or policies since last August, when President Bush was touting them not as terrorist menaces but as "rogue states" whose alleged nuclear missile ambitions justified his antiballistic missile defence project. And nothing has been found in the al-Qaeda camps in Afghanistan that links these countries in any way with bin Laden or the September attacks on the United States.

The last known terrorist attack by North Korea was more than a decade ago, when agents of the late Kim Il-Sung blew up a plane full of South Korean officials. Under his son, Kim Jong-il, North Korea remains a nasty, repressive state, but its people are starving, the economy is wrecked and the regime has been trying for years to bargain away the nuclear weapons program it inherited from Kim Il-Sung (which is a very long way from completion) in return for large-scale economic aid.

Iran's Islamic regime loyally supports anti-Israeli guerrilla groups, notably Lebanon-based Hizbollah (which last year forced Israel to pull out of southern Lebanon after a twenty-two-year occupation). However, the last time Iran was rumoured to be involved in international terrorism outside the Middle East (the "terrorism of global reach" that is the avowed target of Bush's war) was the bombing of Pan Am flight 103 over Lockerbie, Scotland, in 1988—and that allegation was not taken seriously last year by the international court that tried the Libyan agents accused of placing the actual bomb.

Iraq will remain a serious danger to its neighbours so long as Saddam Hussein is in power. Ask the Iranians, who lost hundreds of thousands of soldiers repelling Saddam's forces in the Iran–Iraq war of 1980–88. But there is no evidence that Iraq has sponsored any international terrorist attacks in recent years.

As for Saddam's once-ambitious nuclear weapons program, it was comprehensively dismantled by United Nations inspectors after the 1990–91 Gulf War. He has probably restarted it since UN inspectors were withdrawn three years ago, but he now operates under a strict international embargo: it would take many years for the program to even get back to where it was in 1990.

The notion of an axis of evil, which evokes the great threat posed by the Axis powers in the Second World War, is just silly. The original Axis alliance consisted of three great powers linked by treaty, ideology and purpose. The current "axis" consists of three impoverished, middle-sized, Third-World countries that have almost nothing in common. Iraq is an Arab country run by a dictator whose religious roots are Sunni Muslim, for what it's worth, but whose regime has always been firmly secular. Iran is a non-Arab country whose people are mostly Shia Muslims who hate and fear Saddam's Iraq—and who may soon overthrow the theocracy that continually thwarts their elected government in favour of a fully democratic system. North Korea is a decrepit Stalinist dictatorship at the other end of Asia whose state religion, so to speak, is atheism.

Not only are these three countries not allies, they barely speak to each other. And there has been absolutely no development, no new information that suggests they are one whit more dangerous now, even to their immediate neighbours, than they were a year ago. So what is this all about?

"If you believe the doctors, nothing is wholesome. If you believe the theologians, nothing is holy. If you believe the generals, nothing is safe." Lord Salisbury, three times British prime minister in the late-nineteenth century, left this warning against "experts" to his colleagues in the political trade, but it is a lesson George W. Bush has yet to learn. Bush has fallen into the hands of intelligence agencies that see conspiracies everywhere because that is their "professional deformation," as the French say.

Bush is a willing victim because it serves his purposes to be fighting a war rather than a recession. And it will probably remain a phony war unless some of the tens of thousands of people who trained in the al-Qaeda camps (the vast majority of whom remain at large) succeed in carrying out another major terrorist attack against the United States.

I really didn't get it for a while—which makes me inclined to be forgiving to all the other journalists who didn't get it either. It was easier and more comforting to believe that Mr. Bush was running a bluff, or making a mistake, than to believe that the United States was setting out to overthrow the international rule of law and the entire multilateral system in favour of some resurrected version of Pax Americana. By the spring, however, the evidence that the war on terror concealed a whole new strategy was becoming hard to dismiss.

BORDERING ON OBSESSION
May 14, 2002

One day your sister, who lives in a very safe neighbourhood and doesn't get out much, is burgled. Afterwards she keeps calling you up and she talks of nothing else. What upsets her even more than her actual loss is the fact that her home has been violated; so you install an alarm system, put bars on the windows and listen patiently. She'll get over it in a while.

Only, months pass and she doesn't. She wakes at every sound, she becomes a nuisance to the police with her constant false alarms and she fantasizes about funny-looking people lurking in the neighbourhood. All her other interests fade away and now the world's single real problem is burglars. You try to put up with it, but after eight months you snap. It's time for either frank talk or psychiatric counselling.

Talk is cheaper, so let's start with that. Over three thousand Americans died horribly in the terrorist attacks eight months ago. The US responded by destroying the headquarters of al-Qaeda, the organization responsible for the attacks and the Taliban government of Afghanistan that sheltered it, which made perfectly good sense.

President George W. Bush did talk about launching a "war on terror," which would have been worrying if he really meant it. Terrorism is not a country or an ideology. It's a technique that has been used by a wide variety of ethnic, ideological and religious groups around the world (including many that the US has supported in the past) against an equally wide variety of enemies.

If Bush really intended to take all the world's terrorists on, then the US was entering an unwinnable struggle of enormous dimensions—but he clearly didn't mean that. In his speech to Congress in late September, he actually declared war against "terrorism of global reach," that is, foreign terrorists with the will and the ability to reach out and hurt Americans.

We only know of one such group, al-Qaeda, with probably no more than five or ten thousand active members, so the task rapidly dwindled to a manageable size. Destroying or at least crippling al-Qaeda was an attainable goal, and all of America's friends and allies willingly signed up for it.

But eight months later, even with al-Qaeda's main base smashed and its surviving leaders on the run, the US government is still a gibbering mess of insecurities, obsessions, and paranoid delusions about the "terrorist threat." Here is a partial list from just one day in mid-May.

On May 13, former US president Jimmy Carter was in Cuba touring the Centre for Genetic Engineering and Biotechnology. A harmless visit to a respected research facility—but Carter spent the day fighting off an accusation by John Bolton, undersecretary of state for arms control and international security, that Cuba is helping terrorist groups to buy or develop biological weapons.

It was mere propaganda, designed to perpetuate Cuba's isolation, and eventually Secretary of State Colin Powell was forced to recant: "We didn't say [Cuba] actually had some weapons, but it has the capacity and capability to conduct such research." So what? So do thousands of other biotechnology labs in universities and industrial facilities around the world. The point is that nowadays, the lying allegations are always about terrorist links.

On the same day, US Attorney-General John Ashcroft was in Canada to discuss the "G8 Counter-Terrorism Action Plan." When uppity Canadian journalists suggested that this was all just to reassure nervous Americans, Ashcroft replied that the September attacks had been aimed at "the entire civilized world. . . . It is not how other countries can serve the United States. The question is how we . . . can serve each other in a war against those who would destroy the things in which we believe, namely, freedom, human dignity, liberty and opportunity."

Nonsense. Al-Qaeda's September attacks were aimed at the United States because the militants who planned them hate America's policies, and even its presence, in the Arab world where they come from. They were wicked men, but they didn't spend one second considering whether they should attack Sweden, Japan, Brazil or anywhere else in the "civilized world."

As for "freedom, human dignity, liberty and opportunity," the al-Qaeda terrorists couldn't care less. They are simply not interested in America's domestic arrangements, so long as it goes away and leaves them free to reshape the Middle East in their own warped image. It won't, so it's going to have to fight them, but this is really about regional politics, not high ideology (as the US pretends) or religion (as al-Qaeda pretends).

Also on May 13, in New York City, Democratic Senator Charles Schumer was issuing hysterical warnings about terrorists smuggling nuclear weapons into the United States: "We probably have a year or two before any terrorist gets hold of such a device and smuggles it in." Who told him that? The risk of some terrorist getting control of a nuclear weapon and smuggling it into a US port has existed ever since the '60s, but it has always been tiny—and it hasn't changed a bit in all that time.

Taken a bit at a time, none of this foolishness is very harmful. Cumulatively, however, the obsession with terrorism is distorting American policies, distracting the US government from its real priorities, and driving everybody else crazy. It's time to get over it.

Pathetic, isn't it? By the time I wrote that piece, the United States had been publicly saying that it would invade Iraq for almost four months. Mr. Bush had already popped the question to Britain's Prime Minister Tony Blair during Blair's visit to the Crawford Ranch in Texas six weeks before, and Blair had secretly agreed to commit British troops to the invasion, too. The US administration had done practically everything short of putting up a neon sign saying WE WILL INVADE IRAQ to make its intentions clear, and I still clung to the belief that it was just an emotional overreaction to the shock of 9/11. I simply couldn't make myself believe in the alternative, because it required too radical a re-think of what the United States was actually up to.

At least I noticed that Afghanistan was going wrong.

TICKET OUT OF AFGHANISTAN
June 14, 2002

"This is not democracy. This is a rubber stamp," said Sima Samar, minister for women's affairs in the interim Afghan government. "Everything here has already been decided by those with the power. This *jirga* includes all the warlords. None of them is left out," she continued, looking around the enormous tent. It had been erected in the grounds of the wrecked Kabul Polytechnic to house the two thousand delegates to the *loya jirga*, the grand council called to set up a government until elections are held in late 2003.

She was not exaggerating. There they were in the first and second rows: a roll-call of the thugs and murderers who have ruined Afghanistan. They were there because the United States, at the moment the real ruler of Afghanistan, wanted them to be there. Washington wants a cheap one-way ticket out of Afghanistan, and these warlords are it.

When the Taliban regime was overthrown late last year by an alliance of American air power and these same warlords, the US had a choice: to stay and help build a new Afghanistan, or just to hand over to its warlord allies and get out fast. The British and Russians will both tell you that foreign armies who stay too long in Afghanistan always end up regretting it. Besides, the Bush administration doesn't do "nation-building," so the decision was a no-brainer.

Since President Bush has little else to show for his Afghan expedition—no Osama bin Laden dead or alive, not even Mullah Omar in chains—he needs to show the American public that something positive has been accomplished, so "democracy" has to come to Afghanistan. But not real democracy, because that would take years of effort and billions of dollars of development funds, and even then it might not work. Just a show of democracy, and then out within a year or two.

That is why ISAF, the International Security Assistance Force to which nineteen nations have contributed troops, has never expanded outside Kabul. Nobody wanted to take on the big job of policing the rest of the country even long enough to ensure that the *loya jirga* could be chosen freely. What happened instead was documented in a recent report from Human Rights Watch that was based on a survey of the delegate selection process in six southern provinces. Intimidation was rife, beatings and false arrests were frequent, and the province usually wound up being represented by the friendly neighbourhood warlord and his men.

Meanwhile, the highway banditry and illegal road tolls that were suppressed in Taliban times are reappearing everywhere. The poppy crop that the Taliban successfully banned (Afghanistan used to supply 75 percent of the world's opium) has been replanted, and interim president Hamid Karzai's government is too weak to enforce the law against poppy farmers with warlord backing. Humanitarian aid must now be funnelled through the hands of the local mafiosi in half the provinces of Afghanistan.

Afghanistan was not better off under the Taliban, but it was not a whole lot worse off. To which Americans might reply: too bad, but we didn't really go there to improve life for you Afghans. If that happens, we're pleased, but we went there to root out a terrorist group that inflicted a great hurt on the United States, and was given shelter by the Taliban regime. We destroyed it, and now it's up to you Afghans to pick up the pieces if you can. 'Bye.

Fair enough, if this were the first contact between the US and Afghanistan, and if the Afghans were really an incorrigibly tribal people who have spent their entire history in a low-grade civil war. However, neither of those things is true.

Afghan leaders have been trying to modernize their country for almost a century now, and after left-wing officers overthrew the monarchy in 1973, the new, pro-Soviet regime put the project into high gear. Twenty years ago, there was barely a head scarf to be seen in Kabul, let alone a burqa. The grounds of Kabul Polytechnic, now thronged with the bearded retinues of tribal warlords, were filled with young Afghan women in jeans studying for engineering degrees.

The conservative tribal areas hated modernization, but what turned it into a twenty-two-year civil war was former US National Security Adviser Zbigniew Brzezinski's insight that if he secretly armed the tribes against Kabul, he could sucker the Soviet Union into coming to the Afghan government's rescue. The Russians duly "invaded" at the request of beleaguered Afghan officers in 1979, the US ran even more arms in to the tribes and Brzezinski got what he wanted: "Russia's Vietnam."

Afghanistan's modern infrastructure was destroyed and millions of Afghans were killed or driven into exile, but after ten years the Russians pulled out. Brzezinski boasts that it helped to bring down the Soviet Union, which is rather like the butterfly in Kipling's *Just So Stories* that stamped — and felt responsible because King Solomon's temple then collapsed.

Having helped to wreck Afghanistan, Washington then walked away, abandoning it to a long civil war and the tender mercies of Pakistan's Inter-Service Intelligence (which eventually pacified it, more or less, by creating the Taliban). Now the US is walking away again, behind a flimsy façade of "democratization." But given the dismal record of past interventions, British, Russian, American and Pakistani, maybe this is the least bad outcome to a miserable episode in Afghan history.

By May I had begun writing articles that worried out loud about Bush's intentions, but I'm too embarrassed to put them in this book because they were so timid and tentative. It's not that I was afraid of the repercussions; rather, I was afraid of my own conclusions and what they would imply for the way the world worked. The populist end of the mass media declares a crisis three times a week ("Martians Eat Madonna, Invasion Imminent!"), but at the other end of the spectrum we shy away from that sort of thing even when it's appropriate. Let this be a lesson to us all. I finally got there in print, just ahead of the Senate Foreign Relations Committee, in late July 2002.

PLANS FOR ATTACKING IRAQ

July 30, 2002

"I always kid him and say: Mr. President, there is a reason why your father stopped and didn't go to Baghdad," said Senator Joseph Biden, chair of the Senate Foreign Relations Committee. "He didn't want to stay for five years."

Senator Biden's powerful committee opens hearings this week on the Bush administration's plans for bringing about "regime change" in Iraq, if necessary by a full-scale military attack. It is a striking demonstration of the virtues of a constitutional system of checks and balances: George W. Bush may be the most powerful man in the world, but he can't ignore Congress.

The American public is sleepwalking towards a war with Iraq that it has been told is inevitable, and most of the US mass media have sent their brains on holiday for the summer, but the Congress is doing its job. Biden's committee is actually summoning senior Bush advisers in the midst of a Washington summer to explain what they are planning to do and how they think they can get away with it. Nor is it in the least a partisan attack by Democrats on a Republican administration.

Good journalism can happen in the most unexpected places. Last month it happened in *USA Today*, a down-market tabloid that had the novel idea of asking various Republican

members of Congress what they thought about the enterprise of overthrowing Saddam Hussein.

"You hit the other guy, but only if you know he's going to
hit you," said Congressman Henry Hyde, chair of the House
International Relations Committee. "US forces are already
stretched to the limit," said Senator Trent Lott, Republican
leader in the Senate. "Our focus should be Israel," said
Congressman Dennis Haskert, Speaker of the House. Or as
Senator Biden put it a couple of weeks later: "I want them to
refine their objectives . . . I'd like to know how important our
allies are in this."

He won't find out, of course. The administration witnesses will hide behind "national security," as administration officials always do in these circumstances. But the
Senate hearings might finally open a real debate in the
United States on whether this war, one of the best-advertised
in history, is really such a good idea. Given that the start date
for the war is somewhere between next October and early
next year (depending on which strategy is adopted); this
would not be a moment too soon.

America's friends and allies are close to unanimous in
believing that an attack on Iraq would be stupid, illegal,
costly in American and Iraqi lives and enormously counterproductive in terms of Middle Eastern politics. As Jordan's
King Abdullah said on Monday after meeting with Tony
Blair, "All of us are saying: 'Hey, United States, we don't
think this is a very good idea.'" But Americans don't listen to
foreigners much, so it's really down to the Congress, the
media (when they get back from vacation)—and, remarkably, the US armed forces.

Selective leaking of documents and plans is as much a
part of the Washington political process as harem intrigues

were to the Ottoman court, and recently the leaking has reached flood level. On July 4 the *New York Times* received a five-inch-thick dossier on Pentagon plans for an invasion of Iraq that would involve a three-month build-up and two hundred and fifty thousand American troops—"son of Desert Storm" in the jargon. The leakers were clearly military, and equally clearly thought that the plan was the stupidest idea since Winston Churchill's plan for the Gallipoli campaign.

On July 28, the *Washington Post* told its readers that the familiar "senior officials" at the Pentagon oppose any large-scale campaign to overthrow the Iraqi government. And one day after that, the *New York Times* got a new leak, outlining a plan to destroy Saddam's regime by a blitzkrieg involving a thousand bombers to paralyze Iraqi military communications and a first-day aerial descent on Baghdad by thousands of US troops to capture or kill the monster in his lair. Does anybody imagine that the leakers thought this was a good idea?

The conclusion we may draw from all this is that the "system" is working, after a fashion. When one branch of the system gets a really dumb idea, the other branches respond and try to damp out the aberration. They may not succeed—the executive branch has enormously greater power in today's America than the framers of the Constitution intended—but they continue to fight their corners. And as a backstop, there is always George the First.

However much he hates Saddam, George Bush loves his own family more, and he would not want his son's presidency to end in defeat and disgrace. All the formal evidence points to an all-out US attack on Iraq in the next six months, but it is still not a foregone conclusion.

Seven and a half months, actually, but it was a foregone con-clusion. A brief flurry of articles in the New York Times *in late August and early September cast doubts on the wisdom of the Iraq enterprise. The articles were written by close associates of former president George H.W. Bush, such as ex-secretary of state James Baker and ex-national security adviser Brent Scowcroft, and the pieces would certainly have been vetted by Bush père before publication. But the White House rained all over them, and after that the elder Bush and his friends retreated to a dignified (and useless) silence.*

By now, even the dead should have noticed that American strategic policy had come completely off the rails. And then Tony Blair revealed that Britain was going along for the ride.

THE ARSENAL OF EVIL THE CAT
September 26, 2002

Cartoon villains have no need of complex personalities or even motives; they're just evil, that's all. From the Joker in the old *Batman* comics down to Evil the Cat in *Earthworm Jim*, they seek to destroy our hero and conquer the universe simply because evil is their vocation. Saddam Hussein's image in Western propaganda is a lot like that.

The fifty-page dossier entitled *Iraq's Weapons of Mass Destruction*, published by the British government on September 24, is a major attempt led by Prime Minister Tony Blair himself to persuade the skeptical British public (and the even more skeptical governments of America's other allies) that there is an urgent need to overthrow Saddam Hussein. The document avoids most of the tricks of language and blatant manipulation of facts that contaminate comparable US efforts, trades on the reputation of British intelligence—and still fails to convince.

Nowhere, for example, is there a single mention of al-Qaeda. (But if there are no known links between Iraq and al-Qaeda, then why is dealing with Saddam a more urgent issue this year than last?) It warns that Iraq could build nuclear weapons within a couple of years if it got its hands on fissile material (but fails to mention that so could any other country bigger than Costa Rica, or that there are already elaborate and effective controls to stop fissile materials from reaching Iraq).

The British intelligence analysts did their loyal best to come up with alarming facts to please Mr. Blair and Mr. Bush, but they refused to compromise their basic integrity, so the report is really quite reassuring. For example, on nuclear weapons: "In early 2002 the Joint Intelligence Committee judged that . . . while UN sanctions on Iraq remain effective Iraq would not be able to produce a nuclear weapon. If they were removed or proved ineffective, it would take Iraq at least five years to produce sufficient fissile material for a weapon indigenously . . ."

What the report evades entirely is any analysis of Iraq's strategy: why did Saddam Hussein pursue "weapons of mass destruction" in the first place? By not addressing the question of what rational reasons Saddam Hussein might have for wanting nuclear weapons, the war party in Washington and London hopes to leave the impression that he is like Evil the Cat in the cartoons: pure, unmotivated, boundless malevolence. If he can find a way to do harm anywhere, he will.

US and British propaganda try to reinforce this image by stressing Saddam's unquestioned ruthlessness towards those who oppose him. A favourite accusation is that "he gassed his own people," a reference to his army's 1988 attack on the Iraqi Kurdish town of Halabja, in which between thirty-two hundred and five thousand civilians died. What they omit to mention is that it was the last year of the Iran-Iraq war, and that Baghdad believed that Iranian troops were still occupying the town. Saddam's forces did not know that the Iranians had pulled out and the civilians had returned.

Washington and London also fail to mention that they were both perfectly well aware that Saddam was illegally using chemical weapons against Iran throughout the war, and repeatedly cooperated at the UN to stymie attempts to get Security Council resolutions explicitly condemning their protégé for his crimes.

The whole era when the Reagan administration treated Saddam as a de facto US ally and even secretly lent him US Air Force officers on secondment to help plan his (poison-gas-drenched) offensives against Iran has been dropped down the memory hole. Then he was a useful thug that the US could work with; now he is a berserk monster.

Saddam is indeed a cruel dictator who crushes all opposition, but there is no evidence that he seeks to overrun the region, let alone "destroy civilization" (as one US official recently alleged). His attacks on Iran and Kuwait, criminal and stupid though they were, grew out of border disputes that dated back to long before his seizure of power. As for his quest for nuclear weapons, it makes perfectly good sense in terms of the region's politics.

In his clumsy, brutal way, Saddam Hussein has always aspired to lead the Arab world both against Israel and towards unity: his real dream is to be the new Nasser. The Arabs' biggest perceived problem for the last two decades has been their total, hopeless military inferiority to Israel, and the biggest single reason for that inferiority is the fact that Israel has over two hundred nuclear weapons while no Arab country has any.

A handful of Iraqi nuclear weapons would transform the strategic balance in the region. Given the certainty of massive Israeli retaliation, they would not give Saddam (who has never shown suicidal tendencies) the ability to carry out a first strike against Israel, but they might deter an Israeli nuclear attack in a crisis, and they would make Saddam the most popular man in the Arab world.

This (but nothing worse) might come to pass five or ten years from now if UN sanctions were lifted tomorrow with no further controls, and if Saddam lived that long. But the controls are in place, and a low-risk containment strategy has worked reasonably well for over a decade now. Americans and their allies are being asked to go to war to fix what isn't broken, and the mind inevitably starts to wonder what other agendas are running here.

Well, at long bloody last! But even now, I wasn't sure what the "other agendas" were. It's not that I was afraid of telling the truth for fear of retaliation: no American paper has ever dropped my column for questioning the motives of the US government— it's practically the national sport—and I had already been expelled from most big-city Canadian papers. I just didn't know the truth. Even now, several years later, I'm only operating on fragmentary evidence, logical induction and guesswork.

The reality of the relationship between the modern mass media and the institutions they cover is that everybody spins the story to serve their own agenda, and nobody ever tells you their real strategy and goals. It's much the same in our personal lives, so why be surprised? Out on the far left and the far right there are fringe media that are always sure of the story (though it changes with great frequency) and always in emergency mode, but the rest of us have to deal with complexity and uncertainty. It takes a while to sort through it all and reach our conclusions.

In this case, it took about eight months, while the insiders in Washington who knew what they really wanted had a free run. The chill on dissent after 9/11 helped them, but even in the United States the media had begun to point to the holes in the official story by the autumn of 2002. What the Bush administration was really up to was still unclear. Then along came a terrorist attack, this time in Moscow, to distract us all, and it was at least a month before anybody resumed asking the obvious questions about Iraq.

HOW TO COVER TERRORISM: THE NEW MEDIA RULES
October 27, 2002

Rule One: When covering terrorist attacks, do not discuss the political context of the attacks or the terrorists' motives and strategy. Two generations of comic books and cartoons have accustomed the general audience to villains who are evil just for the sake of being evil, so calling the terrorists "evil-doers" will suffice as an explanation for most people.

Rule Two: All terrorist actions are part of the same problem. Therefore, you can treat this month's bomb in a Bali night club, the sniper attacks in Washington and the hostage-taking in a Moscow theatre as all related to each other in some (unspecified) way, and write scare-mongering think pieces about "The October Crisis."

Rule Three: All terrorists are Islamist fanatics. On some occasions—as when Basque terrorists blow somebody up—it will be necessary to relax this rule slightly, but at the very least any terrorists with Muslim names should be treated as Islamist fanatics.

No journalism school in the world teaches these rules, and they didn't even exist two years ago. Yet most of the Western media now know them by heart. Consider, for example, the terrorist seizure of the theatre in Moscow last week that ended with the death of about fifty Chechen hostage-takers and a hundred hostages. Two years ago, the media coverage of these events, even in Russia itself, would have given us a lot of background on why some Chechens have turned to such savage methods. Didn't see much of that last week, did we?

Nothing about the long guerilla struggle Chechens waged against Russian imperial conquest one hundred and fifty years ago. Nothing about the fact that Stalin deported the entire Chechen nation to Central Asia (where about half of them died) during the Second World War. Nothing about the fact that Chechnya declared independence peacefully in 1991 and that both the Chechen–Russian wars, in 1994 and 1999, began with a Russian attack. In fact, nothing to suggest that this conflict has specific local roots or a history that goes back past last week.

Instead, the terrorists were presented as pure evil, as free of logical motivation as the Penguin or the Riddler in the *Batman* movies. Hardly anybody mentioned the fact that more than four thousand Russian soldiers and at least twelve thousand Chechen "terrorists" (anybody resisting the Russian occupation) have been killed since Russian President Vladimir Putin sent the army back into the Chechen republic in 1999.

Almost nobody refers any more to the suspicion that the apartment-building bombs in Russian cities, which gave Putin his pretext to attack Chechnya in 1999 (and paved his way to a victory in the presidential elections), were actually planted by the Russian secret services. Yet, that was widely suspected at the time: it made no sense for the Chechens, who had won their first war of independence in 1994–96, to start another one—and Russian secret service agents were actually caught by local police planting explosives in another apartment building at that time.

Never mind all that now. The Chechen men and women who seized the theatre have Muslim names, so they must be part of the worldwide network of Islamist fanatics who are driven by blind hatred to commit senseless massacres (or so it says in the script here).

If you like being treated like an idiot child by your leaders and your media, you are living at the right time. The number of people hurt in terrorist attacks is far lower than in the '50s and '60s, when national liberation wars in countries from Algeria to Vietnam took a huge toll of civilian lives. It's not even as high as in the '70s and '80s, when a new wave of "international" terrorists bombed aircraft and even attacked the Olympics. But the world's leading media see the world through American eyes, so the attacks on the United States on September 11, 2001, have utterly distorted people's perceptions of the dangers of terrorism.

In fact, the way terrorism is now being covered closely resembles domestic TV coverage of violent crime in the US, which has gone up 600 percent in the past fifteen years while the actual crime rate fell by 10 to 15 percent (depending on the crime). It has enabled the Russian government to smear the entire liberation struggle of the Chechens as terrorism, and Israel to do the same to the Palestinians. But the truth is that most of the struggles we (retrospectively) see as justified involved a good deal of terrorism at the time.

The controversy that's now starting up about the tactics the Russian authorities used in freeing the Moscow hostages is just the media barking up the wrong tree as usual. The real question is whether Russia should be occupying Chechnya, but in the present media environment we won't hear much about that. So just to check out your sympathies, here's a list of conflicts in which the eventual victors made extensive use of terror (high-tech or low-tech) against the other side.

1) RAF Bomber Command's campaign against German cities
2) US nuclear weapons on Japanese cities
3) the Zionist campaign to drive the British out of Palestine, 1946–48
4) Algeria's independence struggle against France
5) the Mau Mau rebellion against British rule in Kenya
6) Vietnam's independence war against French and American forces
7) Zimbabwe's liberation war against white minority rule

If you approved of more than two, you're obviously a terrorist sympathizer. Turn yourself in to the nearest police station.

Perhaps you sense a certain frustration in these last articles. The American attack on Iraq is inevitable, it will cause untold damage to the international system whose stability we all depend upon, and here we are having to spend our time talking about the "terrorist threat." But that is the way the media works. If you're willing to write about what's on people's minds right now, you can be a journalist. Occasionally, you can call their attention to something that doesn't have an immediate hook in current events, but don't expect too much. And if you can't make that bargain, retire to your study and write books.

CHAPTER SEVEN

ISRAEL AND PALESTINE: THE LONG RUN

It is a reasonable supposition that what I write about Israel and its neighbours is what led to my column being suppressed first in the Jerusalem Post, *once it had been bought by Conrad Black, and subsequently in most big-city Canadian newspapers after he bought up the Southam chain. So the following series of columns are the litmus test, I think, of whether my views are anti-Israel or even (as is sometimes alleged) anti-Semitic. Or just anti-Hamas and anti-Likud.*

In 2001, the beginning of the period covered by this book, the Israeli–Palestinian "peace process" that had occupied the two protagonists and their backers for the previous seven years was finally collapsing. Each side sought to blame the other, and each side was fully entitled to a large share of the blame. But it was over, at least for some years, and blame was irrelevant. Then, in the dying days of the Clinton administration, the two sides met one more time at Taba in the Sinai and defined what a final peace agreement would have to look like.

They could do that because they realized the deal was not going to be put into effect. That freed them to make the concessions that would probably have been politically impossible to sell to Israeli and Palestinian public opinion at the time. That framework of agreement will be there as a point of reference—indeed a point of departure—when the two sides return to the bargaining table at some point in the future.

THE NEXT TWO ROUNDS
January 5, 2001

It's too late already. The past month has seen extraordinary movement from Israel on the terms for a final peace settlement with the Palestinians, but there's no time to sort out what's left.

The final sticking point is the "right of return" of some 3.7 million descendants of the Palestinians who were chased from their homes in what is now Israel in the 1948–49 war. Not all would choose to go back, but enough would do so to destroy the "Jewish character" of Israel.

For Israelis of every political colour, this is truly non-negotiable. Even Yossi Sarid, head of the left-wing Meretz Party and a leading Israeli dove, says that "realization of the right of return means . . . the suicide of Israel."

The right of return is a bottom line for most Palestinians, too, at least in the short run, and this round of peace attempts has run out of long run. On January 20, US President Bill Clinton hands over to George W. Bush, Jr., who is far less willing to spend his political capital on a Middle East peace. So long as Arab oil goes on flowing and there isn't a really big war in the area, he won't lift a finger.

Then, in the Israeli election on February 6, Prime Minister Ehud Barak will almost certainly lose to Ariel "Arik" Sharon, the hardest of hard-liners. As Justice Minister Yossi Beilin bluntly said three months ago, "a government including Arik Sharon will be seen as an Israeli decision to end the peace process unilaterally."

Any deal Barak made with Arafat now would be a post-dated cheque on a crashing bank, for Sharon promises not to honour it if he is elected. The peace process is over, and the near future holds only the killing of more and more Palestinians by Israeli troops, punctuated occasionally by the killing of some Israelis in bombings and ambushes.

But it has not all been a waste, for the Israeli side has moved a lot in the past month. The concessions that the Barak government has made will allow the next round of peace talks to start from a far more realistic point when they finally get underway, some years and some thousands of deaths from now.

At least one assumes that Barak's government has already tacitly agreed to the terms of Clinton's last-ditch peace proposal last month. "The Palestinians always complain that we know the details of every proposal from the Americans before they do," as a senior Israeli official put it recently. "There's a good reason for that; we write them."

The latest US peace terms, implicitly accepted by the present Israeli government, hand over all the Gaza Strip and 95 percent of the West Bank to an independent Palestine.

Most of the Jewish settlers who remain would be regrouped in the suburbs that ring eastern Jerusalem, but the Palestinian state would control Arab areas of East Jerusalem itself.

Barak may even have authorized Clinton's proposal for a deal on Jerusalem's holy places, with the Western Wall, sacred to the Jewish faith, remaining under Israeli sovereignty while the top of the same rock formation, the precinct known as the Haram al-Sharif, would be under Muslim control. But he didn't say that the 1948 wave of Palestinian refugees can return to their homes in what is now Israel, and neither he nor any other Israeli leader ever will.

Several generations of Palestinians have eked out their lives in grim refugee camps, clinging to the notion that they would one day return to their ancestral homes in Israel. But it was never going to happen without an Arab military victory, and it has been clear for more than a quarter-century that that was not going to happen either.

The Arab states bordering Israel, as potential military threats, retained enough leverage to get their own occupied territories back. (Egypt, Jordan and Lebanon have already done so.) Palestinians, while posing no serious military threat to Israel, have enough nuisance value as a restive people under military occupation to get a similar deal for their post-1967 occupied territories—but never for the lands they lost in 1948.

Those lands are now integral parts of Israel, and the continued absence of their former owners is crucial to the maintenance of a Jewish majority in Israel. No more than token numbers of Palestinians will ever be allowed to "return" to Israel proper; the rest will have to be bought off with financial compensation and live elsewhere.

Arafat's more intelligent advisers always knew this, but until mere weeks ago they were still struggling for different concessions from Israel that they believed might actually be attainable. Now, thanks to the draining prospect of an interminable "second intifada" and the volatility of Israeli politics, the Barak government has suddenly put all those concessions on the table and we have reached the final sticking point of the right of return, but it is both too sudden and too late. Arafat can't respond fast enough, and Barak can't deliver the promised concessions anyway.

But it has not been a waste of time. The outline of the final deal is now plain for all to see, and ultimately most Israelis and most Palestinians will find it acceptable. This is where the final round of the peace process will begin under Sharon's successor (and probably Arafat's as well, for he is not likely to live long enough to see it), after the coming round of violence and unreason has blown itself out.

As an exercise in forecasting, not bad at all, but it's one of those cases where you'd rather be wrong. A lot of people were going to get hurt if there was a long delay before the resumption of serious Israeli–Palestinian peace negotiations, and it soon became clear that the delay would last for a very long time. In fact, it was almost unimaginable that any "peace process" would resume until both Arafat and Sharon had lost their grip on power—and for the first time since the early 1990s the possibility that the two sides might never reach a deal re-emerged as a plausible outcome. In that case, Israel was in desperate trouble.

THE LONG TERM

August 12, 2001

Fifteen Israelis, half of them children, were killed by a Palestinian suicide bomber at Sbarro's pizzeria in Jerusalem on Thursday. A comparable number were killed by another suicide bomber at a Tel Aviv disco in early June. These outrages have a far greater impact on public opinion at home and abroad than the appalling daily death toll on Israel's roads—but then, the bombs are *intended* to have a huge impact.

"Nothing is gained by cowardly acts such as this," said US president George W. Bush after the Jerusalem bomb, using a formula that must be pasted on the teleprompter by now. It's what he had to say—what everybody in authority is obliged to say when these things happen—but of course it isn't true.

There is nothing cowardly about blowing yourself up. It may be misguided, vicious, any number of negative things, but "cowardly" isn't one of them. And the twenty-three-year-old man who detonated the bomb in Sbarro's (one Hussein Omar Naaseh, if we are to believe the claim of the militant Palestinian group Islamic Jihad) did expect it to gain something. He may be right.

The point about the bombs is precisely that they have a long-term political purpose. Many of the other killings in the Israel–Palestine arena at the moment have short-term tactical purposes, like the targeted Israeli assassinations of Palestinian militants and the drive-by shootings of Jewish settlers by Palestinian gunmen. But the massacres committed by the human bombs are strategic, not tactical.

The point of the bombs, for those who lead Islamic Jihad, is to prevent a peace settlement between Israel and the

Palestinians that enshrines the current supplicant status of the Palestinians forever. Young "martyrs" like Hussein may not fully grasp it, but they are meant to fill Israelis with such hatred for Palestinians that they reject any peace deal with the likes of Yasser Arafat in this generation. For in the following generation or the next, when the balance of forces has changed, such deals may not be necessary.

The real question, for people who think like this, is whether there will be an Israel in the year 2100. There will almost certainly still be an Israel in 2020, though on current demographic trends its population (within the 1948 borders) will be one-third Palestinian. There will probably still be a Jewish-dominated Israel in 2050, though by then several Arab states will likely have nuclear weapons too and the United States will no longer be the sole superpower. But will there be an Israel in 2100, or will it by then have shared the fate of the various European-run Crusader states that flourished in the region a thousand years ago?

Israelis think like this too. It's clearest in the case of the mostly American settler-fanatics in the settlements of the West Bank, who are prepared to sacrifice not only their own lives but those of the next couple of generations to ensure that this land becomes (or as they would put it, "remains") Jewish. But every prime minister of Israel from David Ben Gurion to Ariel Sharon has also thought about the year 2100, and how to get there without losing what has been gained.

You could even say that the goal of all Israelis is common, and all that differs is the tactics. That does a disservice to many in Israel today who refuse to accept that the end justifies any means whatever. It also omits the huge differences among Israelis about the possible or theologically necessary borders of that long-term Israel. But there is a level at which all Israeli Jews are on the same side.

The goal of all Palestinians is also common: to regain some or all of the historic territory of Palestine as an independent homeland where they can determine their own fate. The differences between the maximalists, such as Islamic Jihad (which still dreams of driving the Jews into the sea), and the pragmatic minimalists, such as Yasser Arafat, remain huge, but in the current environment arguments about tactics slide easily into arguments about basic strategy, and that slide is certainly happening among the Palestinians.

Both sides are easily seduced by the notion that the other side will eventually break if subjected to enough pressure, and this delusion plays a role in the present round of violence. But in fact neither side will break: they are both made up of brave and obstinate human beings. The maximalists on either side try to ensure that they don't make any compromises either. But there is a distinction.

All Arabs, rightly or wrongly, think that time is on their side. A hundred years from now, they assume, Israel's Western friends will be less dominant in the world's affairs and Muslim countries will be more prominent, and the current technological gap will long since have closed.

Many Israeli leaders, including those on the right, make the same assumptions—which makes them ambivalent about a compromise peace now, rather than totally opposed. Even men like Sharon are reluctant to slam the door definitively on a negotiated peace in this generation, though their terms for peace are unlikely ever to be acceptable to Palestinians.

This explains Sharon's surprisingly measured response to the Jerusalem bombing: the occupation of Orient House in East Jerusalem, the Palestinian Liberation Organization's "head office" in the city, is hardly a killing blow. But the bombers (who despise Arafat as much as they do Sharon) are not finished, and the Israelis who voted for Sharon do not take nearly as long a view as he does. In the end, the bombers may win.

Going back through the articles I wrote about the Israeli–Palestinian conflict in this period, I'm struck by how they swing from hope to despair and back again in a matter of months. I returned in early 2002 to the question of what really happened in the Israeli–Palestinian peace talks in 2000. It was a journalist's attempt to counter the Likud Party myth that insists that Israel made an unprecedentedly generous offer for a final settlement to the Palestinians in that year, and that the Palestinian rejection of that offer proved once and for all that they are not interested in a peaceful settlement. Palestinians have shown that they are not reasonable people, goes the story, and so the rest of the world must acquiesce in their continued subjugation by Israel.

It was the journalistic equivalent of spitting into the wind. This myth is now entrenched in mainstream media coverage of the Israeli–Palestinian conflict throughout the West, and cannot be dislodged. Spin sometimes works very well.

ISRAEL AND PALESTINE: THE PEACE TERMS
February 24, 2002

There will be no more peace talks between Israelis and Palestinians until Israel's Prime Minister Ariel Sharon loses power, for he doesn't really want a compromise peace. There may be no successful outcome to peace negotiations so long as Palestinian Authority Chairman Yasser Arafat is in power, for he lacks the courage to take the final step. But neither of these septuagenarians is irreplaceable—and when serious peace talks start again, everybody knows more or less what the final deal must be.

And what is that deal? It is not the "amazingly generous" settlement that former Israeli prime minister Ehud Barak allegedly offered to Arafat at the Camp David talks in July 2000, only to have Arafat reject it. As Robert Malley, President Clinton's special assistant for Arab–Israeli affairs, has repeatedly said, there never was a formal Israeli offer at Camp David. Nothing was written down, and Israel's final position was never clear. The story that Arafat refused an offer that any Palestinian interested in peace would have snapped up is a myth fabricated by Israeli spin doctors.

The real deal was put on the table almost six months later, when the "second intifada" was already well underway. It is the settlement proposed by former US president Bill Clinton on December 23, 2000, as described by Malley and Palestinian negotiator Hussein Agha in the *New York Review of Books* last August, and recently confirmed by then Israeli foreign minister Shlomo Ben Ami in an interview with *Ha'aretz* newspaper.

The "Clinton parameters" outlined a Palestinian state including 94 to 96 percent of the West Bank and the Gaza Strip. Most of the Jewish settlements there would have to go, and Palestine would be compensated for the rest with an equivalent slice of Israeli territory elsewhere. Jerusalem would be the capital of both states, and the sacred sites within the city would be divided: Palestine would have sovereignty over the Haram al-Sharif/Temple Mount complex, and Israel over the Western Wall just below it.

Palestinian refugees everywhere could move to the state of Palestine, but they could return to their ancestral homes within Israel proper only with the agreement of the Israeli government (which would not be forthcoming in most cases). For all the Palestinian refugees who could not go home and all the Jewish settlers who had to move, there would be generous compensation. And everybody would live grumpily ever after.

This deal was on the table at the last serious round of Israeli–Palestinian peace talks, at Taba in Egypt in January of this year. According to Ben Ami, Israel said yes—but Arafat said no. He knew that the Barak government was going to lose the Israeli elections, and would be replaced within weeks by a new government led by Ariel Sharon. Why should he sign away the right of return, selling out millions of Palestinian refugees, when Sharon would just tear up the agreement next month?

It was a classic Arafat blunder, for the Palestinians were always going to have to give up the unrestricted right of return in any peace settlement. Signing the deal would have committed the United States to its terms even under the Bush administration, and it would have put Sharon hopelessly in the wrong. It might have taken years to get a different Israeli government that would finally accept the deal, but it would have been a permanent diplomatic fact.

That sort of deal seems utterly beyond reach at the moment, but the two sides will probably be back at the negotiating table within a year or so anyway because, as Israeli Foreign Minister Shimon Peres said this month: "We cannot keep three and a half million Palestinians under siege, without income, oppressed, poor, densely populated, near starvation." And the talks will be based on the Clinton parameters because "It was a brazen act to invest our national energies in a hopeless settlement project in the heart of an Arab population," as former foreign minister Shlomo Ben Ami puts it.

The Palestinian state that is now waiting to be born will be almost exactly the same as the one that would have come into existence fifty-four years ago if the bits of Palestine remaining in Arab hands at the end of Israel's war of independence had become a state then, instead of being annexed by Jordan (or, in the case of the Gaza Strip, occupied by Egypt).

No Arab state, and few among the Palestinians, still believe that Israel can be driven back from its present borders. Israel can still seize and colonize lands in the occupied territories, but the Palestinians can impose a price that only a dwindling number of Israelis are willing to pay. So it is over, and all that remains is to acknowledge that it is over.

The prediction that the two sides would "be back at the negotiating table within a year or so" was more than a trifle optimistic. (The contacts between the Palestinian Authority and the Israeli government that have resumed since Arafat's death in late 2004 hardly qualify as peace talks.) But I would still stand by the basic analysis.

THE CURSE OF THE SIX-DAY WAR
June 11, 2002

Thirty-five years is not much as anniversaries go, but there are things to discuss so it will have to do. It is just thirty-five years since Israel won a crushing victory in the June 1967 war and quadrupled the amount of territory it controlled in less than a week. It was a calamity for both sides, though only one side realized it at the time.

For the Arabs, the catastrophe was complete, immediate and largely irreversible. In their first two wars with Israel, there had been excuses for defeat despite their huge numerical superiority. This time, there was none.

In Israel's 1948–49 war of independence, its Arab neighbours were just emerging from centuries of colonial rule, and still lived under the rule of corrupt and incompetent monarchs like Egypt's King Farouk. In 1956, when Israeli forces attacked the Suez Canal in secret alliance with Britain and France, the Arabs could blame their defeat on their great-power opponents.

But in 1967 the Israelis were on their own, and revolutionary young officers across the Arab world were promising unification, material progress and, above all, victory over Israel. For ten years these officers made blood-curdling threats about a "battle of destiny"—and then were dumbfounded when the Israelis took their threats at face value and struck first.

The Arab front-line states lost their air forces in the first hour of the war. Over the next 132 hours they also lost the Sinai peninsula and the Gaza Strip (Egypt), East Jerusalem and the West Bank (Jordan), and the Golan Heights (Syria). The despair and psychological demobilization across the Arab world were so great that even the regimes responsible for the defeat were allowed to survive. (Indeed, they survive still.) And that should have been the end of it.

Like most other countries, Israel is built on land that was previously occupied by somebody else. It's no big deal, historically speaking. There is usually a good deal of fighting in the early stages, as the previous tenants resist eviction and their neighbours lend a hand, but then if you win a few wars they accept your borders and the confrontation subsides. By 1967, Israel had effectively reached that stage—so why is there still an "Arab–Israeli conflict" thirty-five years later?

Prime Minister Levi Eshkol understood that the 1967 victory could be the basis of a peace settlement guaranteeing Israel's place as an accepted if unloved neighbour of its former enemies. On June 19, 1967, less than a week after the shooting stopped, his cabinet secretly agreed to withdraw to Israel's prewar frontiers in the Sinai peninsula and the Golan Heights, returning all the captured land in return for peace, diplomatic recognition and demilitarization of the territory that would be returned to Egypt and Syria.

But that offer was never actually sent to the Egyptians and the Syrians, and the cabinet was never able to agree on returning the West Bank, the Gaza Strip and East Jerusalem at all. After four months, it even dropped the idea of a "land-for-peace" swap with Egypt and Syria. "Poor little Samson," as Eshkol put it: the choices opened up by the 1967 victory completely paralyzed Israeli diplomacy.

The problem was that Israel's victory had been too big. Ultranationalist and messianic elements in Israel seized the opportunity to expand into the new territories, setting up settlements everywhere with the explicit purpose of making the conquests politically irreversible by creating "facts on the ground." If anybody objected, they argued that the old borders were unsafe—although Israel had just beaten all its plausible opponents without even working up a sweat.

A surprise Arab attack in 1973, though launched for strictly limited objectives and rapidly defeated by Israel, subsequently persuaded Menachem Begin's government to trade the Sinai peninsula for peace with Egypt, by far the biggest of Israel's Arab neighbours, but all the rest of the land captured by Israel thirty-five years ago is still under its control. Many Israeli leaders have tried to create a domestic consensus on trading it for a lasting peace, but it's just too tempting to hang onto it.

There is no immediate danger to Israel. The guerilla and terrorist attacks carried out by the Palestinians who live under Israeli rule in the occupied territories are only a nuisance, strategically speaking, and no combination of Arab armies would dare to take Israel on. Israel is the regional superpower even without counting its several hundred nuclear weapons, and in the short and medium term it can do whatever it wants.

But the world goes on turning, and circumstances change, and the time will eventually come when Israel is no longer the only great military power in the Middle East, with unquestioning backing from the world's only superpower. It may not happen for many decades, but when that time arrives, Israel's fate will probably turn on whether its Arab neighbours still see it as an enemy.

The window of opportunity that opened thirty-five years ago is not yet closed, but the transition from enemy to unloved-but-accepted neighbour that should have got underway then has not yet even begun. The year 1967 could yet prove to have been an even greater calamity for Israel than for the Arabs.

CHAPTER EIGHT

SOUTH ASIA: DANGEROUS, BUT GETTING BETTER

It's a measure of the sheer parochialism of the Western media that the Israeli–Palestinian problem took up around ten times the space of South and Southeast Asian questions even in 2002, the year when India and Pakistan very nearly went to war—a war that could easily have ended up going nuclear. And even Americans, whose main nightmare was that a nuclear weapon might fall into the hands of Islamist terrorists, ought to have noticed that Afghanistan and the Arab countries don't have any—whereas their new ally in the "war on terror," Pakistan, most definitely does.

This piece was written several years before we learned that the "father of the Pakistani bomb," Abdul Qadeer Khan, had secretly been running an international nuclear-weapons consultancy and spare parts emporium on the side for at least a decade. His customers included North Korea, Iran and Libya. But still . . .

PAKISTAN: CANDIDATE FOR PREEMPTION

November 5, 2001

"Let me say that all our nuclear weapons are in very, very safe hands," said Pakistan's dictator General Pervez Musharraf recently on CNN's *Larry King Live*. But General Richard Myers, chairman of the US Joint Chiefs of Staff, said on Sunday that he is "concerned" about Pakistan's stability and the safety of its nuclear arsenal. The Indian government said nothing at all, but you can guess what it is thinking.

It is thinking that if Pakistan should fall into the hands of Islamic fundamentalists as the result of a revolt against Musharraf, most probably from within his own armed forces, then India will have to "preempt"—destroy Pakistan's nuclear weapons on the ground before it can launch them—within the first hours after a new regime comes to power in Islamabad. And Washington, of course, is thinking exactly the same thing.

Seymour Hersh has just published a report in the *New Yorker* magazine, strenuously denied by the Pentagon (but then it would deny it, wouldn't it?), that the United States already has a secret plan to destroy Pakistan's nuclear weapons immediately if they seem likely to fall into fundamentalist hands. It could end up as a race between the

Indians and Americans to see who can destroy Pakistan's nuclear arsenal first—and Hersh even alleges that a third party, Israeli intelligence's top-secret Unit 262, is collaborating with the US in this contingency plan.

This is insanely dangerous stuff even if it is true, as everybody assumes, that the preemptive attack would be carried out using only conventional, not nuclear weapons. Pakistanis in all walks of life would certainly resist, regardless of their attitudes towards Islamic fundamentalists, because they see their nuclear weapons as their last and maybe their only safeguard against far more powerful India.

And there are no happy endings. A bungled or partial preemption would probably end with the new regime in Pakistan launching its nuclear weapons (or those that remained) while it still could. The targets could be Indian nuclear bases and cities, or even US troops on the ground in Afghanistan.

Even a successful preemption that destroyed all Pakistan's nuclear weapons (not an outcome you could count on) would be disastrous, for at the end of it there would be many dead Pakistani soldiers, and an enraged and terrified country of 140 million people would be solidly behind the new fundamentalist regime.

How real is the danger? It's not so much the civilian fundamentalists demonstrating against the West in the streets who pose the danger, but the generation of fundamentalist officers, brought into the armed forces by the late General (and President) Zia ul-Haq in the 1980s, who have now risen to command key army formations. Together with many senior officers of Inter-Service Intelligence (ISI), the military intelligence agency that basically created the Taliban as a proxy force through which Pakistan could control Afghanistan, they comprise a large fundamentalist presence inside the only Pakistani institution that really works.

If they were to overthrow Musharraf (who has fired or demoted several senior military officers in recent weeks in an attempt to forestall a coup), then that entire institution, including its dozen or so nuclear weapons, would be at their service. They would doubtless issue instant declarations that they wished no war and would never use nuclear weapons first, but neither Indians nor Americans would be willing to take the chance of believing them. In would go the air strikes and/or the special forces, and the fat would truly be in the fire.

Pakistan doesn't deserve this fate, in the sense that the whole nuclear madness that has brought the subcontinent to within hailing distance of a real calamity is not Pakistan's fault. It was India that tested a "peaceful nuclear explosive" three decades ago, prompting Pakistan's then-prime minister Zulfikar Ali Bhutto to promise that Pakistanis would "eat grass" if necessary, but would match India's achievement. It was India that led the dance again two years ago, testing a series of nuclear weapons and effectively forcing Pakistan to follow suit.

In terms of India's long-term strategic interests, it was madness. India has seven times Pakistan's population and an even bigger edge in money and resources, so the *only* kind of war with Pakistan that India could ever lose is a nuclear one. The Indian government's main motive for taking the nuclear lead, on both occasions, was to gain a quick burst of domestic popularity by decking the country out with the symbols of a great power, with little thought to the strategic consequences. But it is having to think hard about them now.

Of all the countries in the regions where the attacks on the United States on September 11 might set in motion the Islamic fundamentalist takeovers that Osama bin Laden craves, Pakistan is by far the most dangerous. It is an almost-failed state teetering on the brink of a cliff, and one good shove could send it over the edge. When bin Laden addressed a special appeal to the Pakistani people to over-throw their government in his most recent videocassette message, he knew exactly what he was talking about.

TERRORIST GAMES

January 23, 2002

"The nuclearization of the subcontinent might have altered the situation, but despite that, the space exists for a limited conventional operation." So said Lieutenant General R.K. Nanavatty, head of the Indian army's Northern Command, about a month before the terrorist attack on the Indian par-liament on December 13 that ignited the current crisis between Indian and Pakistan. Senior Indian army officers continue to believe today that they could get away with a conventional war with Pakistan—which in reality means that a nuclear war between the two is also possible.

Though the last of the three wars between India and Pakistan was over a quarter-century ago, the hostility between the two governments is kept fresh by the Kashmir dispute, and relations often sink to a childish level. In November, for example, General Musharraf and Indian Prime Minister Atal Bihari Vajpayee had a public disagree-ment about whether India was a nation of bangle-wearing women (as General Musharraf claimed) or of tough men who wore metal bracelets (as Prime Minister Vajpayee maintained).

This nonsense would be less alarming if the two parties did not now have eight hundred thousand soldiers deployed on their long common frontier, and at least several dozen nuclear weapons each. But Pakistanis have always been convinced of the Indian "threat," mainly because the justification for carving a Muslim-majority country out of the old Indian empire requires that secular India be seen as a malevolent, anti-Muslim entity. Now many Indians believe in a Pakistani threat too.

A comparable level of Indian obsession with Pakistan has only come about with the rise to power of the Bharatiya Janata Party (BJP), the parliamentary wing of a Hindu nationalist movement with a strong fascist element. Only one-fifth of Indians actually voted for the BJP, and running a coalition government has constrained its leaders from pursuing their more radical goals, but this is a party that wants to end the separate civil code for Indian Muslims and suppress the autonomy of Muslim-majority Kashmir.

The BJP has already changed the political culture of India much for the worse. School texts are being rewritten to reflect Hindu nationalist, implicitly anti-Muslim views of Indian history. Indian crowds at international cricket matches now routinely chant "Down with Pakistan" during dull moments in the game. Last year's biggest box-office success in India was *Gadar*, a film about a Sikh who heroically rescues his Muslim wife from bloodthirsty Pakistanis after Partition in 1947 traps her on the wrong side of the line. He brings her to India — where she gratefully converts to Hinduism.

Indians would be less ready to contemplate a war between two nuclear-armed countries if they understood where it could lead, but most ordinary people don't: Indians have not been through the long consciousness-raising exercise on these matters that North Americans and Europeans underwent during the Cold War. And the Indian government wilfully ignores the likeliest explanation for the current wave of terrorist atrocities: that the Islamic terrorists who once collaborated with Pakistan's Inter-Services Intelligence in launching terrorist attacks into Kashmir are now actively seeking to embroil Pakistan in a nuclear war with India.

Why would they do that? Because they are fanatics who believe that a few million deaths would be worth it if such a war might "liberate" Kashmir, and because they are so ignorant about how large-scale wars work that they imagine a nuclear war might shake up the status quo enough to bring about that result. Or, in some cases, because they are so foolish and so extreme that they dream of re-establishing Muslim rule over the whole subcontinent.

These are not rational people, but there will be a disaster if those in power do not deal rationally with the threat they pose. General Musharraf has made a start by banning all five of the big Islamic extremist groups in Pakistan, arresting hundreds of their members, bringing all mosques and religious schools under government control, and condemning the radicals for promoting "half-baked religious thought" and a "Kalashnikov culture." It is time for India to recognize that Pakistan is (belatedly) doing the right thing, and to make some calming gestures in return.

It took another two years and an election in India that evicted the BJP in favour of a Congress-led government that is still committed to the old ideal of a secular, multicultural India, but the crisis did pass. By 2005, India and Pakistan were even starting to negotiate over the future of a divided Kashmir.

In another generation, with the gradual emergence of both India and China as economic superpowers, Asia is going to be the centre of world politics, so it matters a great deal that democracy is winning most of the time in South and Southeast Asia. Though there remains the bitter case of Burma . . .

THE LADY IS STILL IN JAIL
June 26, 2003

"The military regime is very worried that they are facing a Cory Aquino–type of people-power movement, and basically, they've panicked," explained a foreign diplomat in Rangoon shortly after a mob of government-sponsored thugs attacked Aung San Suu Kyi's motorcade at Dipeyin, northeast of Mandalay, on May 30. About seventy of her supporters were killed, she was beaten up—and she and nineteen members of the National League for Democracy (NLD) who were travelling with her were taken into "temporary protective custody." A month later, "the Lady"—as everyone in Burma calls her—is still in Insein prison in Rangoon.

She has been under some form of restraint, mostly house arrest, for almost all of the past thirteen years, as her children grew up without her and her husband died without even being allowed a farewell visit to Burma, but it has never been as bad as this. The military regime has realized that all its wealth and power are on the line right now, and the gloves have come off. However, alone in her cell, still wearing the same blouse and skirt she was arrested in a month ago, she remains the most influential person in Burma. The generals have the guns and the money, but she has the legitimacy.

She has earned it by her patience and self-sacrifice — but also through the regime's blunder thirteen years ago in allowing free elections in Burma. The generals calculated that they could bribe or bully a majority of Burma's 45 million people into voting for their candidates, but when the counting was over in 1990 Suu Kyi and the NLD had won by a landslide: 82 percent of the votes. The army immediately "cancelled" the results and arrested all the NLD leaders, but it never got over the effects of that mistake. And now it has made the same mistake again.

The confrontation between Suu Kyi and the generals began fifteen years ago, when the original tyrant, the half-crazed Ne Win, precipitated a crisis by resigning after more than two decades in power. His bizarre and isolationist version of "socialism" had reduced the once-prosperous country to penury, and his aim was to transfer formal power to a more respectable elected government while retaining real control. But Aung San Suu Kyi happened to be in Burma in 1988, home from her quiet life as an academic in England to nurse her dying mother.

She had lived most of her life abroad, the inevitable consequence of being the only daughter of Burma's great independence hero Aung San, who was assassinated when she was only two. But in 1988 Southeast Asia was in political ferment: the example of the nonviolent democratic revolution led by Cory Aquino in the Philippines in 1986 had already spread to Thailand and Bangladesh, toppling long-ruling military regimes, and now threatened the control of the Burmese military as well. Suu Kyi's name made her invaluable to the pro-democracy campaigners, and she quickly became the symbol of the whole movement.

After three months the generals, realizing that events were spinning out of control, took back power and massacred thousands of students and other citizens in the streets of Rangoon. Then in 1990 the regime held a carefully stage-managed "election" to gain some international respectability—but the NLD won by a landslide. The regime refused to recognize its victory, and Burma has been in deadlock ever since. So last year a new generation of generals tried to square the circle again: they released Suu Kyi from house arrest in the hope that they could end all the foreign boycotts and rejoin the world without actually giving up power.

It never seemed like a good idea to General Than Shwe, the current head of the junta (who virtually froths at the mouth whenever the Lady's name is mentioned), but he was talked into it by other senior generals led by Khin Nyunt, the influential head of intelligence. Thirteen months after she was released from house arrest, however, it turns out that Than Shwe was right: neither Suu Kyi nor the Burmese people were satisfied with tokenism, and the regime's power and privileges really were at risk.

The NLD tiptoed through the first months after Aung San's release, anxious not to derail the process of democratization by too much open campaigning, but as it became clear that the generals were just looking for political cover it changed its style. In the last six months, Aung San has been making open antiregime speeches up and down the country, and every month the crowds are bigger. The regime had to stop her or it was toast, so a month ago the thugs were unleashed to stage a massacre that would provide a pretext for the Lady's arrest.

That has stopped the protests for the moment, but the regime is back where it was, loathed by foreigners and Burmese alike. How long can it hold out against the united disapproval of practically everyone? Quite a long time, if the past is any guide—and one should not expect a split between the top generals over this bungle. They know that they must hang together or else they will hang separately (probably literally, in some cases, for some of them have much Burmese blood on their hands).

Aung San Suu Kyi will need all her patience.

Note: The renaming of Burma as "Myanmar" and of Rangoon as "Yangon" in 1989 was a cynical ploy by the military regime intended to win the support of Burmese nationalists, and is not recognized by the democratic opposition.

At the time of writing, Aung San Suu Kyi was still under house arrest, and the generals still ruled Burma. But generally democracy was doing fairly well in Asia—if you didn't mind a lot of corruption.

ASIAN DEMOCRACIES: THE HALF-FULL GLASS
May 6, 2004

Twenty years ago, the Philippines, Indonesia, Taiwan and South Korea were all dictatorships. Now they are all democracies, and between March and July of this year they will all have held national elections.

But the president of South Korea is under impeachment, the president of Taiwan was almost assassinated, an alleged war criminal has been nominated by Indonesia's biggest party as its presidential candidate in the July 5 election, and an ex-movie star and high-school dropout, who just mumbles a few well-rehearsed sentences before breaking into a pop song at his rallies, is the leading challenger for the Filipino presidency in the election on Monday (May 10). Is this glass half-empty or half-full?

Fernando Poe, Jr. (FPJ or "Da King" for short) makes Arnie Schwarzenegger look like a serious politician. "He's an actor who has been living in a bubble," said one Filipino journalist. "He has nothing between the ears." But he is an old drinking buddy of Joseph "Erap" Estrada, the film-star president who was toppled in 2001 by street protests against the massive corruption of his administration. Erap is on trial for plundering public funds, but the same wealthy families who backed him have now thrown their support behind Da King, including Imelda Marcos, widow of dictator Ferdinand Marcos. (She also happens to be Fernando Poe's godmother.)

If FPJ wins, he will almost certainly pardon Estrada before plunging his own snout into the trough, and the few hundred families who control 95 percent of the wealth in a country of 80 million people will be safe once more. But their position was not in great danger under incumbent president Gloria Macapagal Arroyo either.

She was not personally corrupt (being wealthy already), but the general corruption that causes an estimated 40 percent of the national budget to end up in the pockets of officials hardly declined at all under her rule. Small wonder that so many of the Filipino poor are inclined to vote for someone who at least seems like one of them.

It's a hell of a way for democracy to end up in the country that pioneered the concept of nonviolent democratic revolution in Asia eighteen years ago—and it's not a lot better in neighbouring Indonesia, where a similar revolution turfed out General Suharto, the long-ruling dictator, only six years ago. Suharto's old party, Golkar, emerged as the biggest party in the parliamentary elections on April 5. It has now nominated General Wiranto, army head in the last years of the Suharto dictatorship, as its presidential candidate in July—even though he is accused of sponsoring atrocities in East Timor in 1999.

Then there is South Korea, where President Roh Moo-hyun faces impeachment on charges of election violations and corruption as a result of a vote in March in the outgoing parliament. And Taiwan, where President Chen Shui-bian suffered a stomach wound in an assassination attempt just before the election on March 20, which he then won by the narrowest of margins on a sympathy vote. The opposition accused him of faking the incident, but he still ended up in office for another four years.

So what was the point of it all? Between 1986 and 1998, every one of these countries, home to more than 350 million people, overthrew corrupt and oppressive dictatorships, mostly by nonviolent public protests. But how much has really changed? Not nearly enough, would be most people's answer: the glass is half-empty.

But who ever believed that democracy would automatically end poverty and corruption (in the Philippines and Indonesia) or political chicanery (in South Korea and Taiwan)? Democracy doesn't make people wise or good. It's just a better tool than any of the available alternatives for choosing people who are wiser and better to run our affairs—but we mustn't expect miracles.

In the end, Filipinos probably will re-elect President Arroyo by a narrow margin, partly because she really is wiser and better than Da King (it isn't hard)—and partly because she has just spent about $25 million in public funds to create temporary jobs in poor areas. And while President Megawati Sukarnoputri will probably lose the July presidential election in Indonesia because of her lacklustre leadership, the likely victor is not General Wiranto but another former general with a much better reputation, Susilo Bambang Yudhoyono.

The recount in Taiwan confirmed the original result, the assassination attempt against President Chen was almost certainly genuine—would you hire someone to shoot at you with a handgun and just graze your stomach while you are in a moving car?—and the opposition now seems to be grudgingly accepting the legitimacy of the outcome.

The impeachment charges against South Korea's President Roh were a cynical political ploy by the opposition parties, who were duly punished by the voters. The liberal Uri Party, which supports Roh but had only 49 seats in the outgoing National Assembly, won 152 seats in the mid-April parliamentary election, giving it a slim majority and guaranteeing Roh's survival.

Sometimes the choices in a democracy are not great, nor do the voters always get it right. But it's a better range of choices than the average dictatorship offers, and people aren't stupid: they do get it right most of the time. The glass is half-full.

Well, they did get it right. The attempt to impeach President Roh Moo-hyun in South Korea failed, Gloria Arroyo was re-elected president in the Philippines and Susilo Bambang Yudhoyono won the Indonesian election. Above all, Indians returned to their traditional democratic and secular values. In fact, they did something absolutely unprecedented in Asia, where ethnic politics is the norm, and voted for a leader who was not Hindu, not male, not even Indian-born: Sonia Gandhi.

In the end she decided that it would be a lot easier to create and maintain a coalition government if she stepped aside and let her Congress colleague Manmohan Singh become prime minister instead. But it was still enormously heartening.

CHAPTER NINE

INVADING IRAQ: THE REASON WHY

By the beginning of 2003 it was clear that the United States was going to invade Iraq in the next few months no matter what anybody said or did. It made no sense in terms of the announced motives, and little enough even in terms of the goals that probably lurked behind them. The media were filled with blatant lies and cynical distortions as the US and British authorities tried to hype their people up for war, and far too many journalists went along with it even though midlevel people in the intelligence world in both Washington and London were privately warning their contacts to take it all with a very large grain of salt. In the United

States, you could excuse some of media's failure in terms of post-9/11 trauma and chill (although after more than two years . . . ?). Elsewhere, there was less excuse.

And the ultimate target of all this activity was a man whom almost nobody knew.

THE JACKAL IN WINTER

February 27, 2003

He's had such a strange life that it's as hard as imagining what it's like to be Michael Jackson, but it's a good deal more important. What is going through the mind of Saddam Hussein as he waits for the American avalanche to bury him?

Like any doomed man, he must entertain occasional fantasies of a miraculous last-minute reprieve, but nobody who has spent thirty-five years at the centre of power in a country where the losers usually die can have many illusions. Saddam knows that he and his sons will almost certainly be dead by April, and his thoughts now are probably divided between wondering where it all went wrong, and figuring out how to play the end-game in a way that enshrines him as an Arab hero.

Being an Arab hero was always important to the abused boy who grew up on tales of Saladin defeating the Crusaders and who dreamed of emulating the great pan-Arab leader of the '50s and '60s, Egypt's Gamal Abdul Nasser. Iraq was definitely the wrong place to be born if Arab unity was your dream, because three-quarters of its people are Kurds or Shia Arabs who don't give a damn for pan-Arab nationalism; but among his own Sunni Arab people it is the dream.

That is why Saddam has always been Israel's most vocal enemy among Arab leaders: hostility to Israel is the one topic that might unite the Arabs under his leadership. His nuclear weapons program, when he still had one, was always about breaking Israel's nuclear monopoly. A few nuclear weapons would not give him the ability to attack Israel, which has hundreds of the things, but it would constitute an Arab deterrent to Israel's first use of nuclear weapons—and catapult him into a position of pan-Arab leadership. But those dreams are gone now.

So is his dream of a rich, powerful Iraq whose people are healthy and well educated. Remnants of it remain, such as a 97 percent literacy rate and a higher status for women than in almost any other Arab country, but the generous welfare state that Saddam built with the help of abundant oil revenues between 1968 and 1979 has long since been swept away by his post-1980 blunders. Iraq today is just another impoverished Arab police state like Egypt or Syria or Algeria, except even more brutal.

Does Saddam understand that his own savage methods made this outcome inevitable? Probably not, for his real role model, Stalin, got away with it. (Visitors report that his personal quarters are furnished with numerous Arabic-language translations of biographies of Stalin.) Like Stalin, he has ruthlessly killed anyone who challenged his power. Like Stalin, too, paranoia has served him well: most of the people he had killed were no real threat, but the slaughter did sweep away most of his genuine enemies along with all the harmless victims.

The real difference between the two men is that Stalin knew the international rules: you can do what you like to your own people, but never attack your neighbours without some legal cover and never attack anyone stronger than you. Saddam, a poorly educated man with little knowledge of the world beyond Iraq, broke the rules twice by attacking Iran and Kuwait.

His attack on Iran in 1980 was not unprovoked (Ayatollah Khomeini tore up the 1975 treaty defining the border and urged Iraq's Shias to revolt), but it was an act of folly which Saddam only narrowly survived thanks to lavish US aid. His 1990 invasion of Kuwait, for which he mistakenly believed that he had clearance from his American ally, turned Washington into his enemy, destroyed his army and led to the UN-imposed sanctions that have had him on the ropes for the past eleven years. Everything he built is wrecked; Iraq's power has never been less—and now the US government is going to kill him.

Saddam must hate the irony that Washington has decided to destroy him as a sort of displacement activity after a terrorist attack against the United States by radical Islamists who also wanted him dead—and that those same Islamists will probably be the main beneficiaries of the chaos that follows. But as a man who is about to die, his main concern will be with his own legacy. How will Arabs see him a generation from now?

The Arabs are one of the last romantic cultures, where people really still believe in heroes and martyrs for the cause. Saddam Hussein is quintessentially Arab in this respect, and he will try to contrive a heroic death amid the ruins that will put his reputation as an Arab nationalist hero on a firm foundation.

If the Islamists actually win as a result of all this, then it will all have been for naught: they will despise and exe-crate Saddam even as they condemn the United States for invading Iraq. But they don't run the Arab world yet, and despite Mr. Bush's unwitting efforts on their behalf they may never do so. Besides, what other goal can Saddam have in his last few weeks of life than a hero's death?

"Washington has decided to destroy him as a kind of displacement activity . . . ?" Can't the clever columnist do a bit better than that? Why is all this happening, o wise one? Do your damn job.

I went back through all the old columns, expecting to find lots of stuff from 2002 in which I provided an analysis of the Bush administration's larger strategic motives for invading Iraq that I would not be embarrassed to stand by today. I didn't find one.

I knew that invading Iraq was stupid and bound to end in tears. I didn't believe any of the reasons that were being publicly advanced for doing so. But I just didn't get it, or at least I failed to put it down on the page. My whole training and inclination drive me to think in strategic terms, and yet the article below, published only two weeks before the United States actually invaded Iraq, was the first in which I actually got to the heart of the matter.

THE SHORT-LIVED AMERICAN EMPIRE
March 3, 2003

Just over two thousand years ago, when the Roman republic turned itself into an empire and extended the *Pax Romana* over most of the known world—western Europe, the Mediterranean and the Middle East, plus the great reservoir of barbarian tribes in eastern Europe and Central Asia—

Rome exercised direct control over about half the total population, and was able to tax them and raise troops from them. So the *Pax Romana* lasted over four hundred years.

Many people in Washington now talk openly of turning the American republic into an imperial power that enforces a *Pax Americana* around the planet, but the United States has only 4 percent of the planet's population, and its people are equally averse to high taxes and US casualties. The demand for US troops and money will rapidly outrun the supply, so the *Pax Americana* will last about twenty minutes—but it may be a hectic and painful twenty minutes.

The dream of American empire has attracted American neoconservatives for decades, but it gained a much broader following after the collapse of the Soviet Union in 1991. The only apparent constraint on US power had been removed, and the idea that the world will be a safer place if it is governed by multilateral organizations under the rule of law began to give way to the fantasy that the United States can and should make the world a safer place (particularly for American interests) by the unilateral exercise of its own immense power.

Official Washington was starting to oppose any new international rules that might act as a brake on the free exercise of US power even in Bill Clinton's administration. It was Clinton, not George W. Bush, who fought an international ban on land mines and tried to sabotage the new International Criminal Court. President Bush's cancellation of the Anti-Ballistic Missile Treaty, the US veto on new provisions for intrusive inspections under the Chemical Weapons Convention, and Washington's more recent rejection of similar attempts to write some provisions for enforcement into the Biological Weapons Treaty simply follow in the same path.

As Boston University professor and retired US army officer Andrew Bacevich wrote in a recent edition of *The National Interest*: "In all of American public life, there is hardly a single prominent figure who finds fault with the notion of the United States remaining the world's sole military superpower until the end of time." This is called hubris, and it is generally followed by nemesis. That will probably arrive during the next phase of the fantasy: the wildly ambitious project to make the conquest of Iraq the cornerstone for a wholesale restructuring of the Arab world along American lines.

"America has made and kept this kind of commitment before, in the peace that followed a world war," said Mr. Bush late last month, comparing the project with the rebuilding of German and Japan after 1945. "We will remain in Iraq as long as necessary." You don't know whether to laugh or cry, but tears are probably more appropriate, for that is where this is all going to end.

Iraq is no more like Germany than Saddam Hussein is like Adolf Hitler. Germany and Japan in 1945 were industrial states with strong national identities, several generations' experience of democracy, homogeneous populations and fully professional bureaucracies. Iraq is an artificial state of competing ethnic identities with no democratic tradition and a deeply politicized, totally corrupt state apparatus dominated by a single ethnoreligious minority. Never mind running the world or spreading democracy throughout the Middle East; merely occupying Iraq is likely to prove too heavy a burden for the US public to tolerate for very long.

The Romans dealt with this sort of stuff all the time. In fact, they often had four or five situations like this going on in various parts of their empire at the same time. They just spent the money, put in the troops, took their casualties and killed enough of the locals to make the rest keep quiet. But does anybody seriously think that the current generation of Americans is going to pay that sort of price for a world empire that nobody except a narrow Washington-based elite really wants? We are probably no more than two years away from a Somalia-style US withdrawal from Iraq.

Well, all right, four or five years away, then. But at least this article is finally addressing what is really going on, rather than simply knocking down the various false motives and justifications that had been advanced to defend the US project. Why did it take me so long to get to this point? Why did it take everybody in the media so long?

Most other journalists have an excuse, in that they tend to turn to "experts" for help in complex matters, and most experts in strategic affairs are "professionally deformed" (as the French would put it) in ways that make them accept official threat assessments at face value. On the other hand, journalists are also trained to apply a certain windage factor to counter professional deformation, and that wasn't happening much. As for me, there was no excuse at all. I had allowed myself to get caught up in the details, bat away at all the lies and distortion, and forget about the big picture. Which is probably just what they wanted us all to do.

PROCRASTINATION
March 10, 2003

Finally we have a hard start-date for the war: March 17. Five thousand or so people will die that day, most of them Iraqi soldiers obliterated by the "shock and awe" blitz of bombing

147

with which the United States plans to begin the invasion. The number of civilian and American casualties in subsequent days is less certain, as it depends on whether the Iraqi army makes a stand in the cities; however, the United Nations relief agencies are planning for up to eighty thousand Iraqi dead. That's quite a few people, but President George W. Bush has run out of patience.

He has waited a long time, but that Saddam Hussein keeps turning and twisting, destroying a few missiles a day and occasionally producing a new document to prove to the United Nations inspectors that he really did destroy his chemical weapons twelve years ago. "Deception and delay" Mr. Bush calls it, and he has had enough of it. It's time to stop the nonsense and start the war.

He's not too happy with his friends and allies, either. They're also into delay, from the French, Russians, Germans and Pakistanis, who keep insisting that the inspectors must be given time to do their job, to the sly Canadians, who have been playing their usual slippery game of trying to broker a "compromise" resolution at the United Nations. They all argue that it is unwise to abandon collective security and let one country attack another preemptively, as if a US attack on Iraq without UN backing (which it is very unlikely to get in the next week) were setting a bad example.

Canada's Prime Minister Jean Chrétien went so far as to worry that other countries might start playing by the new US rules: "China might say, 'Well, we have a problem somewhere, and we don't like the regime, and we're going to change the regime.'" Don't these people understand that international law is only there to restrain the bad countries, not to hamper the good ones? How can any self-respecting democratic superpower let itself be Gulliverized by these pygmies? They don't understand how urgent this is.

Only, there's a nagging little question in many people's minds. Why wasn't it urgent to sort Iraq out a year and a bit ago, when President Bush first nominated Saddam Hussein's fiefdom as lead villain in the "axis of evil" in his State of the Union speech on January 29, 2002? If the man is that dangerous, why did the Bush administration do absolutely nothing about him then?

Why did the great debate on "the war" begin only last September, when (by sheer coincidence) it diverted public attention from tedious domestic issues, like the recession and corporate scandals, during the campaign for the midterm congressional elections in November? And why did the US not start to call up reservists and move major military units towards the Gulf until after the elections were over?

Saddam Hussein, if you believe the Bush administration, is not just another Middle Eastern dictator weaving his bloody way through the shoal waters of the region's cutthroat politics. He is a maniac with a fanatical hatred of the United States (and never mind the fact that he was quite cheerfully allied to the US during the 1980s). He has "weapons of mass destruction" and might give them to Islamist terrorists for use against the United States (though the International Atomic Energy Agency's chief inspector, Mohammed El Baradei, says there has been no Iraqi nuclear weapons program since 1991, and the Islamists constantly call for Saddam's overthrow).

Well, then, he has chemical and biological weapons—not currently in production, perhaps, but he surely has some hidden away from the 1980s war with Iran, when he relied on US-supplied aerial and satellite intelligence to drench

Iranian trenches with nerve gas. (Q: Mr. President, how can you be sure that Saddam Hussein has chemical and biological weapons? A: We kept the receipts.) Except these are the sort of weapons that any halfway-competent terrorist organization can make in its own labs (as the Japanese cult group Aum Shinrikyo did in 1994–95). Nobody needs to go to Saddam Hussein for them.

The reason that Washington feels such great urgency about launching an attack on Iraq is not Iraqi weapons. It's just that it was ruled by the domestic political cycle for the nine months between the "axis of evil" speech in late January 2002 and the midterm congressional elections in November, and didn't want to alarm American voters by mobilizing for war in that period.

So here we are with the summer heat approaching, and a lot of US reservists who need to get back to their civilian jobs soon, and US popular support for the war getting steadily softer — and that's why there is now a great urgency in getting it started. There is certainly no urgent threat from Iraq (the overwhelming majority of people and governments outside the United States would say there is no threat at all), but some other timetables are running out, so the killing has to start next week.

The final delay was at the United Nations. The Bush administration was not interested in a UN resolution authorizing the United States to attack Iraq for its own sake, but a large portion of the American population was deeply uneasy about the enterprise and wanted at least one traditional US ally to go along with it for reassurance. Britain was the only available candidate, but the British public would be very hard for Prime Minister Tony Blair to bring along without a UN resolution, so the attempt had to be made. It failed, of course.

THE UNITED NATIONS: THE DAMAGE DONE
March 16, 2003

In the end, it wasn't the wicked French and their veto who deprived the US and Britain of a second United Nations resolution authorizing them to attack Iraq; the Bush administration couldn't even come up with a majority of "yes" votes that would trigger a French veto. But it's a safe bet that when the bombs start to fall on Iraq, the Security Council will not pass a resolution condemning the US attack either. The American veto will not be needed.

The long propaganda campaign to link Saddam Hussein to the Islamist terrorists of al-Qaeda has persuaded about half the American public that there must be some connection, but it has been a purely domestic campaign based on endless naked assertions by local pundits and authority figures (including President George W. Bush) whose credibility stops at the US border. Nowhere else on the planet is this alleged linkage widely believed, so Washington was bound to find it hard to get UN support for its Iraq adventure.

The anti-French hysteria that has been whipped up by sections of the US media helps to distract American public attention from the fact that there are strong popular majorities against this war in virtually every country in the world outside the United States. If you're busy shaking your fist against the "cheese-eating surrender monkeys" and renaming French fries "liberty fries," you're less likely to notice that even the few governments that back the US attack on Iraq (Britain, Spain and Italy) do so in the teeth of their own public opinion.

On the other hand, nobody wants the United States to abandon the UN: President Bush is quite right in saying that if the US rejects the UN's authority, then it will become, in his word, "irrelevant." Other countries would not give legal cover to a "preemptive" US attack on Iraq that most of them see as grossly premature and a terrible precedent, but they will not deepen the rupture with the United States by passing resolutions against it.

The war in Iraq will duly end in an American victory, but how much damage will Mr. Bush's decision to go it alone do to the UN, to America's alliances, and to international law? If things work out as well as the White House serenely expects (and Tony Blair desperately hopes), then the damage may not be all that great.

Imagine that the fighting in Iraq ends in a week, with Saddam Hussein and perhaps ten thousand other Iraqis dead—and that little of the carnage is seen by the Arab public because Washington persuades Qatar to pull the plug on al-Jazeera for the duration. There are no eruptions of violence leading to Islamist takeovers in other Arab countries or Pakistan, and resistance to the US occupation of Iraq doesn't start right away.

Pigs may fly, I hear you cry, but remember that the United States is the most powerful nation in world history, run by people who are quite competent at the operational level even if the strategic direction leaves something to be desired. With sufficient thrust, as a friend of mine frequently observes, pigs fly just fine. They have real problems with aerodynamic stability and in the end they tend to crash and burn, but that could be several years down the road from here.

The United States could get away with the conquest of Iraq without big negative side effects, at least in the short term, in which case it can return to the UN next month, magnanimously forgive all who doubted it and get them to do much of the dirty work of postwar reconstruction. An *ex post facto* Security Council resolution would legalize the conquest, France and Russia would sulk for a bit and then normal service would be resumed. Happy ending, at least for a while.

But if the fighting in Iraq takes several weeks, and the death toll climbs into the tens of thousands, and al-Jazeera stays on the air, then there could be calamitous upheavals elsewhere in the Arab world and a much grimmer start to the US occupation of Iraq. As American casualties mount and the whole enterprise turns sour, the natural response of the Bush administration would be to blame it all on the perfidious foreigners who sabotaged the US crusade— which could have profoundly negative consequences for the UN and NATO.

Nobody would miss NATO all that much, but wrecking the UN would be a very different matter. For all its flaws, the United Nations is a serious attempt to substitute the rule of law for the age-old rule of the strong as a way of running the world. That attempt is now several generations old, and it has made as much progress as you could hope for in the first half-century.

However, it would not survive the defection of the United States, so Washington must be persuaded to remain an active UN member even if it spins out for a while. This doesn't mean that everyone else must adopt the Bush administration's view that the UN has "failed" whenever it does not agree with current US policy—but if things go badly wrong for the US in Iraq, what will be needed is not scorn and recrimination but sympathy and understanding. Somehow or other, America must be kept in the system.

Although there were not "calamitous upheavals elsewhere in the Arab world," the Iraqi resistance did turn out to be a good deal tougher than the people around US Defense Secretary Donald Rumsfeld had expected, and Rumsfeld's policy guaranteed that the occupation would face huge problems because of a sheer lack of manpower. (I'm omitting the pieces that simply analyzed or second-guessed the strategy and conduct of the war because they are only of specialist interest now, and concentrating on those that dealt with the broader and longer repercussions of the war.)

RUMSFELD'S WAR
March 30, 2003

American generals are not political innocents, though they have to act as if they were. When Lieutenant General William Wallace, the commander of American ground forces in Iraq, ruefully told journalists last Thursday "the enemy we're fighting is different from the one we'd war-gamed against" and predicted a much longer war, he was launching a (deniable) cruise missile straight at the US secretary of defence, Donald Rumsfeld. Everybody in Washington knows that it was Rumsfeld who ignored professional military advice and insisted on "War Lite" in Iraq.

Rumsfeld and his civilian allies control the upper echelons at the Pentagon, and the war on Iraq was a chance for them to prove that they could carry out overseas interventions at low cost. (They have a long wish list of such interventions: last month, John Bolton, under-secretary of state for arms control, told Israeli officials that it would be "necessary to deal with" Iran, Syria and North Korea after the war in Iraq.) So when US professional soldiers who respected the Iraqi army's capabilities insisted that to invade Iraq they needed "heavy" forces as large as those used in the first Gulf War in 1991, Rumsfeld simply overruled them.

The head of the US army, General Eric Shinseki, a twice-wounded Vietnam veteran, wanted to move the 1st Cavalry Division from Texas and the 1st Armored Division from Germany to the Gulf for the invasion, but Rumsfeld refused to send them. He wanted to prove that his project for re-ordering the world to America's taste by force could be done on the cheap, exploiting the military superiority that he and his neoconservative cronies believed that US forces, thanks to new technologies, now had. If you have to send most of the US army just to deal with a country like Iraq, then it's such a big deal that you won't get to do it very often—but if you can do it with "light" forces, then it could become an almost annual event.

The conflict between the ideologues and the military professionals became so acute that Rumsfeld, unable to fire the army chief, took the unprecedented step of announcing Shinseki's successor's name eighteen months in advance. By last December, the US armed forces were so alarmed by Rumsfeld's strategy that former Marine Corps commandant General James Jones, now commanding US forces in Europe, took the risk of publicly criticizing "those who seem to think this is pre-ordained to be a very easy military operation" in an interview with the *Washington Post*.

In January General Norman Schwarzkopf, commander of US forces during the 1991 Gulf War, worried aloud in the same paper "when [Rumsfeld] makes his comments, it appears that he disregards the army." But Rumsfeld was the boss, which is why there are now fewer than one hundred thousand US combat troops in Iraq, why the operation has stalled before Baghdad, and why the Pentagon has belatedly ordered another one hundred and twenty thousand troops to the region (while insisting publicly that plans have not changed).

As General Shinseki told a congressional committee in February, the United States will need a force in the hundreds of thousands to police postwar Iraq. Rumsfeld immediately denied it, saying that the army chief was "far off the mark," and a "senior administration official" told the *Village Voice* newspaper that Shinseki's remark was "bullshit from a Clintonite enamored of using the army for peacekeeping and not winning wars." So General Shinseki, in an act of insubordination that stunned his colleagues, went right out and told another congressional committee the same thing.

The rupture between the ideologically driven civilians who run the Pentagon and the professional military is now almost complete. That is a recipe for a longer and messier war, leading to a postwar occupation regime that promises to be an utter nightmare. Welcome to Iraq.

War over, America victorious. Distinct shortage of flowers being strewn under the feet of conquering GIs, but the show's over in Iraq and it's time for the world to move on. Except it doesn't. It still hasn't. This is not about Iraq, really; it's about the way we run the world.

THE US AND THE UN
May 25, 2003

"The French foreign minister . . . said he was not completely satisfied with the resolution but supported it in the interests of 'unity of the international community.' Translation: we give up, you're bigger than we are." That was how the *Los Angeles Times* greeted the UN Security Council resolution of May 22 recognizing US control of Iraq, but it isn't quite that simple.

The debate in the Security Council before the war was not about whether President Bush should attack Iraq or not: he was obviously determined to do that anyway. It was about whether the UN system would be more damaged by defying American power and risking a US boycott, or by cynical complicity in an American attack that most members saw as unjustified. A large majority of the members—eleven out of fifteen, including all the major powers except the US and Britain—decided to take the risk and defy Washington.

That didn't stop the war, but they got away with it, more or less. President Bush no longer takes phone calls from French President Jacques Chirac, but he will show up for the G8 summit meeting in France this week and smile with Chirac for the cameras—and the US and Britain have already had to go back to the UN Security Council to get some legitimacy for their occupation of Iraq. Once again, the question for the other Security Council members was how to minimize the damage to the UN.

Should they grant the invasion a kind of postdated legality by ending the UN sanctions against Iraq and recognizing the "occupying powers" as legitimate, so that they can get on with selling Iraq's oil, rebuilding the shattered economy and creating some sort of government? Or should they stonewall on the issue and push the Bush administration into an outright rejection of the UN's authority? Put it that way, and the answer is obvious: the Security Council members had to swallow their principles and give the US what it wants. But how deeply does the UN want to get involved in Iraq?

On the surface, the UN seemed to be demanding serious authority over Iraq, in which case it was almost entirely unsuccessful. The oil-for-food program will end in six months rather than four, which gives Russia more time to be paid on existing contracts, and the UN "special co-ordinator" in Iraq has been marginally upgraded to "special representative"—like being promoted from "head janitor" to "building maintenance supervisor"—with the vaguely defined job of facilitating "a process leading to an internationally recognized, representative government of Iraq." But there is no timetable for that process, nor any UN veto over how it unfolds, nor even a commitment to allow UN arms inspectors to return. Game, set and match to the US.

But hang on a minute. Are we really supposed to believe that the Russians and French and Germans and Chinese were all itching to send troops to Iraq to share the load that the United States and Britain have chosen to bear? And that they really wanted to help pay for it too? If they didn't, then they probably weren't very serious about wanting the UN to take over in Iraq either, for even if Washington had been open to such a deal, that would surely have been the quid pro quo.

The reality of the matter is quite different. Most members of the Security Council see the US occupation of Iraq as a disastrous mistake that will probably end by destroying the Bush administration. A month and a half after the end of the fighting, basic services have still not been restored in much of Iraq, no-go areas are proliferating in Baghdad and other cities, plans to create an Iraqi transitional government within a month or two have been scrapped, and the first American proconsul has already been fired and sent home. It may be only a matter of months before armed resistance to the American occupation begins.

Why would France or Germany want to send troops into that? Why would Russia or China want the UN to take responsibility for it? The default position would be to say to the US and Britain (and Australia and Poland), "You made your bed. You lie in it." The reason they don't say that is that they all know there will be a post-Bush United States at some point, and that it will be necessary to persuade Americans (who will probably be feeling pretty battered and unloved by then) to come back to the UN system.

So don't alienate American public opinion, which remains doubtful about the whole Bush administration project to destroy the existing international system. Don't stand on legality, and don't give the hawks in the current administration an excuse to abandon the UN entirely. The more you can limit the damage now, the less you have to rebuild later. It's a holding operation based on the assumption that the Bush administration has fatally overreached itself in Iraq already, or if not will do so in the next war.

The UN is not finished. It couldn't stop the US invasion on Iraq, but it has gained enormous credit in the 96 percent of the world that is not American by its refusal to go along with it. Now it has made a compromise that will distress the purists, but it has to keep its popular support in America, too. And it still has a lot of support in the US. After all, Americans practically invented the UN.

THINGS WE DIDN'T KNOW AT THE TIME: *We didn't know that Jay Garner, the retired US army general who had been chosen to run the occupation regime in Iraq and was then summarily dismissed within weeks of taking charge in early April, lost his job because he was insisting on early elections in Iraq. The neocons who were running the Pentagon were confident that they had years to reshape Iraq at their leisure, and they didn't want any elected Iraqis interfering in the process. They explained Garner's sacking with the usual leaked slanders about incompetence, and his soldier's reflex of obedience kept him from going public with the truth.*

Then things started to fall apart in Iraq. First, the pretexts for the war vanished . . .

THE "WEAPONS OF MASS DISAPPEARANCE"
June 1, 2003

"We know where [the weapons] are. They're in the area around Tikrit and Baghdad and east, west, north and south somewhat."

—*US Defense Secretary Donald Rumsfeld, March* 30, 2003

"It is . . . possible that they decided that they would destroy them prior to a conflict."

—*Donald Rumsfeld, May 27, 2003*

Sure, Don, that's probably what happened: "They're going to attack us, boys. Quick, destroy all our weapons." The issue of the missing "weapons of mass destruction" that were used to justify the invasion of Iraq is not going to go away, even though all the American and British leaders who hammered away on this issue before the war now just sound irritated when you bring it up.

"It's not crucially important," said British Foreign Secretary Jack Straw on May 14, but it is. And although the political uproar over the lies and distortions that were used to manoeuvre the public into supporting the war is much greater in Britain at the moment, with allegations that Prime Minister Tony Blair's office "sexed up" the intelligence reports on Iraq and deliberately misled Parliament, the furor will grow in the United States as well. Probably just in time for the presidential election campaign.

Insiders always understood that the WMD issue was a red herring. Nobody really believed that Iraq had nuclear weapons, and its alleged chemical and biological weapons, if they existed, were the sort of thing that every country with pretensions as a power has been messing around with for generations. Iraq had no way to deliver them over long ranges even if it had them, and the terrorist issue was irrelevant. There were no known ties between Iraq and al-Qaeda, and besides, if terrorists wanted such weapons, they could just cook them up themselves. It isn't hard.

The WMD story was needed to scare the US public into supporting the invasion, but also to give Britain some legal cover for taking part in the war. Americans were not much concerned about the legality of invading Iraq, but it was crucial for Blair to have UN cover in order to retain the support of his own Labour Party—and the war would only be legal under United Nations rules if Iraq were violating the UN resolutions that ordered Saddam Hussein to get rid of his WMD.

When the Security Council, unconvinced of the urgency of attacking Iraq to "disarm" it, refused to support an invasion, Blair took Britain to war alongside the United States anyway, but it left him horribly vulnerable, particularly within his own Labour Party. Over a quarter of the Labour Members of Parliament voted against an attack on Iraq, and as many more only backed it because of Blair's blood-curdling accounts of Iraqi WMD "ready to launch within forty-five minutes."

So now, seven weeks after the war's end, with no WMD found in Iraq and British intelligence sources protesting to the media about Blair's misuse of their reports, his position has become very difficult—but his worst problem is what they are saying in Washington. Consider US Deputy Secretary of Defense Paul Wolfowitz's cynical remarks in the forthcoming issue of *Vanity Fair*: "For reasons that have a lot to do with the US government bureaucracy, we settled on the one issue that everyone could agree on, which was weapons of mass destruction as the core reason."

It makes perfect sense for the neoconservatives in the Bush administration who cooked up the war on Iraq to admit now that it wasn't really about WMD. Their real purpose, after all, was to scare all America's rivals and enemies into submission by demonstrating US military power and making it clear that no considerations of international law would stand in Washington's way. But they are putting Blair into a dreadful corner, and storing up trouble for Bush as well.

A great many Labour MPs deeply resent having been lied to by their own party and government, and neither they nor the British press will let the matter drop. For the moment, there is much less outcry in the US, but the smarter Democrats are just biding their time. Right now questioning the wisdom of the war would still leave them open to the charge of being unpatriotic, but as Iraqi resistance and American casualties grow—five US soldiers killed and thirteen injured last week—that calculation will change.

By next winter, Mr. Bush will be facing harsh questions about why it was necessary to invade Iraq. With the US economy unlikely to recover dramatically in the next year, that could spell electoral disaster unless he wraps himself in the flag again, so another war before November 2004 and a "khaki election" are not out of the question. The likeliest target would be Syria, which could be conquered quickly and cheaply, rather than Iran or North Korea—but whichever it is, he should not expect to have Britain along next time. Tony Blair has not enough credit left.

In the end, there was no need for another war to ensure Mr. Bush's re-election because the Democrats chose the hapless John Kerry to run against him. And besides, the Iraqi resistance was soon growing so fast that the US army simply couldn't spare the troops for another invasion.

CHAPTER TEN

THE STATE OF EUROPE

Because Europe ruled most of the world for the past few centuries, it is somehow seen as "older" than other places, though of course it is not. Because it seems to be past its wars and is now mostly democratic, it is also sometimes seen as more mature, or at least more sedate. This leads to a curious kind of reporting on European issues in the global media, as if the European countries were not populated by people just as ambitious, greedy and foolish as those elsewhere.

They are.

WHO'S A BANANA REPUBLIC NOW?

January 31, 2002

Is corruption a Third-World disorder? Not if the French are any guide.

"France is not a banana republic," insisted former prime minister Raymond Barre last year, as the financial scandals surrounding President Jacques Chirac grew ever more damning. "You must not believe that all French politics or that all French politicians are corrupt." But most French people believe exactly that.

Judge Eric Halphen, who spent seven years investigating the French president's alleged crimes, only to have France's highest court rule last October that "the president of the republic cannot be questioned as a witness . . . or charged with any infraction," has come to the same conclusion.

Halphen finally quit his job as investigating magistrate two weeks ago. Claiming that he had been bugged and followed, subjected to threats and a sting operation, and obstructed at every turn, he said that in France "political investigations are just like mafia investigations. No one speaks. . . . People who embezzle huge sums escape all judgement . . . but the man who steals a handbag on the Métro is not so lucky. He gets six months."

To be fair, former French foreign minister Roland Dumas was sentenced to six months in jail last June for receiving kickbacks through his former mistress Christine Deviers-Joncour, the self-described "whore of the republic," that were worth up to $4 million. They don't all get away. But it is still largely true that in France "the law is for little people," not for the elite. And the "little people," remarkably, generally go along with it.

That is certainly the case in Italy, where Prime Minister Silvio Berlusconi has led a counteroffensive against the attempted clean-up of Italian politics by crusading magistrates in the latter 1990s. The *"mani puliti"* (clean hands) investigators actually broke the astoundingly corrupt Christian Democratic Party, which had dominated Italian politics for forty years, but Berlusconi, who owns or strongly influences all six of Italy's national television channels, has now persuaded many Italians that it was all just a left-wing plot.

Berlusconi deals with the various bribery charges he faces himself by endless delaying actions—one case has already expired because it passed the legal deadline before getting to court—or by simply changing the law. For example, there is now a proposal to downgrade false accounting (a charge that is, by coincidence, facing his own Mediaset Corporation) from a felony to a noncriminal misdemeanour. Italians still vote for him.

Nor is it just some Latin thing. In 2000 Germany watched former chancellor Helmut Kohl feign memory loss whenever he was asked about illegal campaign contributions to his Christian Democratic Party. (He admitted to receiving over nine hundred thousand dollars in 1993–98 alone, but investigators suspected far larger sums.) And Ireland recently went through a two-year drama while a special tribunal examined how Charlie Haughey, four times prime minister, had accumulated a fortune more than a hundred times greater than his highest annual salary.

How does this compare with poor countries in the developing world? It's not as bad as African kleptocracies such as Congo under Mobutu or Nigeria under Abacha, where the rulers stole literally billions of dollars. It doesn't even rank with Peru, where Vladimiro Montesinos, for ten years disgraced ex-president Alberto Fujimori's closest adviser, had twenty-four hundred videotapes showing the country's political and business elite accepting bribes.

But even poor democracies with free media, such as India (where former prime minister Narasimha Rao got a three-year jail sentence for bribery in 2000), sometimes get it right. Corruption is everywhere, but so is retribution. India's defence minister George Fernandes had to leave the cabinet last year after an upstart website called tehelka.com sent out journalists disguised as British businessmen seeking an arms contract and secretly filmed Indian generals, politicians and senior officials accepting large sums of cash from them.

Or take the Philippines, whose people elected a charming scoundrel, Joseph "Erap" Estrada, to the presidency—and then overthrew him last year when his influence-peddling and bribe-taking got too public and too embarrassing. Crime, but also punishment—a great deal more punishment than France's President Chirac expects to receive.

The most recent and in some ways the worst of the many scandals that dog Chirac is the revelation that he paid for three hundred and fifty thousand dollars worth of air travel in 1993–95, including private trips to places like New York (by Concorde), Mauritius and Japan for himself, his family and friends, with brown envelopes stuffed with 500-franc notes delivered to the travel agency by his chauffeur.

The assumption is that this money is part of the kickbacks he received on almost all city construction projects while he was mayor of Paris, but if he is re-elected president this year it will be another five years before anybody can even question him about it. And he probably will win: French voters don't seem upset about it.

On an index devised by the anticorruption crusaders at Transparency International, the cleanest countries are predictably in northern Europe, from Finland at 9.9 to Britain at 8.3, while the very lowest scores are registered by big, poor countries like Bangladesh, Indonesia and Nigeria. But France gets only 6.7. (The United States gets 7.6.)

Many people think there's a simple equation: rich countries are honest, poor ones are corrupt. But it's much more complicated than that. Some cultures secretly despise rip-off artists even when they become the rich and the powerful, as they so often do. Other cultures, however, secretly admire them—and let them get away with it.

The flip side of Europe is that it is the site of the boldest political experiment in the world today. The idea that you can and should unify all of Europe in a single postmodern state—not a traditional nation-state, in other words, not even a federal one, but nevertheless an entity that deals with its own citizens and the rest of the world in a way that becomes increasingly coherent and consistent over time—has grown from the far narrower concept of the early 1950s into a genuine political enterprise of astounding ambition.

WHERE DOES EUROPE END?
April 26, 2004

As of the 1st of May, the European Union's easternmost land border will be with Russia, and its sea frontier will be halfway between Cyprus and Lebanon. The entry of ten new member countries in eastern Europe and the Mediterranean (Estonia, Latvia, Lithuania, Poland, the

Czech Republic, Slovakia, Hungary, Slovenia, Cyprus and Malta) brings the EU up to twenty-five countries and 450 million people, but it's not finished expanding yet.

Romania and Bulgaria, with 30 million more people, are working towards entry in 2007, Croatia has also joined the queue, and Turkey hopes to get a green light for entry negotiations this December. If Turkey eventually joins, the EU's easternmost borders will be with Iran and Iraq. Where exactly does Europe end?

The traditional geographer's answer is that Europe ends at the Ural Mountains, but that is not a national frontier at all, just a not very dramatic mountain chain that divides "European Russia" from western Siberia. The problem with Russia is the same as with Turkey, where Europe technically ends at the Bosphorus Strait that runs through Istanbul, leaving most of Turkey in Asia. Only in Russia's case, including the whole country in the EU would give "Europe" a short common border with North Korea—and a three-thousand-kilometre (two-thousand-mile) frontier with China and Mongolia.

It sounds preposterous, and yet both Turkey and Russia have been part of the European great-power system for centuries. The expansion of the EU from its original six-member core in the 1950s has been relentless: three more members in the 1970s, three more in the 1980s, three more in the 1990s, and now ten more at once. With each expansion it becomes more complicated—EU documents must now be available in Latvian, Maltese and Hungarian, together with over a dozen other languages—but new candidates keep banging on the door, and Europe finds it hard to say no.

It's hard to say no because the EU's real purpose is not merely economic (though it spends much of its time squabbling over budgets and subsidies). It grew out of a "European Coal and Steel Community" that was initially created in 1951 not just to produce cheaper coal and steel, but also to bring together France and Germany, two countries that had fought each other three times in seventy years. Economic integration was supposed to make wars between the partners impossible.

It worked: nobody today could imagine France and Germany going to war with each other again. The same now applies to Britain, Italy, Spain and all the other European countries that have been at one another's throats for centuries. The more recent creation of a common European currency, the euro, was likewise driven more by the desire to make the union indissoluble than by strict financial logic (though Britain, Denmark and Sweden remain outside the euro zone). But if the goal is to turn the "cockpit of Europe" into the garden of Europe, how can you freeze any European country out? Which brings us back to the question of where Europe ends.

It will take the EU some time to digest the ten new members (whose 75 million citizens will not enjoy unrestricted freedom to move to any other EU country for another seven years). The business of running such a complex assemblage of still-sovereign states gets ever more cumbersome, and while a new constitution to streamline the workings of the EU will probably be agreed in June, it must then run the gauntlet of as many as half a dozen national referendums, with a single "no" being enough to sink the whole project. And yet, however haltingly, the expansion will continue.

Romania, Bulgaria and Croatia are shoo-ins, and some of the smaller Balkan fragments left over from former Yugoslavia will doubtless join once they establish a stable democratic order. Which leaves three big steps: Turkey (75 million people), Ukraine and Belarus (60 million) and Russia (145 million).

Turkey is the most democratic and probably the most prosperous of these potential candidates: its government has turned itself inside out to meet EU standards, and entry negotiations should be a cinch. They will not be, mainly because almost all Turks are Muslims, and their entry would mean that almost 20 percent of the EU's total population is Muslim. That should not be an impediment, but in central Europe there is still a folk memory of the time when Turkish armies were beating at the gates of Vienna, and in western Europe there is already prejudice against the large Muslim immigrant populations in most major cities.

Yet Turkey probably will gain entry in the next ten years, and Ukraine and Belarus may not have to wait much longer (although the latter would first have to get rid of its dictator, Alexander Lukashenko). Which leaves Russia, the biggest and most indigestible lump that the EU might ever try to swallow. Given a big democratic deficit in Russia, the war in Chechnya, and half a dozen other major obstacles, that question isn't on the table yet, or anywhere near it.

But even Russia will probably join in the end. It will join a lot sooner if the Bush administration's unilateralism wrecks the NATO alliance and ruptures Europe's transatlantic bonds. One way or another, it will probably be possible by 2020 or 2025 to drive from Portugal to the Pacific Ocean without passing through a single border checkpoint. Who would have believed that in 1945, or even in 1990?

Croatia turned out not to be a shoo-in: Brussels suspended its entry talks because of the Zagreb government's failure to deliver to the Hague tribunal a suspected war criminal, a Croatian national hero from the war with Serbia. Croatia will doubtless be allowed back in the queue to join once it has complied, but it is important that the legal and human rights standards required for EU membership are not being weakened as the Union expands into the newer democracies of eastern Europe. And of course, the new European "constitution" hit a brick wall in the French and Dutch referendums in spring 2005, leaving the EU to stumble along with the old rules for years to come.

The trickiest bit, however, is to keep the United States, which increasingly sees Europe as a potential strategic rival, from splitting the EU between "old Europe" and "new Europe." The game is already afoot.

POLAND'S DILEMMA
July 15, 2004

"We're interested in becoming a concrete part of the arrangement," said Polish Foreign Ministry spokesman Boguslaw Majewski, after it was revealed on July 10 that Poland has been in secret talks with the United States for the past eight months on locating elements of the US ballistic missile defence system, including interceptor missiles, on its territory. Then it came out that the US has also been talking to the Czech Republic, Hungary, Romania and Bulgaria about it, but Poland is definitely the leading candidate.

Poland's main problem has always been its geography: sandwiched between Germany and Russia, it was regularly conquered by them or partitioned between them. Poland lost 20 percent of its population in the Second World War, mainly in Nazi death camps, and then spent the next forty-five years under a Communist dictatorship imposed by its Russian liberators. You can see why it wants close links with a great power that isn't in Europe, and giving the United States military bases that Washington sees as important is one easy way of doing that.

The project to protect the United States from ballistic missile attack is one of the great boondoggles of all time. After twenty years of development, there is still no evidence that it will ever work reliably—even though the Pentagon is going ahead with the construction of two missile interceptor sites in California and Alaska, presumably to shoot down the ICBMs that North Korea doesn't have, tipped with the nuclear warheads that it probably doesn't have either. The main function of "Son of Star Wars" in the US political system has been to serve as a kind of social welfare system for needy aerospace companies and recently retired Air Force generals.

The Poles don't care whether the missiles work or not, and most of them don't even believe the story that the Pentagon wants a site in eastern Europe to intercept nuclear missiles fired at the United States by Iran or Syria. (Iran and Syria don't have missiles that could get even a quarter of the way to the US, or any nuclear warheads to put on them, either.) They suspect that Washington really wants to intercept Russian missiles just after they launch, but that's okay with them, too. Poles mistrust the Russians almost as much as they do the Germans.

All the Poles want is an important American base on their territory, so that Washington doesn't forget about them in a crisis. They'll make do with radar stations if they have to, but, as former defence minister Janusz Onyszkeiwicz put it, "an interceptor site would be more attractive. It wouldn't be a hard sell in Poland." It's a very understandable Polish reflex, given the history—but it could greatly complicate Poland's foreign relations closer to home.

Germany and France are not at all pleased to see the US seeking missile bases in eastern European countries that have become, since this spring, part of the European Union. They see it as part and parcel of Washington's strategy of splitting off the recently ex-Communist countries of eastern Europe that Defense Secretary Don Rumsfeld described last year with typical sensitivity as "new Europe" (good and strongly pro-American), to be distinguished from France, Germany and other parts of "old Europe" (bad and allegedly anti-American).

It's working, too. Most of the eastern European states have sent token contingents to Iraq to curry favour with the United States, and most of them would be happy to have American bases on their soil (though they'll never outbid the Poles). And it's practically a cost-free strategy at the moment: the Germans and the French haven't been nasty to them, and the Russians have been positively saintly about it all. But it could get ugly further down the line.

If the United States remains on a unilateralist course after this November's election, failing to consult with allies, ignoring the United Nations whenever it gets in the way, and frequently violating international law, all the other great powers will start to respond by trying to create counterbalancing centres of power. They are on hold for the moment, because none of them really wants to go down that road, but it's clear what they will do if they conclude that it is necessary.

They will start building up their arms, of course, and in the case of China that is probably all they will do. In Europe, however, the great powers will also start to come together in what won't be called an alliance, but will gradually become exactly that—and its chief members will be France, Germany and Russia. That's the only combination big enough to say "no" to overwhelming American power.

If it comes to that, five years down the road, life will get very hard for eastern European countries that have become too closely bound to the United States—especially if they have American missile interceptor sites on their territory. And if you think that this scenario hasn't already occurred to the chief American negotiator on the potential deal with Poland, Under-Secretary of State for Arms Control John Bolton, then you are seriously underestimating the man.

The real question is whether it has occurred to the Poles.

That is a worst-case analysis. There is an expanding zone of peace, democracy and prosperity on the European continent, and people's ideas of what is possible are being profoundly affected by the fact that they might one day join it. The Serbian and the Georgian revolutions would probably not have happened without that promise shining in the distance; the Ukrainian revolution certainly would not have. And it may not stop there.

EU: THE HALO EFFECT
December 20, 2004

"The Islamic world, the Islamic extremists, even bin Laden, rejoice for the entrance of Turkey into the European Union. This is their Trojan horse," warned Libyan dictator Muammar Gadafy on December 17. The EU's decision on that day to open membership talks with Turkey would eventually lead to Muslim domination of Europe, he explained.

It was an encouraging outburst, in a way, for Gadafy is almost always wrong: if the Sage of Tripoli is predicting disaster, then it should be all right in the end. Turkey's eventual membership (still ten or fifteen years away) will not transform the EU; rather, Turkey will be transformed by its membership. The influences travel outwards, not inwards.

There is a kind of halo effect around the European Union. Even though the EU doesn't actively push its values on its neighbours, the mere fact that a majority of Europeans already live in this zone where democracy works and civil and human rights are genuinely respected is transforming expectations and behaviour in the rest of Europe. Take Turkey, for example.

The 70 million Turks have practically turned themselves inside out in their effort to meet the standards on democracy, human rights, and legal and fiscal propriety demanded of countries seeking to open membership negotiations. Turkey has changed more in the past three years than in the previous thirty, and almost entirely for the better.

Or consider the re-staged second round of the Ukrainian presidential election next Sunday, which will almost certainly be won by reformist candidate Viktor Yushchenko. The weeks of nonviolent mass protests in Kiev that forced the cancellation of the rigged election results and a re-run under intense international scrutiny would probably not have happened without the hope of eventual EU membership for Ukraine.

The EU has done nothing to encourage this hope. It has just taken in ten new members and another three countries in the Balkans will probably be joining in 2007. Most EU leaders would have dodged a decision on Turkey's candidacy this year if they were not trapped by promises made long ago. No EU government wants to start entry negotiations for 50 million impoverished Ukrainians on the borders of a resentful Russia any time soon—but Ukrainians simply ignored that.

A majority of Ukrainians, who have lived for the past thirteen years in a post-Soviet morass of arrogant corruption, brazen election-rigging and sold-out media, took to the streets because they believed that there could be an alternative future for their country in the EU. Ukrainian entry into the EU may be even further away than Turkey's, but it was that vision of honest government, free media and fair enforcement of the law glimmering on the horizon that made the Orange Revolution in Ukraine possible.

The same was at least partly true for the Rose Revolution in Georgia last year, and it was wholly true for the other "Orange Revolution" of the past month—the one that happened in Romania. In every case the initiative came from local people demanding the same rights and values that EU citizens enjoy, not from the EU trying to export its values to the east. In fact, if it had been left to the governments that are allegedly the guardians of the EU's democratic values, it wouldn't have happened at all.

Romania had the most oppressive Communist Party in eastern Europe before 1989, and the revolution there in December of that year was largely a fake. Leading regime members, seeing which way the wind was blowing, launched a coup, stood dictator Nicolae Ceauşescu and his wife against a wall, and shot them. But then they just renamed themselves Social Democrats and went right on ruling the place.

They have been in power for most of the past fifteen years, enriching themselves shamelessly and manipulating the media and the electoral system to stay in charge. Corruption is so bad that an estimated 10 percent of the average Romanian's income goes to bribing public officials. Romania was much less qualified for EU membership than Turkey—it even has a lower per capita income—and yet the EU was pushing entry negotiations through to an early conclusion.

The 22 million Romanians are not Muslims, so there was no popular anxiety in existing EU members about letting them in. EU officials were deeply cynical about the possibility of real reform in Romania, and decided to let it in anyway. Prime Minister Adrian Nastase, once a fervent supporter of Ceausescu, seemed to be cruising smoothly to another term after the first round of elections in early December, although monitors from the Organization for Security and Cooperation in Europe reported multiple voting frauds. (The EU did not bother to send monitors.)

In effect, practically everybody had written off democracy in Romania—except the Romanians. In the second round of voting on December 12, with much closer monitoring of the polls, they voted Nastase out and elected Traian Basescu, a former ship's captain with no links to the ex-Communist oligarchy. It will take Basescu years to loosen the grip of the oligarchs on Romania's economy and its media (as it will for Yushchenko in Ukraine, too), but the Romanians have decided that if they are going to be in the EU, they want the whole package.

Given the choice, people know what they want.

CHAPTER ELEVEN

MISCELLANY I

Do two columns a week for twenty years — or three a week, as I did for quite a few years before that — and you will become familiar with the problem we experts call Nothing's Happening. Nothing new on the international scene of a political or military nature, that is to say, or in my case, nothing that can reasonably be represented as interesting and relevant to people in every continent. It doesn't occur that often, but when it does, that's when you turn to new science, or sociology, or economics or even history. And it's usually a lot more fun to do. You can get very sick of politics.

BUGS IN THE SKY

July 31, 2001

The biggest news so far this year is not George W. Bush's plans for intergalactic defence, or even the Code Red virus that is going to eat our computers and then our brains. It is the discovery of bugs in the upper atmosphere.

"There is now unambiguous evidence for the presence of clumps of living cells in air samples from as high as forty-one kilometres, well above the local tropopause above which no air from lower down would normally be transported," Professor Chandra Wickramasinghe told the International Society for Optical Engineering in San Diego last week. Wickramasinghe's home base, Cardiff University, says it is "the first positive identification of extraterrestrial microbial life."

According to Wickramasinghe's ten-person team of scientists, there are living cells in the upper atmosphere of this planet that probably come from space. They are also suggesting that living cells arriving from outer space are the mechanism by which life first arose on this planet—with the further implications that life exists on almost every planet, and that all life in this galaxy is genetically related.

That is rather a lot to deduce from a balloon collecting air samples in the stratosphere, even if it went twice as high as any balloon on such a mission has ever gone before, but the Cardiff University team were not surprised. "We have argued for more than two decades that terrestrial life was brought down to Earth by comets," said Wickramasinghe, "and that cometary material containing micro-organisms must still be reaching us in large quantities."

The hypothesis of the Cardiff University team, originally

led by brilliant cosmologist Sir Fred Hoyle, has never been completely dismissed by more orthodox scientists because their credentials were so strong (Hoyle was the man who worked out how the heavier elements in the universe are created in the hearts of dying stars). But what they were saying was so contrary to conventional scientific wisdom that they were mostly politely ignored.

The conventional wisdom states that life on Earth arose from the soup of organic chemicals that existed on the primordial surface of the planet. Simple chemical experiments have shown that the gases that then made up the Earth's atmosphere, when zapped with electrical charges of the sort that lightning would have provided, combine readily into organic molecules. It's a very long way from those to the first living cell, but there were several billion years for evolution to work its magic.

Hoyle and Wickramasinghe began suggesting, as long ago as 1974, that while the evolutionary process leading to the first living cell undoubtedly happened somewhere, sometime, it probably occurred far, far away, long before the Earth had even cooled. Their starting point was the then-new observation that even the interstellar gas clouds contain organic molecules. Their radical suggestion was that the millions of comets that shuttle between the interstellar depths and the inner solar system were the conveyor belt that brought this organic material, perhaps including even living cells, to the Earth.

At the time, it was an unprovable theory, but recently space probes have found evidence that comets contain chemical material similar to the cell walls of living organisms. Meanwhile, Wickramasinghe's team reasoned that if comets are constantly delivering living cells to the inner solar system that are then swept up by the Earth as it orbits the sun, then we should be able to find those cells in the upper atmosphere. So let's go look for them.

The consensus among meteorologists is that there is normally no mixing between the lower atmosphere (the troposphere), where all earthly life exists, and the upper atmosphere or stratosphere. If you did find living cells above the tropopause (the barrier between the two), they would likely have come from space, not from the Earth. So the Cardiff team sent up giant balloons from a research base near Hyderabad in India, collected air samples at altitudes of up to forty-one kilometres and found what they were looking for—bacteria.

"Clumps of living cells were found at all altitudes using this technique," they wrote in their report. "Since the 41-km sample was collected well above the local tropopause, a prima facie case for a space incidence of these micro-organisms is established."

If Wickramasinghe's conclusion is correct, then this is one of the most important discoveries of all time. It would mean that throughout this galaxy and beyond, all environments even marginally hospitable to life are actually inhabited by living things, because the microbial seeds fall from space on every available surface (which probably means hundreds of millions of planets in our galaxy alone). And it would also mean that all these life forms—you, me, the cloud-creatures of Betelguese and even the dread Bugblatter Beast of Rigel X, having a common origin in space-borne micro-organisms, are intimately related to one another.

And sometimes, there's nothing going on even on those fronts.

SUMMERTIME BLUES

August 25, 2002

First I thought that I'd write an article called "Death Watch at Marbella," about the last days of the Saudi king at his palace in Spain, and the exciting things that might happen in the Middle East after his death. But then my elder daughter's boyfriend, who's looking after our house in London, called to say my younger daughter's rabbit had been found dead in the garden, surrounded by five rather puzzled but pleased-looking cats. (The rabbit actually bit through a cable and electrocuted herself, but the cats would certainly have killed her if they thought they could get away with it.)

Kate is only ten, so it took a while to break the news that her rabbit was dead and get her through the worst of it. By that time I had lost my enthusiasm for the Saudi article — truth is, the king may last for years yet — so I started to write a piece on Burma instead.

It's over three months since the military regime that has ruled the country for the past forty years was forced by international pressure to free Aung San Suu Kyi, Nelson Mandela's only real rival as a living hero of nonviolence and democracy. Surely there must be some signs of movement there by now. But then I was interrupted by a man at the door who had come to tell me that replacing the roof tiles on our house in France is going to cost us an arm, a leg and several vital organs.

The house is very small, it's in a deeply unfashionable part of France, and we only use it two weeks a year, but it's been in the family since my wife's grandmother's time, so we can't just walk away from it. We can't argue much about the cost of the roof either, because the roofer is the son-in-law of our next-door neighbour, and this is a very small village.

By the time all that was dealt with, the whole idea of writing about Burma had lost its charm. There will be big things happening there one of these days—the nonviolent democratic revolution that was put down with machine-gun fire in 1988 is not dead, it is only biding its time—but at the moment there is no hook at all. Nothing newsworthy is happening in Burma.

I could go on, but I won't. The point is obvious: it's late August, almost all the world's troublemakers are on holiday, and there isn't enough news to go round. Journalists still have to write articles, because papers need something to hold the ads apart, but frankly there is hardly anything that couldn't wait for next month.

What can we usefully say about this phenomenon? First of all, we must apologize to the southern hemisphere, where it isn't summer and nobody's on holiday. (I'm personally very conscious of this because I have close family in Argentina, South Africa and Australia.) But less than a fifth of the world's population lives south of the equator, and it's a relatively civilized fifth. In terms of global news, it's the summer doldrums.

Next week, of course, the wicked northerners will come back from their holidays, reinvigorated and ready for fresh trouble. As soon as the kids go back to school and the grown-ups go back to work, the wheels will start to turn again, and in a couple of weeks there will be enough crises and confrontations and emergency summits to fill a column a day, with plenty left over. You must recognize the pattern, but you may not have noticed that it's telling you something.

When all the presidents and prime ministers and tinpot dictators of the northern hemisphere go off on holiday, the world manages to run itself without them—and it runs so well that it fails to generate the usual headlines. The caretakers who have been left in charge take no new initiatives on their own, so everything suddenly goes very quiet.

You could call it the "Putin's at his dacha, all's well with the world" phenomenon. Americans like George W. Bush even more when he's in Crawford, Texas, than when he's back in Washington, DC. The Chinese people perceptibly relax when the Communist Party's senior leadership goes off to its weird collective summer camp on the Shantung coast. If they never came back, would anybody mind?

Cheap shots, I admit. Countries do have to be run, decisions have to be taken, changes sometimes have to be made. Somebody has to take the responsibility for doing all that, and even in the most democratic systems the people who volunteer for the job are often the last ones you'd want to give it to—but you have to give it to somebody.

I'm not recommending anarchy as a substitute (though I would if I could figure out how to make it work). I'm just pointing out that the reason the world seems less crazy and dangerous than usual is that our leaders are on holiday.

The one that follows is a political story, but you never know where to put Australia, do you?

THE REAL AUSTRALIA

August 23, 2003

They sent Pauline Hanson to jail for three years last week on charges of electoral fraud. The One Nation Party that she founded did not have the five hundred members that she claimed when she registered it in 1997, but only five hundred signatures from an unofficial support group. She also got half a million Australian dollars from the state of Queensland by fraud to fight the 1998 election there. Bad Pauline—but she has changed the country anyway.

"The reason why I got into politics was to make a difference," Hanson said earlier this year, when her challenge to the established Australian parties had already faded. "When you have the government and the Prime Minister take up your policies, I think you have made a difference." And that is just what has happened: John Howard, Australia's second-longest-serving prime minister, has ensured his longevity by becoming Pauline Hanson in drag.

Hanson herself is a familiar phenomenon in democratic politics: a right-wing populist who exploits the issues of race and immigration to create a following. She first ran for Parliament in 1996 as a candidate of Howard's Liberal Party, but was "de-selected" when they realized how extreme she was: Asian immigrants were synonymous with crime and disease, she said, and she wanted to slash government spending on health, education and housing for the desperately poor Aborigines.

It turned out that a lot of other Australians felt the same way. Hanson won her seat as an independent in 1996 and founded "One Nation" the following year. In its first national election, in 1998, it won an astonishing 8 percent of the vote.

Those who voted for One Nation were mostly rural people who were losing their place in the world because of changes in the global market and city-dwellers who were being left behind by an increasingly knowledge-based economy. Hanson offered them scapegoats: Asian immigrants who were stealing Australians' jobs (she wanted immigration stopped until unemployment fell to zero) and ungrateful Aborigines who scrounged a living off the welfare system.

Politicians of this ilk are part of the political ecology in every country: they come along every week or so, like cold fronts. So why did Hanson first take Australia by storm, and then find the country's leading mainstream politician stealing her clothes? Because Australia is not the country it thinks it is, or would like to be. It is a much more old-fashioned, conservative place with a few big cities that seem cosmopolitan—but even in Perth or Brisbane you'll often hear casual racist remarks of a sort that died out a generation ago in big cities elsewhere in the English-speaking world.

All the major Australian political parties used to cooperate to keep people like Paula Hanson off their candidates' lists, but once she demonstrated how big the market for racism was, their common front broke. The first sign of what was to come was Prime Minister John Howard's refusal to condemn Hanson's One Nation Party in the 1998 election.

Howard is not a racist; he is just a skilled political operator who recognizes what works, and he is not hampered by a serious case of scruples. His Liberal Party began to steal bits of Hanson's agenda—and then two years ago came the golden opportunity of the *Tampa*, a Norwegian freighter that rescued 434 Afghans from a sinking ship in the Indian Ocean and headed for Australian territory with them.

The Afghans had been heading for Australia anyway, with the intention of claiming asylum. But international law obliged Australia to allow these survivors of shipwreck, huddled together on the deck of a freighter in the tropical sun, to come ashore at the nearest port. Howard, only weeks away from an election and lagging in the polls, refused to let them land—and when the captain of the *Tampa* ignored Canberra's instructions and kept steaming towards Australian territory, Howard sent the Australian Navy and SAS (Special Air Service) troops to seize the ship.

Most Australians cheered his action because they had already half-accepted the line peddled by Hanson and echoed by dozens of "shock-jock" radio call-in hosts that the country was being inundated in illegal immigrants. In fact, Australia only gets a few thousand "illegals" a year, far fewer than most other rich countries (and it takes in a smaller share of legal immigrants than most of them, too). In matters of this sort, however, perception is everything—and the perception is that Australia is being overrun by nonwhites.

The Afghans on the *Tampa* were dispersed to various Pacific islands without ever touching Australian soil, there to be held in camps and sorted through by Australian immigration officers. A few weeks later Howard won the election, collecting most of the votes that once went to Hanson's party (which had virtually destroyed itself in vicious internal battles in the meantime). And now Hanson has gone to jail, but she has left Australia a changed place.

What was once redneck talk shunned by educated people is now part of the national political discourse, and the lurid fears of the racists are seen as reasonable concerns that need to be addressed. The principal beneficiary of this shift is none other than Prime Minister John Howard, whose Liberal Party disowned Hanson and her ideas only seven years ago. As one Australian commentator said: "He is a genius of sorts. He looks this country in the face and sees us not as we wish we were, not as one day we might be, but exactly as we are."

John Howard was re-elected for a fourth term as prime minister in 2004.

WAITING FOR THE CANADIAN HORDES
March 15, 2004

Dr. Samuel P. Huntington, chairman of the Harvard Academy for International and Area Studies and co-founder of *Foreign Policy* magazine, is like a dog that has only one trick: we've all seen it before, but he won't stop doing it. We're going to have to stop giving him biscuits.

Dr. Huntington's trick is to identify some alleged new threat to US security, dress it up in academically respectable language and inflate it to bursting point. He did it in 1993 with his essay "The Coming Clash of Civilizations" and recycled it as a best-selling book in 1996; but now it's time for a new threat. This time it's the Mexican hordes coming from the south. In the most recent issue of *Foreign Policy*, he poses the questions: "Will the US remain a country with a single national language and a core Anglo-Protestant culture? (Or will) Americans acquiesce to their eventual transformation into two peoples with two cultures (Anglo and Hispanic) and two languages (English and Spanish)?"

Don't confuse Dr. Huntington with the foul-mouthed bigots who usually rant on about the Mexican Peril: his usual habitat is Harvard University's dreaming spires, not some down-market drinking establishment on the wrong side of town. But his article "The Hispanic Challenge" is a trailer for his new book *Who Are We? The Challenges to America's National Identity,* and one suspects that his definition of "We" does not include African-Americans, Muslim

Americans or Mexican-Americans. In fact, it doesn't really even include Catholic Americans.

Dr. Huntington is not exactly predicting that Mexican-Americans will grow into a permanent Spanish-speaking minority as important as French Canadians in Canada, with a territorial base in the Southwest, a culture that profoundly diverges from the traditional white, Protestant culture of the United States, and the political clout to impose bilingualism nationwide. He's just warning about it, that's all (and he's too cunning to court charges of extremism by suggesting specific policies to avert this dreadful fate).

It would be a waste of time to go through his arguments piecemeal, but a couple of examples will convey the style. He admits that the share of Mexican immigrants in current US immigration is lower than that of Irish immigrants in the period 1820 to 1860 or of German immigrants in 1850 to 1870, but insists that the danger is greater now because Mexicans won't assimilate.

Then he quotes a study showing that more than 90 percent of second-generation Mexican-Americans in Los Angeles speak fluent English and that over 60 percent of them speak either no Spanish or worse Spanish than English, but promptly frets that "with the rapid expansion of the Mexican immigrant community, people of Mexican origin would have less incentive to become fluent in and use English in 2000 than 1970." Yes, they might, but where's your evidence? There is none; just false parallels, unsupported conclusions and a lavish use of the conditional mood.

Yet, there is more to Huntington than cynical careerism; you sense a genuine cultural and racial panic in what he writes. He talks of the "distinct Anglo-Protestant culture of the founding settlers" as "the bedrock of US identity," and lists its key values: "the English language; Christianity; religious commitment; . . . the rule of law, including the responsibility of rulers and the rights of individuals; and dissenting Protestant values of individualism, the work ethic, and the belief that humans have the ability and the duty to try to create a heaven on earth, a 'city on the hill.'"

Anybody who does not live in the United States would reel back in disbelief at the arrogance and naïveté of that list, as if France and Japan didn't have the rule of law and the work ethic, or as if the British and the Spanish couldn't really manage democracy because so few of them ever go to church. But Dr. Huntington seems genuinely to believe that what most other people see as human values are uniquely American values, and that people who aren't white Protestant Christians and don't speak English have no access to them.

He really ought to get out more. He might start in a small way by visiting Canada, which takes in proportionately twice as many immigrants as the United States, picking them by rules that give every region of the world an equal chance. As a result, about a quarter of its immigrants are Chinese, and Chinese is already the third most widely spoken language in Canada. Old-stock Canadians, whether English- or French-speaking, seem remarkably unalarmed by this, and most nonwhite Canadians will tell you that they live in a less racist society than the one next door.

If nothing else came out of his Canadian trip, Dr. Huntington would come home with two good ideas. One is how to solve the "Mexican problem": open up America's doors to immigration from all over the world at the same per capita rate as Canada, and Mexican immigration would shrink to relatively insignificant proportions. Alternatively, when he needs a topic for his next scare book, he could write about the hordes of black, brown and yellow Canadians, some of them French-speaking, who are about to inundate the United States from the north.

CHAPTER TWELVE

IRAQ: VANISHING WMD, RISING RESISTANCE

The naked triumphalism of the first weeks after the fall of Baghdad—epitomized by a flight-suited President Bush announcing the end of "major combat operations" on an aircraft carrier with a banner declaring "Mission Accomplished" carefully framed in the background of the shot—did not last very long. The first thing to fall apart was the main pretext for the invasion: the notorious "weapons of mass destruction."

WAITING FOR THE TOOTH FAIRY

July 13, 2003

Every night when they go to bed, just after they've said their prayers, US President George W. Bush and British Prime Minister Tony Blair each tuck a tooth under their pillows. They've been good boys and they won their war fair and square, so surely one of these days the tooth fairy will come and leave some Iraqi weapons of mass destruction in its place. But the days turn into weeks and months, and still the tooth fairy doesn't come.

Meanwhile, the crowd outside is getting ugly — especially in Britain, where Blair's credibility has been severely damaged by the perception that he distorted what the intelligence services actually said about the alleged threat from Iraq in order to manufacture a case for following the United States into war. Public outrage in the United States is still at an earlier stage and will probably only grow in step with mounting American casualties in occupied Iraq, but some awkward questions are being asked at last.

So, one cheer for the fact that (some of) the truth is finally coming out, but where were all these newspapers and politicians in the months leading up to the invasion of Iraq? You had to be wilfully blind not to know at the time what they are now discovering in such breathless shock — that the US and British governments were telling brazen lies in order to manipulate their peoples into supporting the war.

Even now, the new doubters confine themselves to specific issues like Tony Blair's claim that Iraq could deploy chemical and biological weapons in forty-five minutes and George Bush's reference to (forged) documents about alleged Iraqi attempts to buy uranium in Africa. In both cases, the official defence has been to blame the intelligence services for the false information (which is a fine reward for serving up the conclusions that the governments wanted). But never mind the details: the whole story was incredible.

Nobody in their right mind would have believed that the Iraqi nuclear weapons program, completely dismantled by United Nations arms inspectors in the early '90s, could have revived since the UN teams were withdrawn in 1998. How could the program have advanced so fast, despite continuing sanctions, that it already posed an urgent threat to America and Britain by 2003? How did thousands of journalists swallow the story that Iraqi nuclear weapons were a threat so urgent that they justified defying the UN, aborting the renewed inspection process, and launching a "preventive war"?

Disbelieving such a fantastical story was not an ideological choice; it was just common sense. As for chemical and biological weapons, it turns out that Saddam Hussein was telling the truth when he said Iraq had destroyed them all in 1991–92, but it wouldn't have mattered much if he had been lying. He had no delivery vehicles to get them beyond his immediate neighbourhood if they had existed, nor were terrorists going to deliver them for him. Quite apart from the lack of a plausible motive for such an attack, there was no evidence that Saddam Hussein's Iraq had ever had any connection with Islamist terrorism. Three months after the war, there still isn't.

And by the way, any journalist with decent contacts in Washington or London would have been aware that people high up in the intelligence world were desperately signalling from behind the curtain that the story being peddled by their political masters was not what the professionals really believed at all. The CIA and MI5 were leaking on an Amazonian scale—it was practically coming out by list-serv—but the leaks just weren't being followed up by most of the mainstream US and British media. Why not?

The whole cover story to justify the invasion of Iraq was ridiculous, nonsensical, patently untrue—and occasionally very funny, like the tale of the balsa-wood drones with which Saddam Hussein was going to spray us all with poison gas. So the real question, once again: why did most US and British media, including serious newspapers like the *Washington Post* and the London *Times*, treat this farrago of transparent misrepresentations as serious news?

In the United States it's mostly down to post-9/11 chill: most American journalists were reluctant to question their government's truthfulness in a perceived time of crisis. Dissent was widely seen as unpatriotic, and so the most blatant lies went unchallenged. Despite the recent flurry of reporting on the bogus uranium purchase that featured in Bush's eve-of-war speech, this chill still restricts the range and tone of stories in the US media, and will probably continue to do so unless the aftermath in Iraq gets completely out of hand.

In Britain it was always more nuanced. Of the nine daily national papers, only the four whose owners have strong North American ties and large interests there—the ex-Australian Rupert Murdoch (now a US citizen to get around US media ownership laws), and the ex-Canadian Conrad Black (who traded in his Canadian citizenship for a British title)—blindly supported the Bush–Blair line. British-owned papers and the BBC were more doubtful from the start, and by now the rest of the media has been forced to follow suit: the story is just too big to ignore.

It's impossible to say if the progressive unravelling of the lies will ultimately ruin Mr. Bush or Mr. Blair: they are both adroit politicians who know how to turn the public's short attention span to their advantage. But the tooth fairy is clearly not going to show up—and the truth fairy is on her way at last.

The truth fairy did show up, but she didn't make a lot of difference. The Bush administration never formally acknowledged her arrival, American public opinion was too deeply split on ideological grounds to respond to mere factual evidence—and soon all the attention shifted to the growing resistance war in Iraq.

IRAQ: LA POLITIQUE DU PIRE
August 19, 2003

United Nations Secretary-General Kofi Annan is outraged. US President George W. Bush makes his usual clumsy attempt to paint the Iraqi resistance as just another bunch of "terrorists," and to link them with some worldwide conspiracy of terrorists who attack the United States because "they hate freedom." All the usual suspects express their shock that the United Nations headquarters in Baghdad has been bombed. And you wonder: can they really be surprised?

To adapt Bill Clinton's famous phrase: it's a war, stupid. In the first phase of the war, cluster bombs were the weapon of choice, and so the United States won. Now we have moved into the phase where the dominant weapon is the truck bomb, and that levels the playing field. A classic guerilla war is taking shape in Iraq, and such wars are a contest not of technology but of will.

In this sort of struggle guerillas have several inbuilt advantages. They are at home, among friends and relatives, with all the local knowledge (starting with language) that the foreign troops lack. They can wrap themselves in the local flag (or increasingly, in the case of the non-Baathist resistance in Iraq, in the green banner of Islam), options that are simply unavailable to the occupying forces. And there is something more: the occupiers have to build; the resistance only has to destroy.

There is a key concept of revolutionary guerilla warfare which has, oddly, no standard translation in English: *la politique du pire*. Literally, it is the strategy of (making things) worse. The idea is that the guerillas, who lack the military strength to beat their opponents in open battle, should concentrate instead on destroying the structures and services on which the population depends.

If their attacks and sabotage make the lives of ordinary people awful, the people will not blame the guerillas. They will blame the authorities whose duty it is to provide those structures and services—the occupation authorities, in this case. This is already happening in Iraq, where the failure of the US forces to restore power and water four months after the fall of Baghdad contrasts sharply with Saddam Hussein's rapid restoration of essential services after the heavy bombing of the 1991 Gulf War.

In this context, attacks on infrastructure like the recent bombings of oil and water pipelines make perfect sense. The wholesale looting of copper cable that is the largest single reason for the US failure to restore electricity supplies in Iraq is mostly a freelance activity undertaken for profit, but certainly the resistance forces have no objection. And the bombing of the UN headquarters will not be unpopular in Iraq either.

Iraqis who watched their once-comfortable living standards collapse over the past twelve years under the impact of UN sanctions have a rather different perspective on that organization than the rest of the world. Saddam Hussein's regime brought those sanctions upon itself by its invasion of Kuwait in 1990, but since Iraqis never chose Saddam in any meaningful sense, they feel no blame for that crime—and they certainly bore the punishment. The Iraqi resistance does not discredit itself at home by attacking the UN.

On the contrary, it furthers its principal strategic goal, which is to demonstrate that the US cannot bring even security and prosperity to Iraq, let alone democracy. The US is already having immense difficulty in persuading other countries to send troops to Iraq to share the burden of the occupation, because in addition to their original misgivings about the wisdom and legality of the invasion they now have to worry about a significant toll of casualties. All the more is this true of international organizations.

For all the rhetoric that ricochets around Washington about building democracy in Iraq the way the US and its allies built German and Japanese democracy after World War II, this is an administration that does everything on the cheap, and there is no Marshall Plan in the offing. On the contrary, the Bush administration was hoping to pay much of the cost of the occupation out of Iraqi oil exports (which is why pipelines are being attacked), and to unload a lot more onto the UN and the alphabet soup of humanitarian aid organizations that generally follow in its wake.

It was never likely that the UN would let itself be used in that way: the mistrust of US motives and tactics goes too deep in a lot of the members. But Iraqi guerillas are not up on the latest intrigues in the Security Council, so to them it makes sense to bomb the UN's headquarters in Baghdad. And the bombing is also meant to tell all the international aid organizations that they are vulnerable to attack and to scare them off: exactly what the *politique du pire* is all about.

The US-backed "contras" in Nicaragua followed this strategy, as did the Viet Cong in Vietnam and the FLN in Algeria, and it worked for all of them. It did not work, on the other hand, for the Montoneros in Argentina, the IRA in Northern Ireland or the New People's Army in the Philippines. There are no foolproof, one-size-fits-all strategies in guerilla/terrorist campaigns; the specific context always makes a difference. But at the moment, the Iraqi resistance is on a roll.

THE FUTILITY OF INQUIRIES
August 28, 2003

"The government lied every time it skewed, misrepresented, used selectively and fabricated the Iraq story," said Andrew Wilkie, a senior intelligence officer in Australia's Office of National Assessment until he resigned last March in protest at the way the Australian government was distorting intelligence to justify its attack on Iraq. "Key intelligence assessment qualifications like 'probably,' 'could' and 'uncorroborated evidence suggests' were frequently dropped," he told a parliamentary inquiry in Canberra last week. "Much more useful words like 'massive' and 'mammoth' were included."

The same process is underway in Britain, where two weeks ago the Hutton inquiry began taking public evidence about whether the British government deliberately "sexed up" intelligence reports about the threat posed by Iraq in order to bamboozle the British public into backing an attack on Iraq. It's a much bigger deal in London, because the trigger for the British inquiry was the suicide of a senior government expert on Iraq's "weapons of mass destruction," Dr. David Kelly, who had been linked to leaks to the BBC.

Prime Minister Tony Blair denied any government meddling in the intelligence process in his testimony to the Hutton inquiry on Thursday, admitting that it would have "merited my resignation" if he had lied to the British public about the "serious and current" threat posed by Saddam's alleged WMD, but insisting that the available intelligence backed it up. A torrent of testimony and an avalanche of official e-mails submitted to the inquiry show that it did not back it up, really, but Blair still walked away from the witness box seemingly unscathed.

Australia's Prime Minister John Howard won't even have to appear in person before his country's parliamentary inquiry, and it won't be able to pin anything specific on him either. In response to Andrew Wilkie's accusations, he simply said: "If he has got evidence of that, let him produce it. Otherwise, stop slandering decent people." As if there might be a document somewhere in which Howard instructed his minions to "sex up" the intelligence in order to trick the Australian public into going along with his war. Things don't really work like that.

Of the three countries that sent actual combat troops to invade Iraq last March (not counting the marching band from Ruritania and the typing pool from Lower Slobbovia), both Australia and Britain are conducting public inquiries into the government's alleged subversion of the intelligence process to justify that deed, whereas the United States is not. Many Americans lament this fact, imagining that a proper congressional inquiry would make the Bush administration come clean about the imaginary WMD and the supposed links between Iraq and al-Qaeda that were used to sell the war to the American public. They are dreaming.

Lots of interesting details are coming out at the Hutton inquiry, of course. We learn that Blair's chief of staff, Jonathan Powell, commenting on the "Iraq dossier" being prepared by the government last September, wrote: "the document does nothing to demonstrate a threat, let alone an imminent threat from Saddam. . . . We will need to make it clear in launching the document that we do not claim that we have evidence that he is an imminent threat."

That was just what Mr. Blair did claim in his famous September dossier, referring to Iraqi WMD that could "be ready within forty-five minutes of an order to use them." This was a key factor in persuading many Labour MPs to back Blair in going to war, but it came out in the inquiry that these alleged WMD were just short-range shells and rockets that couldn't even reach Iraq's neighbours. No risk of the great British public realizing that, however: Blair's comment in the draft version of the foreword saying "The case I make is not that Saddam could launch a nuclear attack on London or another part of the UK (he could not)" was removed from the published version.

Even the short-range shells and rockets were a fiction, and many in the British intelligence world suspected it at the time—like Dr. Kelly, who thought that there was only a 30 percent chance that Iraq had resumed production of WMD after 1991, and Air Marshal Sir John Walker, a former chief of Defence Intelligence, who said in a confidential note to the Foreign Affairs Select Committee last month that the claims about Iraqi WMD were "not the reason to go to war, but the excuse to go to war."

All fascinating stuff, but will it make any difference to out-comes? Not likely: around half of the British public now believes it was lied to in the run-up to the war, but around the same proportion believed it at the time and the war happened anyway.

About a third of Australians think their government lied to them, which is also largely unchanged over the past ten months. And in America, despite all the recent revelations in the media about how the administration massaged the evidence, around half the population still goes on believing Mr. Bush's brazen assertion—or rather innuendo, for he never quite says it straight—that Saddam Hussein was an ally of al-Qaeda.

Inquiries and revelations about the past will not change these beliefs much. A large part of the public simply doesn't care if their country launched an illegal war of aggression on faked evidence, so long as the price for doing so stays low. So what might decisively turn public opinion in the "coalition countries" against the occupation of Iraq? Oh, the usual: the cost and the casualties.

OLD AMERICA
October 2, 2003

Lying in bed just after 7 a.m., listening to the radio. The rain is pouring down, my youngest child has decided that she'd rather be driven to school today and the BBC's *Today* program, which completely dominates serious morning radio news, is discussing the closing day of the Labour Party conference.

This gathering is a major event in the British political cal-endar, similar in tone though different in purpose to the four-yearly national conventions at which the Republican and Democratic parties nominate presidential candidates in the United States—and the presenters are being remarkably cheeky, especially given recent history.

It was the *Today* program, a few months ago, that reported that the British government had "sexed up" last year's dossier on Saddam Hussein's alleged weapons of mass destruction, setting in motion a train of events that led to a senior official's suicide, the Hutton inquiry and huge damage to Prime Minister Tony Blair's reputation. Blair has just made a speech to the conference defending his motives in attacking Iraq alongside the US and asking the delegates for understanding. Most of them heartily disapprove of the war, but they give him a standing ovation nevertheless. So how do the presenters deal with the gap between the public displays of unity and the seething dissent beneath the surface?

By talking about the decision to bring back the practice of singing "The Red Flag" at the end of the conference. The old socialist anthem was dropped in the '80s, when Labour realized that luring middle-class voters was not fully compatible with songs about class war ("The People's Flag is deepest red / It shrouded oft our martyred dead . . ."), but now that Blair has led the party into the sunlit capitalist uplands of privatization and foreign invasions, the problem is how to keep the old left-wing stalwarts from rebelling. A little socialist window-dressing helps.

So the *Today* program had some fun with that, and then offered helpful hints about less antiquated songs that might capture the essence of the proceedings. How about something that said what was really on the delegates' minds? Cue the Vietnam-era song "War! Unh! What is it good for? Absolutely nothing!" Or maybe something from The Animals to sum up Tony Blair's state of mind? "I'm just a soul whose intentions are good. / Oh Lord, please don't let me be misunderstood." Then on to the next item of news.

And it struck me (still lying there) that no serious American radio or television broadcaster would ever take the mickey out of a US major-party convention like that. The US news media generally treat political figures with the utmost reverence, no matter how few clothes the emperor in question may be wearing on a given day. Which leads to some further thoughts about the nature of the political process in the United States.

A couple of weeks ago I was at a professional conference of several hundred American newspaper journalists, and to my astonishment the opening session was devoted to three history professors who gave talks on the "Founding Fathers" (Washington, Jefferson, Franklin, et al.) and their relevance for Americans today. Good talks, actually, but can you imagine a couple of hundred British or Australian journalists—or Russian or Indian ones—voluntarily sitting through an hour's discussion of eighteenth-century history at their professional convention? It would never happen.

Is this because American journos are more patient and more scholarly? On the contrary. When they started asking questions, it was clear that the ideas and intentions of the Founding Fathers mattered to them because in their daily working lives they have to navigate all sorts of tricky political and constitutional issues with their roots in a very distant past. Which makes perfectly good sense, because the United States is one of the oldest countries in the world.

Americans are brought up to think of their country as "new" and Europe and Asia as "old," but there are few nations in Eurasia where the constitutional arrangements are even one century old. Most countries go back no further than 1945 in their current political incarnation—whereas the United States has had the same constitution and political system for two and a quarter centuries. It has also been largely spared the calamitous wars that smashed the old structures and the mindset that went with them in every other great power during the twentieth century.

It goes directly counter to the prevailing domestic ideology to say this, and it frequently infuriates Americans who mistake it for criticism, but the United States is a very old-fashioned country compared to the other industrialized democracies. It's visible in the overt nationalism and religiosity of public debate, in the huge role that lawyers and litigation play in a society based on a two-hundred-year-old constitution, and in the reverence Americans have for their ancient political institutions. It makes for a society that is instinctively conservative in both social and political matters (apart from a few big cities on the coasts).

This does mean that Americans are significantly slower to change their minds on major issues than the febrile French and the volatile Germans—let alone the flibbertigibbet British—but they do generally get there in the end, and it is generally the same "there." At the moment, the post-Iraq collapse of public trust in the government in Britain is about three months ahead of the parallel process in the United States, but Americans are catching up fast.

You wish. Some Americans were catching up—and a brave handful were well ahead of the crowd—but my mistake was to assume that the argument about the war would be conducted as a separate event. It was in most other countries, but in the United States opinions about the war in Iraq largely mapped onto existing ideological divisions over domestic issues. If you believed Mr. Bush on other things, then you believed him on this one too, and vice versa. And never mind the evidence.

THE TRIALS OF SADDAM HUSSEIN
December 18, 2003

"[Saddam Hussein] was wise not to wait too long," said Colonel James Hickey, commander of the American forces that took the former Iraqi leader prisoner on December 14. "We were about to clear that [underground facility] in a military sort of way," he added, explaining that "things like that are cleared with hand grenades, small arms, things like that." But Hickey's instructions were to "capture or kill" Saddam, and the latter managed to get his hands up in time.

The Bush administration is probably wishing quite hard by now that Saddam had waited a little longer and been killed in his hole. While others debate where he should be tried and by whom, and whether he should face the death penalty or not, President Bush's people will be realizing just about now that they can't afford to give him a fair trial at all.

He would certainly be convicted in the end: the evidence of Saddam's crimes over the years is overwhelming. But in a fair trial, with normal rules of evidence and reasonably competent defence lawyers, it would be impossible to stop the defence from pointing out that every US administration from 1980 to 1992 (all Republican administrations, as it happens) was directly or indirectly complicit in his crimes.

During Saddam's quarter-century of power in Iraq, every year saw tens of thousands of people tortured and killed, for that is the nature of absolute dictatorships of any political ideology. Mao Tse-tung, the Argentine generals and Idi Amin all did it, the Algerian regime, the Burmese generals, and Kim Jong-Il are all doing it today. But nobody would try Mao for the routine fifty or hundred thousand people killed by his regime in an average year such as 1962; they would focus on the millions who were exiled, tortured and/or murdered during the Cultural Revolution.

Saddam's career includes three great crimes: the use of poison gas against Iranian troops during the 1980–88 war; the slaughter of rebellious Iraqi Kurds towards the end of that war and just afterwards (again involving the use of poison gas); and the massacres of Kurds and Shia Arabs who rebelled against his rule after the Gulf War of 1991. After that, his misdeeds fall back to a more mundane level.

These three great crimes, committed between 1983 and 1991, would be the primary focus of any trial. The problem for the US government is that it was directly implicated in the first two, and largely though indirectly responsible for the third as well. A truly impartial court might even lay charges against senior American political and military figures (including some in the present administration) who assisted Saddam in his war crimes. At the least, the whole process would be acutely embarrassing for the United States.

US involvement with Saddam's regime began in 1983, when his ill-advised invasion of Iran had backfired spectacularly and Iraq was facing defeat at the hands of Ayatollah Khomeini's radically anti-American regime in Iran. The US knew that Saddam was already illegally using chemical weapons against Iranian troops on an almost daily basis, but in December 1983 the Reagan administration sent Donald Rumsfeld (now US defence secretary) to Baghdad to tell Saddam that it was willing to help and wanted to restore full diplomatic relations.

In the following years, the US government allowed vital ingredients for chemical weapons to be exported to Iraq, together with dozens of biological agents, including anthrax. It also supplied Iraq with intelligence information on Iranian troop movements and positions, and from 1986 even sent US Air Force officers to Iraq to help interpret US-supplied satellite and aerial photos to plan attacks against the Iranian trenches—in which it was clearly understood by Washington that huge quantities of poison gas would be used.

The Reagan administration used its influence to kill a Senate bill banning the export of US military technology to Iraq to punish Saddam for using chemical weapons against Iran. When Saddam used poison gas against his own Kurdish population at Halabja in 1988, killing thousands of innocent people, US diplomats were instructed to blame the incident on Iran. All this would come out in gory detail (and perhaps much more besides) if Saddam ever got a fair and public trial.

The third great crime of the Saddam years was the massacre of rebellious Shia Arabs and, to a lesser extent, of Kurds, after Saddam's defeat in the 1991 war. The massacre occurred because President George H.W. Bush urged the Iraqi population to revolt against Saddam—but when they did, he withheld US military support, even allowing Saddam's helicopter gunships to range freely over the rebellious areas. It was not complicity, but it was at least great carelessness.

This is why there will probably be no public trial at all. It has already become clear that the ousted Iraqi leader, contrary to Washington's first statements, will not be treated as a prisoner of war although he is technically the captured commander-in-chief of a defeated national army. Instead, he will be assigned to the same legal limbo shared by the hundreds who have been imprisoned in Guantanamo for the past two years, suffering perpetual interrogation without the protection of the Geneva Conventions and beyond the reach of any national law including that of the United States.

Nobody at Guantanamo has yet been brought to trial. Saddam will be the same.

Or maybe they will bring him to trial under the same conditions that prevailed at his one-day arraignment hearing in late 2004—with his microphone muted so that nobody except the court officials could hear what he said. It would still be a lot more convenient if he just died.

TERRORISTS WITH NINJA STARS
December 27, 2003

Joe Foss died early this year, but he lived long enough to see things get really foolish. Travelling through Phoenix airport last year, he was stopped by security guards who made a great fuss about a five-pointed metal star he was carrying, which they feared was some sort of weapon. ("Last week the terrorists were trying to smuggle nose tweezers onto the planes, and this week it's these ninja stars.") Foss was eighty-six at the time, and the star in question was the Congressional Medal of Honor that President Franklin D. Roosevelt gave him sixty years ago, but they wouldn't believe him.

You couldn't be more All-American than Joe Foss, a farm boy who put himself through university by waiting tables, became a Marine Corps fighter pilot, and shot down twenty-six Japanese planes in a few hectic months on Guadalcanal in 1943 to become one of America's leading aces. In later life he was twice elected governor of South Dakota, and ended up as president of the National Rifle Association. We don't know the details of what passed between him and the fools at security, but he was upset enough that the story got out.

You can imagine what he must have thought. His war had been a real war in which an average of twenty-five thousand people were killed every day for years on end. His own friends died in burning airplanes with awful regularity. The "war on terror," on the other hand, is a vastly overblown media event that bears no relation to the real size of the threat. It gives bumptious officials and cynical politicians a licence to inflate their own importance and hide their mistakes, and ignorant journalists an excuse to pontificate about how the world has changed forever. It is mostly lies and distortion, and the ignorance is not innocent.

The Catch-22 of covering terrorism in the media is that it seems indecent to say the truth about it when an attack has just killed some people and everybody is expressing shock and horror—but when there hasn't been an attack recently, there's no hook for the story. So here it is, with no hook to speak of: terrorism is a really small problem.

Terrorism is a technique, not a country or an ideology, and having a war on terrorism makes about as much sense as having a war on carpentry. In practice, the current "war on terror" is mainly about fighting terrorists who attack Americans, although others who are waging wars against rebellious Muslim subjects—Russia, Israel, India—have tried with some success to hitch their local struggles to the American wagon.

Global casualties each year in all the conflicts where the weaker side uses terrorist methods are running at around ten thousand a year, roughly the same as annual traffic deaths in France or Spain, but at least half of the deaths from terrorism involve Nepalese, Colombian and African peasants that nobody except their families cares much about. The other half are mostly Muslims killed by the "counterterrorist" forces: three Palestinians die for every Israeli killed in the local struggle there, and ten Chechens for every Russian. But every year, a few hundred of the victims are from (self) important places like the United States, western Europe and Japan.

Those are the people—Australian tourists in Bali, American families in Saudi Arabia, the British consul in Istanbul—whose deaths really matter. Only, they wouldn't matter at all if they died in a less politically sensitive way, such as falling off a ladder. More Americans die each year from falling off ladders than from terrorism, and you could halve the death rate from falling-off-ladderism at about one-thousandth of the annual cost of fighting terrorism. You wouldn't even have to attack civil liberties to do it, apart from banning people over seventy from climbing ladders unsupervised. But since their deaths don't matter, nobody bothers.

Terrorism is a form of political judo in which small, weak groups kill relatively small numbers of people in deliberately spectacular ways. The al-Qaeda attacks in September 2001 killed three thousand Americans, but they attracted a thousand times as much attention as the similar number of Americans who died in firearms incidents that month and every month. The goal of such attacks is to provoke much larger organizations, such as governments, into overreactions that will ultimately serve the terrorists' cause—like invading foreign countries, for example.

But here's the thing: everybody in the military and law enforcement has known this for at least a generation now—they even teach it in the staff colleges—and most journalists and politicians understand it too. So when they overreact anyway, and use the attacks to launch foreign wars and whip up hysteria about security issues, it is reasonable to assume that they are doing so for cynical and self-serving reasons. Unless they are truly, deeply stupid, of course, but it is generally reasonable to assume that they are not.

So keep your head down and your mouth shut at airport security, because if they can treat Joe Foss like that, imagine what they can do to you. But when you are not isolated and vulnerable in a security queue, treat the whole war on terror and those who claim to be fighting it with the contempt they deserve. Unless you happen to live in Nepal, Colombia, Kashmir, Israel or Chechnya, you are likelier to drown in the bath than you are to die in a terrorist attack.

There is virtually no correlation between the real level of international terrorist activity and the level of media coverage—but there is a high correlation between the number of American victims and the level of media attention worldwide. Thus, for example, the US government's own statistics record more people killed and injured in attacks by international terrorists in 1998 than in 2001 (although the collapse of the twin towers on 9/11 produced an unusually high proportion of fatal casualties). International terrorism was not seen as an urgent global problem in 1998, however, because 80 percent of the victims in that year were Africans and most of the rest were Europeans.

The peak period for international terrorist activity was actually in the mid-1980s. There has been a steady fall in the annual number of attacks since then, interrupted by only two blips on the graph: 1991 and 1998–2001. In 2003, the number of attacks was less than a third the number of those in 1986. Nor, with the devastating exception of the one-off of 9/11, has the average number of victims in these attacks risen over the years.

CHAPTER THIRTEEN

CATASTROPHES OLD AND PENDING

Over the past quarter-century, but with accelerating speed over the past ten years, we have been discovering just how precarious "normality" is on this planet. First, we began to climb the learning curve about climate change and ice ages, then we discovered catastrophic asteroid strikes, and now we also have to worry about potential epidemics that could decimate the population of the entire planet. But things aren't actually getting worse; we are just beginning to understand the situation.

ANOTHER NEAR MISS

January 10, 2002

The journalists called it a "near miss," but asteroid 2001 YB5 didn't really come close to the Earth. It was around six hundred thousand kilometres away when it whipped past our planet last Tuesday. Given that it was not much bigger than an aircraft carrier (though a lot heavier), it was like having somebody fire a .22 bullet at you and miss by about ten kilometres.

The experts did their best to whip up alarm. "Such an object could wipe out a medium-sized country if it impacted and lead to a global economic meltdown," warned asteroid expert Benny Peiser of John Moores University in Liverpool. But the human race refused to get excited: you can safely ignore a bullet that misses you by ten kilometres.

But suppose that the maniac with the .22 got a free shot every year or so. In fact, imagine that there were thousands of near-sighted maniacs with .22 rifles, each taking a shot at you from time to time, plus seven-hundred-odd drunken lunatics with rocket-launchers who also get a free go at you every year or so. Sooner or later, something's going to hit you, and even a .22 bullet can hurt. A rocket-propelled grenade can ruin your whole day.

There are an estimated seven hundred asteroids, give or take a couple of hundred, that are big enough to change the whole fate of life on Earth if they struck it—between 1 and 10 kilometres across—and in orbits that could one day lead to a collision. There are literally thousands of others, ranging down to the size of 2001 YB5, that could wipe out a country the size of France or Korea if they hit the Earth.

The problem is the time-scale of the threat: "long-term planning" in most human contexts is five to ten years.

No country-killer asteroid is likely to hit our planet in the next decade; indeed, there's only a 1 percent chance that it will happen any time in the next century. As for the really big strikes that could wipe out the human race, only two such asteroids have hit in the past 251 million years. In debates about next year's budget, preventing that huge but unlikely catastrophe will always tend to lose out to more urgent priorities.

Yet, there is no reason to despair. Given that nobody had any idea of the scale of the asteroid threat only twenty-five years ago, the way we have climbed the learning curve in a series of huge intellectual leaps is actually quite impressive.

First, there was the whole idea of a "nuclear winter": the hypothesis, first put forward by Carl Sagan et al. during the 1970s, stated that explosions that lift large amounts of dust high into the atmosphere could have planetwide effects (the dust would stay up there for years, blocking sunlight, killing crops and changing the whole climate).

Sagan and his colleagues were mainly concerned about the effects of thousands of thermonuclear weapons being exploded near the ground, which seemed alarmingly likely during the Cold War. But then in the early '80s the father-and-son Alvarez team—physicist father Luis and geologist son Walter—looked at the thin layer of iridium found worldwide in geological strata that are about 65 million years old. They surmised that it could not have a terrestrial origin, and suggested that it was due to a giant asteroid strike—which also wiped out the dinosaurs by causing a prolonged nuclear winter.

The dates matched, and only a few years later the discovery of a giant crater of the right age off Mexico's Yucatan peninsula gave the theory added credibility. Doubters pointed to the enormous volcanic eruptions of the same time that covered much of southern India with a thick layer of lava (the "Deccan Traps") as a rival cause of global climatic disruption and the extinction of the dinosaurs, but now it seems that the asteroid strike and the intense volcanic activity may actually have been connected.

There was an even larger calamity 251 million years ago: the "Great Dying," when 70 percent of land vertebrates and 90 percent of all marine animals suddenly became extinct. Last year, scientists at the universities of Rochester and Washington published a paper in the respected journal *Science* identifying geological evidence of a massive asteroid or cometary strike at that time too. No crater for this strike has been identified yet, but once again it coincides with an unprecedented period of massive volcanic activity, this time in Siberia.

In only twenty-five years, therefore, we have changed our Darwin-based ideas about evolution to include rare but massive changes caused by asteroid strikes. We have begun to suspect that these huge strikes trigger volcanic episodes that disrupt the planetary environment for long enough to cause mass extinctions worldwide. And we have identified and plotted at least a significant fraction of the most dangerous objects in the solar system.

We have not yet developed the technology to divert them, but the average secondary-school graduate today is likely to understand the nature of the threat. Far more than gestures like the creation of a "Planetary Protection Office" at the US National Aeronautics and Space Agency, it is this planet-wide raising of consciousness that will eventually create the political basis for a real planetary defence program.

THE RETURN OF THE PLAGUES?
February 21, 2003

On January 28 an eight-year-old girl from Hong Kong visiting relatives in southern China fell ill with influenza and was admitted to hospital. A week later she died, and since then her father has died of the same flu, while her nine-year-old brother lies gravely ill in an isolation ward in Hong Kong. The virus is outwardly similar to the A (H5N1) strain, also known as "bird flu," that killed six of the eighteen people who were infected in the last outbreak in Hong Kong in 1997.

New strains of viral diseases that can kill human beings generally emerge by mutation as they hop back and forth between people and their domesticated animals. This exchange of viruses goes on all the time in farming areas — but it's only when a lethal new virus crosses the species barrier *and then starts to pass from one person to another* that the alarm bells start to ring. They are ringing now.

"If this virus is transmissible from human to human then it is far more serious," said a spokesperson for the World Health Organization in Geneva on February 19. The 1997 flu virus was stopped by slaughtering the 1.4 million chickens, ducks and geese in Hong Kong, but if the new virus is already loose all over southern China that solution will not really work.

Even the normal wave of flu that circles the world every year, slightly changed genetically each time, exacts a serious toll in lives, but once in a while something really lethal comes along. This could be one of those times.

The "Spanish flu" pandemic of 1918 infected between 20 and 40 percent of the world's population and killed 20 million people in four months, twice as many as died in the

First World War—and the majority of the victims were young, healthy people who died of complications such as bronchitis and pneumonia. If a flu virus like that appeared now, could it do as much damage?

Certainly the two subsequent flu pandemics, occurring after the development of antiviral medicines, did not cause the same carnage. The impact of the 1957 "Asian flu" pandemic was greatly reduced by mass vaccination: only one human being in six caught it, and it killed an estimated 2 million people worldwide. The 1968 "Hong Kong flu" pandemic killed only a million people and, as in 1957, most of the victims were elderly. But viruses are not impressed by medical technology.

Despite the far higher standards of sanitation and medical care in the developed world, influenza death rates there have not been significantly lower than in poorer countries. Viral diseases mutate fast, antibiotics are no use against them, and good hygiene is no protection either. Bacterial diseases like cholera, anthrax and malaria have complex life cycles and mutate only slowly, so they are easy to contain— but if the latest version of bird flu is transmissible between people, we could be looking at millions of deaths over the next year. Nor is that the worst that could happen.

The true nature of the "Black Death" was long a mystery, but early in the twentieth century, after doctors had found and described bubonic plague in India, experts jumped to the conclusion that a more virulent form of that disease, endemic in rats and transmitted to humans by their fleas, was the real culprit. This was a comforting conclusion, because it meant that it was a bacterial disease with a complicated life-cycle, easily contained by hygiene and antibiotics, that would never come back to trouble modern human beings.

But it never actually made sense, because the standard treatment for the Black Death, tried and tested over three hundred years, was to quarantine affected families and villages for forty days. That could not have worked if it were carried by rats, which do not respect quarantines. So two years ago, professors Christopher Duncan and Susan Scott of Liverpool University suggested in their book *Biology of Plagues* that the Black Death was really an Ebola-like virus, a hemorrhagic fever transmitted directly from person to person. It is frighteningly plausible.

There were actually two Great Pandemics, and the first hit Europe and the Middle East in AD 541. The Roman Empire had been relatively unharmed by great plagues, apart from bouts of smallpox in 170 and measles in 250, which killed mostly children and left survivors immune; but the new plague was different. It returned about every ten years for the next two centuries, and reduced the population of the Mediterranean area by between 30 and 50 percent. Large parts of the Middle East and North Africa did not recover their pre-540 populations until about one hundred years ago.

The plague called the Black Death appeared in Mongolia in the 1320s and killed two-thirds of China's population between 1330 and 1350. It reached Europe in 1347 and killed between 30 and 40 percent of the population in the first onslaught. It returned at intervals of about a decade, with gradually diminishing lethality, until it disappeared at the end of the seventeenth century. The aching, the bleeding from internal organs, the red blotches on the skin caused by the effusion of blood under the skin, were all typical of Ebola-style fevers. Besides, bubonic plague, unlike the Black Death, did not disappear. There was an outbreak of bubonic plague in Glasgow as recently as the 1890s.

If Duncan and Scott are right, therefore, there is a virus out there somewhere, dormant for the moment while it tries out mutations that might break through the genetic defences that human beings evolved to defeat it last time, which could kill a significant portion of the human race in a year. The Black Death is not dead, it's only sleeping. And in the meantime, the bird flu may be coming.

Duncan and Scott have more recently suggested that the genetic defences that Europeans evolved to deal with the Black Death (or rather, the residue of those defences) may also explain why between 5 and 20 percent of Europeans appear to have some immunity to HIV/AIDS.

WITH A LITTLE WARNING . . .
January 3, 2005

"We may have severely underestimated the level of the tsunami hazard along the margins of the Atlantic Ocean," said an unnamed researcher at the Benfield Hazard Research Centre at University College London (quoted in the Financial Times of January 2). Scientists do jump on the bandwagon at times like these, but you can hardly blame them; it's the only time they can really get our attention.

By the end of this year, the countries of South Asia will almost certainly agree to install a system to give advance warning of tsunamis like the one that killed an estimated one hundred and fifty thousand people on December 26. A similar system has been operated by the countries around the Pacific Ocean since 1968, and one could be installed around the Indian Ocean for about $10 million, although individual countries would then have to spend further amounts to get warnings to their people who live in low-lying coastal areas in a timely fashion.

Such a system wouldn't have saved many people in northern Sumatra, where the tsunami struck within half an hour of the massive earthquake (at 9.0 on the Richter scale, the biggest in forty years) that occurred just off the west coast. But it would have given people in Thailand and Malaysia over an hour to get to higher ground, and well over two hours in Sri Lanka and India.

The property damage would have been the same, and 5 or 6 million people would still be homeless, but even this time as many as fifty thousand lives could have been saved by a proper warning system. Another time, when the under-sea quake didn't happen so close to a densely populated coast, the great majority of the lives at risk might be saved — so why is there no system in place? Basically, because big earthquakes are very rare in the Indian Ocean.

The Pacific Tsunami Warning System has been in business for almost forty years because the Pacific rim—the "ring of fire"—has over half the active volcanoes and earthquakes on the planet and an average of ten tsunamis a year. No quake has caused a big tsunami in the Indian Ocean since Krakatoa exploded in 1883, and human beings don't readily respond to merely theoretical dangers.

Which brings us to the Atlantic, an area of even less seismic activity. The last subsea earthquake in the Atlantic that caused major loss of life was the great Lisbon quake of 1755, whose sixty thousand victims included tens of thousands killed by the tsunami that struck the city only minutes after the original shock-waves. But there is another problem in the Atlantic—La Palma, in the Canary Islands.

It was Dr. Simon Day of University College London's Benfield Hazard Research Centre, in cooperation with the Swiss Federal Institute of Technology in Zurich, who modelled what will happen when one day, probably during a volcanic eruption, Cumbre Vieja, the western half of La Palma, falls into the sea. Five hundred cubic kilometres of rock (125 cubic miles) weighs about 500 billion tonnes, and when it plunges into the ocean, the model predicts, it will cause a mega-tsunami. It will be 650 metres high in the Canaries themselves, and still "several tens of metres high" when it strikes the east coasts of the United States, Canada, Cuba and Brazil eight to ten hours later.

"There's no 'if' about it," says geophysicist Dr. Bill McGuire, also of the Benfield Centre. "It will happen; it's just a question of time." But although La Palma is the most volcanically active place in the entire Atlantic region, it could still be quite a lot of time before Cumbre Vieja falls off.

The volcano has erupted in 1470, 1585, 1646, 1677, 1712, 1949—that was when the whole western side of La Palma slid down four metres, alerting the scientists—and most recently in 1971. It has probably been erupting every century since long before people started recording it. Yet Dr. Day estimates that there is only a 5 percent chance that Cumbre Vieja will collapse in any given century—so what do you do if the volcano erupts again?

You certainly don't evacuate the whole east coast of North America, most of the Caribbean and northeastern South America, plus all the coastal areas from Guinea to Morocco in West Africa and from Spain to Ireland in Europe. You can't make hundreds of millions of people refugees for months or years and cripple entire national economies just because a volcano is erupting in La Palma and there's a 5 percent chance of disaster. But a warning system that gave people a decent chance of survival if the worst happened would certainly help.

In many coastal areas, a couple of hours' warning of a tsunami is all that would be needed for people to make it to higher ground. In some large coastal cities, where traffic bottlenecks prevent rapid evacuation, refuges in the upper stories of tall buildings that can withstand a tsunami might be needed, but nothing too expensive or elaborate. We are talking about human nature here, and against a low-probability catastrophe people will only pay for low-cost insurance.

CHAPTER FOURTEEN

AFRICA'S TRAVAILS

An admission: my wife is South African, and I have come to care about Africa, too—not as much as she does, I'm sure, but too much to maintain the emotional distance that is best if you want to do really good analysis. I try not to let it show, but when I write about Africa, I'm often angry. Sometimes, I see hope where there probably isn't any. I am not entirely to be trusted when it comes to judging African events, but I do the best I can.

ZIMBABWE: THE SCOUNDREL, THE FOOL AND THE HIT-MAN
February 28, 2002

American hit-men are expensive, but they're efficient, and they do take credit cards. Russian hit-men are cheaper and also quite reliable, though their work is sometimes untidy. A South African hit-man would do the job for five thousand dollars or less, and he would be less obvious on the streets of Harare. But a *Canadian* hit-man?

The story that Morgan Tsvangirai, ex-trade union leader and candidate for the presidency of Zimbabwe in the elections on March 9–10, tried to hire Canadians to kill President Robert Mugabe has dominated the state-controlled media there for the past two weeks. Television has been running the same six-minute clip showing the key meeting in Montreal several times a day, and Tsvangirai has officially been charged with treason.

Yet Mugabe's police didn't keep Tsvangirai in jail, as you would expect with such a dangerous character. They let him out within two hours, as if this were a charge they want to hold over Tsvangirai in case he wins the election, not one they really believe in.

"The message they are trying to send to the voters," said Lovemore Madhuku, chairman of Zimbabwe's National Constitutional Assembly, "is they should not even bother supporting the MDC because their leaders are going to be jailed. Unfortunately, we have a number of illiterate and gullible voters who will buy this propaganda."

The MDC (Movement for Democratic Change) is only a few years old, but it came within a hair's breadth of winning last year's parliamentary elections, and Tsvangirai would probably beat the seventy-eight-year-old Mugabe in the presidential election if the votes are counted properly. But that is the problem: Mugabe has no intention of leaving power after a mere twenty-two years, and as the opposition's credibility has grown, so have the violence and trickery of the ruling Zanu-PF.

Draconian new press laws have been passed, foreign election observers have been expelled, voter lists have been tampered with—and still Mugabe and his cronies are running scared. Which probably explains the weird scene with the alleged Canadian hit-men.

The Australian program *SBS Dateline* first ran the tape of the meeting between Tsvangirai and the Canadian "assassins" as a documentary on February 13, reassured by the sterling reputation of journalist Mark Davis (who also got an interview with Mugabe). Since then, Zimbabweans with televisions have seen the key six-minute clip twenty or thirty times. That has given them time to notice that the time-codes (which were left on by the bungling editors) jump all over the place.

In one case, a sentence Tsvangirai says is immediately followed by another from twenty minutes earlier. What seem on the soundtrack like straightforward and incriminating statements turn out, when you watch the time-codes, to be a cynical scissors-and-paste job. And then it turns out that the Australian reporter, Mark Davis, was given the tape by the man whom Tsvangirai purportedly approached in search of a hit-man, Ari Ben-Menashe—who has been doing work for Mugabe's government for years.

Ben-Menashe is an Israeli-born Canadian who has dabbled in the spy world for decades and was once described by the *Jerusalem Post* as "a notorious and chronic liar." His Montreal-based firm Dickens and Madson has recently been involved in marketing the illegal diamonds with which Congo pays the Mugabe regime for the loan of thousands of Zimbabwean soldiers to back it in the Congolese civil war — a bloody business that is making some senior military and party officials in Zimbabwe disgustingly rich.

The current story appears to have begun when Ben-Menashe's firm of "political consultants" approached Tsvangirai offering him advice on how to deal with the press and political issues in America. (Ben-Menashe's version is that Tsvangirai approached him, but why would somebody living in Zimbabwe look in Montreal either for advice on US media or for hit-men? Even Ben-Menashe's wife says she does not believe a word he says.)

So Tsvangirai meets with these nasty but stupid people three times: twice at the Royal Automobile Club in London (Groucho Marx's famous line about club memberships comes to mind) and then the key meeting in Montreal on December 4, where Dickens and Madson secretly videotaped the whole session. Tsvangirai admits that he was there, but he denies that they were there to plot Mugabe's assassination.

The time-codes bear him out. He never says anything directly incriminating, and his answers to incriminating questions have been cobbled together from various remarks that he made over the course of an hour's tape. The leading questions are so clumsy and obvious that even Tsvangirai twigged eventually. When the others began talking openly about killing Mugabe, he says, he jumped up and left the room.

Thus is the fate of over 10 million decent people decided. Tsvangirai will almost certainly win the vote, but even if he also wins the count, he will not assume the presidency. The treason charge will be activated, and he will be thrown in jail instead. This whole story is the script not of a coup against Mugabe, but against the next elected president of Zimbabwe.

And what are we to make of the major players? Mugabe is a scoundrel, of course, but we knew that. Tsvangirai is a fool, and that is a very unhappy discovery. Mark Davis is a fool too, which is probably less serious. And the Canadian hitman? In the world of crime, what Canadians are revered for is not being good hit-men, but the world's best con-men.

THE AFRICAN UNION

July 6, 2002

This week in Durban, South Africa, more than fifty African heads of state are gathered for the launch of the African Union. The idea is that in time it will come to resemble the European Union.

It sounds crazy. Half a dozen of those fifty states have bitter civil wars underway, and half a dozen more are just emerging from them. Fewer than half of them have democratic governments, and most of those are deeply corrupt. Africa is the poorest, worst-educated, most disease-ridden continent— and it has been getting steadily worse for several decades.

Yet they want to create an African version of the European Union. How can those fifty-odd rulers talk about a central bank and monetary union, a peace and security council modelled on the UN Security Council and a standby military intervention force, an African Court of Justice—even a united, federal Africa if the visionaries get their way—when they can't even save their own people from war, famine and disease?

Time for some analogies. The European Union grew out of the European Economic Community, which was founded in the 1950s by impoverished countries that had just emerged from a war that killed around 10 percent of the continent's population. The idea was partly mutual economic aid, but more important always was the goal of ending the dictatorships and the wars.

The eastern half of Europe languished under Communist tyrannies until 1989, but when the Communists fell, the EEC rose to the occasion. It renamed itself the European Union, and set out on the road of monetary union and political expansion to take in the eastern European countries, with the ultimate goal of a genuinely federal Europe.

The Organization of African Unity was about political solidarity, not democracy or economic progress, when it was founded in 1963, because Africans were still trying to drive the European imperialists out. But the independence struggles are long over, and solidarity has come to mean simply that brother African rulers never criticize one another no matter how badly some behave. The leap to the idea of the African Union is huge, comparable to the declaration of the European Union after 1989. Whether it will work remains to be seen, but this is a serious initiative.

Everybody has their own theory about "what is wrong with Africa," but these days there is surprisingly broad agreement among African leaders and thinkers that most of the solutions probably lie above the level of the individual state. Hence the African Union.

I think they're right, and I even think I know why. Consider those fifty African heads of state. Why does a continent with just over 10 percent of the human population have almost a third of the world's countries?

The North African countries, mostly white, Muslim and Arabic-speaking, match the global norms: average population around 25 million, and one minority language or none. But south of the Sahara the average population drops to around 10 million per country and the ethnic complexity soars: ten, twenty, even fifty languages within the same border. That is sub-Saharan Africa's core problem: an amazingly large number of small ethnic groups, and hardly any big ones.

Five hundred years ago, the Eurasian continent contained all the biggest and most technologically advanced civilizations in the world. Africa came next, with ironworking in most places and some fairly large urban centres. Bringing up the rear were the Americas and Australasia, where most tools were of stone and the wheel was high technology.

Then the Europeans burst out of Eurasia and overran the rest of the world. They encountered a few larger societies and literally thousands of little ones (there were six hundred languages in Australia alone), and in short order they exterminated most of them and subjugated the survivors. Some of the killing they did by hand, but mostly the highly infectious diseases endemic in Eurasian mass societies, to which people living in smaller groups had no immunity, did the job for them.

So the Americas and Australasia have seen almost a complete change of population in the past five hundred years. Africa got conquered too, but its population survived. Why? Because its people had been in constant trading contact with Eurasia and over the centuries had gradually developed Eurasian levels of immunity to all the quick-killer diseases that devastated the rest of the world. So the Africans are still there—all of them, in their hundreds and hundreds of different ethnic groups.

Good. Survival is better than subjugation or extinction. But it means that Africa has to build modern states out of the most ethnically diverse populations in the world. It's been getting nowhere fast. But if five or ten or fifteen ethnic groups find it hard to coexist in the same state, the solution is not to subdivide it further. Africa will not be better off if it has three hundred countries with an average population of 2 million. Perhaps the answer is to submerge them all in a sea of other ethnic groups, none of them big enough to dream of dominating the rest.

Nobody will say that this is what the African Union is about, but of course it is. It is the first attempt to solve Africa's problems by moving beyond the postcolonial states. It will be decades before we know if this green shoot can grow into something strong and useful, but at least they are barking up the right tree.

The present is a good deal less hopeful, shall we say.

AFRICA'S THIRTY YEARS WAR
May 29, 2003

In the next few days a French-led multinational force will begin arriving in the Congo's northeastern Ituri province, empowered by the UN Security Council to use "all necessary means," including force, to stop the bloody struggle between the rival militias of the Lendu and Hema tribes that has killed an estimated fifty thousand people and driven half a million from their homes in the past four years. It will have just over a thousand troops, and it will stay only until a Bangladeshi force of similar size arrives in August. It is, in other words, a very small drop in a very big bucket.

The fighting in the Congo since the death of long-ruling dictator Mobutu Sese Seko in 1997 has been called "Africa's First World War," with up to six other African armies and dozens of local tribal militias involved in a many-sided struggle for control of the country's rich resources. The International Rescue Agency, an American aid group, estimated in April that between 3.1 and 4.7 million people have died because of the war, mostly from famine and disease. How are a thousand troops for three months going to cope with a tragedy on this scale?

Well, first of all, it is not like the First World War at all. It is more like the Thirty Years War that killed up to a third of the population of Germany between 1618 and 1648. Like the Congo now, Germany then was more a geographical expression than a real country, with no central authority and no way of protecting itself from rapacious outsiders. The Germans were at each other's throats, with religious differences playing a similar role to tribal rivalries in the Congo now, but military interventions by foreign powers—the Swedes, the French, the Spanish—made things far worse.

It took longer in seventeenth-century Germany than in the twenty-first-century Congo to reach the point where whole cities were depopulated and reports of cannibalism became commonplace (the Pygmy communities of the northeastern Congo recently protested to the UN that their people were being "hunted and eaten literally as though they were game animals" by both government and rebel troops), but Germany also got there in the end.

There is nothing uniquely African about this tragedy, and no particular mystery about how to stop it. It just takes political will on the part of the international community, and a sufficient number of peacekeeping troops with the authority to use "all necessary means" to stop the killing.

An emergency force of a thousand troops in one province isn't enough. Neither is the larger Monuc force that the UN has maintained in the Congo since the first ceasefire agreement in 1999. It only has thirty-eight hundred troops scattered in small packets across the centre and east of the country (its authorized strength is eighty-seven hundred, but too few countries were willing to contribute troops), and in any case it is an observer force with no right to conduct military operations. But forty or fifty thousand troops with a mandate to use force and to stay for at least two years would probably do the job.

Most of the UN force on the ground could be provided by Africans, even though it would be vital to exclude troops from the countries—Rwanda, Uganda, Zimbabwe and Angola— that were most heavily involved in the fighting over the past four years. Western and Asian countries would need to provide communications, logistics, engineering and other specialist units and, above all, the money to pay for the operation. A few billion dollars over two years would cover the cost—the equivalent of one day's expenditure in the recent war in Iraq.

It would be the biggest UN operation for many years, but it wouldn't be starting from scratch. There is a formal ceasefire in place, and even an agreement to hold a free election in two years' time. Most of the foreign armies have already withdrawn—indeed, it was the departure of some six thousand Ugandan troops from Ituri province in March that unleashed the most recent round of carnage there, as the Hema and Lendu tribal militias originally armed by the Ugandans and their Rwandan rivals fought for control of Bunia, the provincial capital.

Rebuilding the Congo after thirty-two years of corruption and neglect under the Western-backed Mobutu regime and over four years of civil war and foreign intervention is a generation's task, but ending the fighting and starting it down the right road could be done cheaply and quite quickly. Both the African Union, which would supply most of the troops, and the countries of the European Union, which would probably supply most of the money and the military expertise, would gain some sorely needed cohesion by collaborating in the task, and the UN could win back some respect after a very bad season.

Or, alternatively, we could all let the tragedy drag on for another decade or so.

I have been hopeful about South Africa ever since I went through the end of apartheid and the transition to majority rule there being told by everybody I met, "There's going to be a civil war." They always said that in the former Soviet Union in the last couple of years before the fall of Communist rule, too, and it was my job as a foreigner to tell them that it wasn't going to happen. After a while, I even came to believe it, and in the end I turned out to be right. So I was in good practice for doing the same job in South Africa, and the magic worked there too. By now, it's just got to be a habit.

SOUTH AFRICAN ELECTION
April 11, 2004

Patricia de Lille, leader of South Africa's Independent Democratic Party, took a very public HIV test as part of her campaign—and challenged all the other candidates in the country's third democratic election (on April 14) to do the same. Not many will, for fear of embarrassing senior colleagues who dare not do so: more than one in nine South Africans is HIV-positive. But then de Lille's whole campaign is based on outspoken and sometimes brazen challenges to the more established parties, and she stands no chance of winning a share of power anyway.

Everybody knows who is going to win this election: the African National Congress (ANC). What's more, it's going to win with about two-thirds of the votes, so President Thabo Mbeki won't need to share cabinet posts with any other party—and it's been that way since the end of apartheid ten years ago. Yet, neither the United Nations nor the European Union is even bothering to send election monitors to South Africa; they know that the vote will be above suspicion.

By every conventional measure, this is not a country where a party that has been in power for ten years should get two-thirds of the votes in a free election. Quite apart from the AIDS plague, which is now killing at least six hundred South Africans a day, there is 40 percent unemployment, the murder rate is still the highest in the world (though it is down by almost a third from its peak) and half the population lives on less than a dollar a day. Where is the impatience? Where is the anger?

The ANC is very lucky: it still basks in the afterglow of having been the steadfast and finally triumphant opponent of the apartheid regime. Most of the country's black majority (about three-quarters of South Africa's 44 million people) still give the ANC full marks for trying, and forgive it for its failures. But it's not just the ANC that's lucky; South Africa is too, for superhuman patience was definitely what was needed after thirty-six years of apartheid.

When the ANC took over in 1994, there was no money to provide all the services to the black majority that had long been neglected under apartheid. The siege economy run by the white minority regime was teetering on the brink of collapse and the state's coffers were empty.

Nelson Mandela, the first post-apartheid president, used his immense popularity to make the ANC accept a policy of tough budget discipline and fiscal orthodoxy, but its real architect was his then-deputy Thabo Mbeki. Because of the austerity, the ANC has built only 1.6 million houses for the poor and fifty-six thousand new classrooms in the past ten years: a lot, but not nearly enough. It has done better on services: the number of people who have electricity has doubled to over two-thirds; 85 percent of households now have running water; and almost two-thirds have proper sanitation. Mere statistics, but they change people's lives.

What the ANC could not deliver was jobs, because Mr. Mbeki's first priority was to stabilize the economy. Ten years of that would have ruined any other government, but now the task is accomplished, and Mbeki says the economy is ready to grow fast and produce jobs. Everybody hopes he's right, and they are willing to give him a chance because they understand, despite all their grousing, that they are living through a miracle.

The "rainbow nation" was just a hopeful phrase ten years ago; the reality was a country so deeply divided by race, language and tribe that people talked freely about civil war. When I visited with my family five years ago, we stayed with black friends in Pretoria and whites in Cape Town. Our black friends saw only other black families and the whites saw only whites, and my youngest daughter, then six, came home believing (as I discovered only later) that we had visited two different countries.

There's still far too much of that: the races mix at work and in public, but not at home. But the real hope lies with the mall rats. It's probably too late for most of the adults to change their ways, but the schools were desegregated ten years ago, and most of the whites are not rich enough to put their kids in private schools, so in many urban areas the schools are racially mixed, and the kids who started in those schools a decade ago are now teenagers hanging around the shopping malls. In racially mixed groups. History is not fate.

I used to believe that South Africa's long, tangled, bloody history was its fate. But at least it *has* a real history, and everybody's past connects (though often in painful ways). There is a South African identity that transcends race, tribe and language emerging out of all that pain, and that's a start. I think they're going to make it.

And finally, the most worrisome political development in Africa in a long time. If it saves Sudan from another decade of slaughter, good. But if the precedent is followed elsewhere, then God help Africa.

PANDORA'S BOX IN SUDAN
January 13, 2005

If the peace agreement signed in Kenya on January 10 really ends the twenty-one-year-old Sudanese civil war, the killing will stop and millions of refugees will be able to go home — but the deal carries a big risk for Africa. As the *Nation* in

Nairobi put it: "One of the elements of the settlement is that the south has the right to secede after six years. This is the first time in Africa that a peace settlement has recognized the right to secession."

That's not strictly true, since the almost equally long war in Ethiopia ended in the early '90s with independence for Eritrea. But Eritrea could be treated as an exception because it had already been a separate entity in colonial times; the Sudan deal is different. The basic rule that Africa's old colonial borders must never be changed, adopted by the Organization of African Unity (OAU) (now the African Union) at the dawn of independent Africa, is starting to break down.

The OAU declared Africa's borders sacrosanct not because they made good sense, but precisely because they didn't. They were arbitrary lines on maps that bundled peoples of different languages, cultures and religions within the borders of a single state, and divided others between several states. If you let anybody get away with changing just one of those borders, you would be opening Pandora's Box—because there's hardly a border anywhere in Africa that somebody couldn't make a good argument for changing.

Fifty-one African countries (or fifty-two, or fifty-three—it depends how you feel about Somaliland and Western Sahara); around two hundred separate ethnolinguistic groups of more than half a million people each; no more than five or six groups south of the Sahara that number over 10 million: Africa is the last place in the world to start trying to draw rational borders. Leave them alone!

That was the rule from the start, and it probably saved millions of African lives over the decades, in wars that were not fought because even if you won them you couldn't change the borders. Yet the wiser men among the OAU's founders probably secretly knew that the rule couldn't last forever. Never mind. It would keep big inter-African wars at bay for at least a generation, and by that time surely economic growth and education would have eroded the old ethnic divisions. With luck, African borders would matter no more than Scandinavian borders by then.

It seemed a plausible hope at the time. Africa's living standards and education levels were much higher than Asia's in the '60s, and most people expected the kind of rapid development in Africa that subsequently did happen in Asia. If that had actually come to pass, African borders really wouldn't matter much by now. But it didn't happen, so they matter a lot.

The Sudanese peace deal makes perfect sense from the point of view of the Sudanese. Neither side can win the war, which has killed 2 million people and displaced another 4 million in the past two decades, and the country's oil reserves can only be developed if the two sides stop shooting and share the profits. So President Omar al-Bashir's regime, which controls the Arabic-speaking, mostly Muslim north of the country, has agreed to share power with the Sudanese People's Liberation Army (SPLA), which runs much of the black African, mostly Christian and animist south.

The leader of the SPLA, John Garang, will become first vice-president to President Bashir, the two armies will be integrated (in theory, though probably not in practice), and oil revenues, mostly generated in the south, will be evenly shared between north and south. There is even hope that the new, integrated government in Khartoum will take a saner approach to the rebellion in the western region of Darfur.

Khartoum's current approach, which has been to unleash a brutal militia called the *Janjaweed*, recruited from Arabic-speaking pastoral tribes in the north of Darfur, to terrorize the more "African" farming communities of southern Darfur from whom the rebels are drawn, has been as vicious as it was ineffective. It has cost seventy thousand lives in the past year and made almost 2 million people refugees, and still the rebels have not been defeated.

The rebels in Darfur are trying to emulate the success of the SPLA, but without either oil or religion to strengthen their hand—everybody on both sides in Darfur is Muslim—they stand little chance of success. A less violent approach from Khartoum and some oil money to lubricate a peace deal there could cut the ground right out from under them.

But the price of all this has been that the non-Muslim southerners (around a third of Sudan's 30 million people) will be able to secede legally in six years' time if they still want out. The hope is that a share of the oil money will reconcile everybody to a more or less united Sudan, but it's unlikely that there will be enough money, fairly enough distributed, to transform opinion in the south (which has been separatist since before independence) in only six years.

If the south chooses to become a separate country in 2010, under an agreement and procedures that have the official approval of the African Union, then the rules in Africa would well and truly have changed, and Pandora's Box would be open at last. This is a very big gamble.

CHAPTER FIFTEEN

IRAQ: SHIA PRESSURE, AMERICAN ABUSE, SUNNI REVOLT

The United States had a year to make good in Iraq: restore public services, restart the economy, deal with the worst of the unemployment and above all, make visible and rapid steps towards handing the country back to Iraqi rule. The invasion would still have been a breach of international law and a potentially fatal challenge to the multilateral system, but at least Iraqis would have got something out of it and some thousands of people now dead would still be alive. Instead, the occupation regime threw several million more people out of work by dissolving the army and most of the civil service; it failed to restore public services because it insisted on giving the work to American firms; and it resisted early elections in an attempt to keep its tame Iraqis recently returned from exile in the key positions.

The first half of 2004 is when all those blunders came home to roost, and the US lost control of the agenda in Iraq. It wasn't being too clever on the terrorist front, either.

WHAT THE TERRORISTS WANT

January 18, 2004

I have always admired Edward Luttwak, one of the clearest American thinkers in the strategy/security game, and I have nothing but contempt for the US Homeland Security Department (*Heimatsicherheitsabteilung* in the original German) and its ridiculous colour-coded threat levels. So I started reading a recent article by the former on the latter with genuine pleasure, anticipating that Luttwak was going to condemn Homeland Security for its habit of running up the levels from puce to magenta and back down to mauve, shredding Americans' nerves with warnings nobody can respond to in a useful way, for no better reason than to cover its own bureaucratic behind.

That's just what he did, and the article was rollicking along with me cheering Luttwak on every line of the way—when his whole argument suddenly veered off into the ditch, rolled three times and lay there bleeding. What he said was: "The successive warnings of ill-defined threats that frighten many Americans are achieving the very aim of the terrorists. Terrorism cannot materially weaken the United States, so their entire purpose is precisely to terrorize, to make Americans unhappy, *in the hope that this will induce them to accept terrorist demands"* (my italics).

If one of the cleverest security analysts in the country has got no further than this in his thinking about what the terrorists want, then it's no surprise that 60 or 70 percent of Luttwak's fellow-countrymen believe that Saddam Hussein sent the terrorists. He thinks that the terrorists are trying to make Americans unhappy in order to "induce them to accept terrorist demands"? What demands could the Islamist terrorists of al-Qaeda possibly make that the United States could conceivably grant?

Fly them all to Havana? Convert to Islam? Put the money in unmarked notes in a brown paper bag and leave it behind the radiator? The whole notion that this is some sort of giant extortion operation is as naive (or as wilfully ignorant) as the Bush administration's pet explanation that the terrorists attack the US because "they hate our freedoms." Unfortunately, the post-9/11 intellectual climate in the United States has prevented any serious discussion of the terrorists' goals and their strategies for achieving them.

In the post-9/11 chill, even conceding that the terrorist leaders are intelligent people with rational goals seemed somehow disloyal to America's dead. Instead, it was assumed that their fanaticism made them too blind or stupid for purposeful action at the strategic level. Even terrorist groups as marginal and self-deluded as the Baader-Meinhof Gang and the Weathermen had a more or less coherent analysis, political goals and some notion of how their attacks moved them towards those goals, but the public debate in the US grants none of that to al-Qaeda.

Yet, the Islamist radicals have always been completely open about their goals. They want to take power in the

Muslim countries (phase one of the project) and then unite the entire Muslim world in a final struggle to overthrow the power of the West (phase two). They are still stuck in phase one, with little to show for it despite thirty years of trying, so in the early 1990s Osama bin Laden and his colleagues switched from head-on assaults on the regimes in Muslim countries to direct attacks on Western targets. Yet, their first-phase goal remains seizing power in the Muslim world, not some fantasy about "bringing the West to its knees."

Terrorists generally rant about their goals but stay silent about their strategies, so now we have to do a little work for ourselves. If the real goal is still revolutions that bring Islamist radicals to power, then how does attacking the West help? Well, the US in particular may be goaded into retaliating by bombing or even invading various Muslim countries—and in doing so, may drive enough aggrieved Muslims into the arms of the Islamist radicals that their long-stalled revolutions against local regimes finally get off the ground.

Most analysts outside the United States long ago concluded that that was the principal motive for the 9/11 attack. They would add that by giving the Bush administration a reason to attack Afghanistan, and at least a flimsy pretext for invading Iraq, al-Qaeda's attacks have paid off handsomely. US troops are now the unwelcome military rulers of more than 50 million Muslims in Afghanistan and Iraq, and people there and elsewhere are turning to the Islamist radicals as the only force in the Muslim world that is willing and able to defy American power.

It is astonishing how little this is understood in the United States. I know of no American analyst who has even made the obvious point that al-Qaeda wants George W. Bush to win next November's presidential election and continue his interventionist policies in the Middle East for another four years, and will act to save Mr. Bush from defeat if necessary.

It probably would not do so unless Mr. Bush's number were slipping badly, for any terrorist attack on US soil carries the risk of stimulating resentment against the current administration for failing to prevent it. Certainly another attack on the scale of 9/11 would risk producing that result, even if al-Qaeda had the resources for it. But a simple truck bomb in some US city centre a few months before the election, killing just a couple of dozen Americans, could drive voters back into Mr. Bush's arms and turn a tight election around. Al-Qaeda is clever enough for that.

As the armed resistance in Iraq grew, the American briefers in Iraq stopped insisting that the resistance was coming mostly from "Baathist dead-enders." They found a new bogeyman: Abu Musab al-Zarqawi.

LETTER FROM IRAQ
February 12, 2004

"Dear Mom:

Iraq is really fun, and us guys from al-Qaeda are doing great work. I personally have organized twenty-five suicide attacks already, and Osama bin Laden himself wrote to thank me. It's a great pity that our ally Saddam Hussein didn't get his weapons of mass destruction finished in time for us terrorists to start using them against the infidels, but that's how the cookie crumbles. The dumb Iraqis are all grateful to the Americans and won't help us, but with the help of other foreign terrorists I am now trying to get a civil war going between the Sunnis and the Shias in order to defeat the Americans and their stupid democracy. Gosh, how I hate their freedoms.

Your loving son,

Ahmed

P.S. Thanks for the clean socks."

I am not at liberty to reveal how the letter came into my possession—let's just say that it came from a highly reputable US intelligence agency whose title includes the letters C, I and A. According to what they told me, it was written by a well-known al-Qaeda terrorist from Jordan, Abu Musab al-Zarqawi (real name Ahmed Fadil al-Khalaylah), and like the seventeen-page letter of his to al-Qaeda's leaders that was leaked to the *New York Times* recently, it proves that US President George W. Bush was absolutely right to invade Iraq. The Iraqis love Americans, and the problems there now are all caused by foreign terrorists.

I must confess that I did wonder for a moment if the intelligence service in question might just be trying to help the government that employs it, but that way lies doubt, disillusion and the deadly sin of cynicism. These spies have professional standards, and they would never cook the intelligence they provide just to suit the needs of some passing administration.

Same goes for the soldiers. When Brigadier-General Mark Kimmitt, US deputy chief of operations in Iraq, said last Wednesday that the suicide bombing outside a police station in Iskandariya the previous day that killed fifty people had "al-Qaeda's fingerprints all over it," you just had to believe him. I mean, why would any Iraqi target a police station just because the people inside were collaborating with foreign occupation forces? And who else but al-Qaeda carries out suicide attacks (apart from Palestinians, Tamils, Chechens and a few others)? "When you see . . . these kinds of attack," as Kimmitt put it, "one has the tendency to look at foreign fighters."

OK, enough sarcasm. What kind of idiots do these people take us for? Having failed to find the weapons of mass destruction they allegedly invaded Iraq for, having failed to be greeted with open arms by grateful Iraqis and having arrested only a handful of foreigners among the thousands of suspects they have rounded up since the resistance movement began blowing up American soldiers and local collaborators, do they really think they can persuade us that this "foreign terrorist"—they have just increased the price on his head from $5 million to $10 million—is the source of all their troubles in Iraq?

"Al-Zarqawi" is not really very foreign to Iraq—he is a Jordanian citizen, but he belongs to the Bani Hassan tribe that straddles the Iraq–Jordan border—and he is not very important either. He is a rather obscure member of al-Qaeda who was in Afghanistan during the period when the 9/11 attacks on the United States were planned and carried out, and there is no evidence that he or any other al-Qaeda member was in contact with the ruling Baathist Party in Iraq before Saddam Hussein's regime was destroyed in the US invasion.

If he is in contact with underground members of that party now—for which there is also no evidence—that would hardly be surprising: the enemy of my enemy is (for the moment) my friend. But the notion that he and al-Qaeda are behind the Iraqi resistance is purely an ideological fantasy. There are plenty of Baathists in Iraq who hate having been driven from power, plenty of Islamists unconnected with Osama bin Laden's crowd (including even some Kurds) who hate the presence of arrogant infidels in their country, and plenty of plain Iraqi nationalists who regard the occupation as an intolerable national humiliation.

Unemployment has soared from 50 percent to 80 percent since the US invasion; it is no surprise that desperate Iraqis are willing to join the new police and army that the US occupation authorities are building to serve as sandbags between American soldiers (who have largely been pulled off the streets to minimize casualties) and the resistance. But it is equally unsurprising that the resistance ("anti-Iraqi forces," in the US briefers' jargon) regards these Iraqi police and soldiers in US pay as collaborators and high-priority targets. Still, you can see why "foreign terrorists" is the preferred explanation in an election year. It makes the whole invasion of Iraq look less like barking up the wrong tree.

If there is only one article that people read in the whole book, this next one should be it. It's what this is all really about, though pitifully few of the players seem aware of that fact.

THE UN IS NOT A MORALITY PLAY
March 7, 2004

"It may well be that under international law as presently constituted a regime can systematically brutalize and oppress its own people and there is nothing anyone can do. . . . This may be the law, but should it be?" asked Prime Minister Tony Blair last Friday in a speech that tried to persuade skeptical British voters that he was right to attack Iraq at President George W. Bush's side. He didn't answer his own question, assuming that everybody agrees the answer is no. The correct answer, however, is yes.

Mr. Blair and Mr. Bush have both ended up arguing the moral case for invading Iraq, though it didn't get mentioned much before the war. Having found no "weapons of mass destruction" nor any connection between Saddam Hussein and the Islamist terrorists who attacked the United States, their sole remaining justification for the invasion is the fact that it removed a vicious dictator. The problem is that it is not a legal justification.

It seems so obvious: there's a wicked regime; we have the power to destroy it; let's do those people a favour and invade. We need to change international law so that we can legally invade "when a nation's people are subject to a regime such as Saddam's," as Mr. Blair put it.

Who would be the targets? Any regime that is judged to "systematically brutalize and oppress its own people"—North Korea, or Burma, or Zimbabwe, or even China, depending on which countries set themselves up as the judges. That should keep us all busy until the End of Time.

Mr. Blair's argument has a strong emotional appeal. It would be nice if there were some impartial and all-powerful force in the world that would unerringly punish all the wicked, while sparing all the innocent. The traditional name for this force, however, is God, and even He has chosen not to act within history in quite so hyperactive a way, postponing the sorting out of the good and the evil to a time shortly after the End of Time. Mr. Blair's offer to bring the Last Judgment forward by a billion years or so is doubtless well-meant, but it is ill-advised.

Even well-educated people such as Mr. Blair profoundly misunderstand the nature of the United Nations. They imagine that it is a sword of Justice, and maybe even an instrument of Love. They do not understand that the heart of the United Nations enterprise is a brutally realistic attempt to change international law in order to prevent the Third World War. The UN is a nuclear blast shelter, not the international equivalent of a refuge for battered women.

When was the UN founded? 1945. What was the situation in 1945? The biggest war in history had just ended: 55 million people were dead, most of the cities of the industrialized world had been bombed flat, and nuclear weapons had just been dropped on cities for the first time. What was the prognosis? Another world war eventually, with every great power holding hundreds or thousands of nuclear weapons on Day One. Five hundred million dead in the first week. So right there, in 1945, the countries of the world decided to try to change that future. They created the United Nations, a new institution whose Charter declared that henceforth war is illegal.

It did not say that henceforth tyranny is illegal, because enforcing such a rule would mean endless war. (First we attack Stalin, then Mao, then . . .) It was a hundred-year project at the very least because human beings have been fighting wars since the dawn of civilization eight thousand years ago, or even before. But it was necessary, because the only alternative, sooner or later, was the Third World War with nuclear weapons.

The basic UN rule is that you can no longer legally attack another country, and no excuses are accepted. The fact that their ancestors stole some of your country's territory a hundred years ago doesn't justify it, nor does a suspicion that they are planning to attack you, nor even the fact that their government wickedly oppresses its own people. Allow those exceptions, and clever lawyers will find a way to argue that every aggression is legal. So the law says no exceptions.

During the 1990s, when the international environment was relatively benign, attempts were made to get round this rule in order to justify humanitarian military interventions to stop genocides in Bosnia and Kosovo. The interventions were actually done by NATO on a nod-and-a-wink basis, with the UN renaming the attacking troops as blue helmets as soon as the fighting ended, and legalizing things post facto. The actions were well meant and they saved lives, but after Iraq that kind of intervention won't soon happen again: it opened doors that should have stayed shut.

Mr. Blair isn't really trying to change the basic UN law; he's just trying to justify why he broke it last year by invading Iraq. It is unlikely that he or Mr. Bush will be urging us all to invade Burma later this year. But the law is there for a reason, and it is still a good reason.

Countries should be left to deal with their own dictators—and these days there are even techniques available that will let them do so nonviolently, if they have the patience to work at it. Foreign invasions are not the solution.

On March 11, 2004, just before the Spanish general election, terrorists set off a number of bombs on commuter trains in Madrid. Two days later, Spaniards voted out the conservative Aznar government that had backed the US invasion of Iraq and later sent Spanish troops to help with the occupation. It's doubtful that many Spaniards actually changed their voting intentions as a result of the bombs, but many younger people who had not been expected to vote (but would vote Socialist if they bothered) actually went to the polls because of the intense sorrow and anger that seized the entire national community. It was their votes that tipped the balance and elected a Socialist government committed to pulling Spanish troops out of Iraq.

DIALOGUE OF THE DEAF: THE WIDENING ATLANTIC
March 17, 2004

The new Spanish prime minister, José Luis Rodriguez Zapatero, was very careful in his choice of words. "Military intervention in Iraq was a political mistake," he said on March 15. "It divided more than it united; there were no reasons for it. Time has shown that the arguments for it lacked credibility. . . . Mr. Blair and Mr. Bush must do some reflection . . . you can't organize a war with lies. The Spanish troops will come back (from Iraq)."

Mr. Zapatero made exactly the same argument a year ago, when the United States was about to invade Iraq and then-prime minister José Maria Aznar was cheering it on. More than 80 percent of the Spanish people agreed with Zapatero about Iraq then, and they still do today. He did not say a single word about appeasing terrorism, and nor does anyone else in Spain want to do that after a terrorist attack that killed over two hundred commuters in Madrid. They are just sick of being lied to, and they don't believe that Iraq had anything to do with terrorism.

The reaction in the United States, however, has been distinctly ungenerous. "The plain fact is that the Spanish electorate displayed craven cowardice by electing the Socialists. It embraced the wrong-headed notion—so dismayingly popular in Europe—that to adopt any policy more resolute than abject appeasement of terrorists is to invite terrorist attacks," wrote the *New York Post*.

The *Post* is a Murdoch paper and has to say that sort of thing, but what about the *New York Daily News* writing that the terrorists "must be big fans of the democratic process after watching the lemminglike Spaniards do their bidding," or David Brooks writing in the *New York Times* that Spanish voters had chosen to "throw out the old government and replace it with one whose policies are more to al-Qaida's liking. What is the Spanish word for appeasement?" Or the *Washington Post* editorializing: "The danger is that Europe's reaction to a war that has now reached its soil will be retreat and appeasement rather than strengthened resolve."

On the contrary. The real "danger" is that those European governments that were always able to tell the difference between fighting terrorism and invading Iraq—"old Europe" in US Defense Secretary Don Rumsfeld's contemptuous phrase—are growing in number at the expense of those who went along with Washington in blurring the distinction between the two. Italian Prime Minister Silvio Berlusconi faces an election in the next year and runs a similar risk of a rebellion by voters who overwhelmingly opposed his support for the invasion of Iraq. Even British Prime Minister Tony Blair, whose day of reckoning is a bit further off, must be feeling apprehensive.

He is right to be, for the Madrid events have only deepened popular doubts about Mr. Blair's Iraq venture. The Murdoch-owned *Sun* predictably praised Mr. Blair for his unquestioning support of the Bush administration's actions, but Steven Glover in the *Daily Mail*, traditionally the conservative voice of "middle England," wrote, "Mr. Blair . . .

has succeeded in making things worse than they would otherwise have been. . . . This is the story of how a sophisticated modern democracy has been misled by one misguided messianic figure. . . . I do not think that the British people will spare, or forgive, Mr. Blair."

Is there a risk that al-Qaeda would try to deepen this growing alienation from the current governments in London and Rome by "doing a Madrid" on the eve of the next Italian or British elections? Of course there is, for part of its strategy is to isolate the United States from its traditional European allies. It undoubtedly wants Mr. Bush re-elected in the United States, since that would perpetuate the US foreign policy of "preemptive" military interventions that is the main recruiting tool of radical Islamists in the Muslim world, but it would quite like to break the old transatlantic alliance between the various "Crusader states."

Does that mean that those European countries whose governments backed Mr. Bush last year must stick with that policy forever or else end up "appeasing the terrorists"? Obviously not, although that is the rhetoric that Bush supporters apply to the question. The alliance really is weakening, and the culprits really do live in the White House, not in Europe.

It is generally forgotten in Washington, but all the allies and friends who refused to support the invasion of Iraq willingly backed the counterstrike against terrorist bases in Afghanistan in the first days after 9/11. Germany, France, Canada and even Russia offered troops (although in the end everybody decided that it would be untactful to let the Russians invade Afghanistan twice in twenty years). It's only when the subject changed from terrorism to Iraq that the divisions started growing.

Now the transatlantic alliance is at its weakest in fifty years: "old Europe" is growing, and in two years "new Europe," the Bush administration's uncritical ally, may include only a handful of eastern European countries. The *Los Angeles Times* is a long way from Europe, but it got it exactly right: "The US should read the results (of the Spanish elections) as demonstrating anew that most of the world does not see the Iraq campaign as part of the global war on terror. . . . The sympathy that much of the world felt for the US after the 9/11 attacks has been squandered by invading Iraq with too little global support."

THE EX–MAD DOG OF THE MIDDLE EAST
March 24, 2004

Start running with the wrong crowd, and pretty soon you'll be meeting some very unpleasant people. Britain's Prime Minister Tony Blair spent Thursday visiting with Libyan dictator Muammar Gadafy, once described by Ronald Reagan as "the mad dog of the Middle East." But that was then and this is now.

Mr. Blair was hot on the heels of US Assistant Secretary of State William Burns, who flew into Tripoli on March 23 to welcome the original comedy terrorist back into the community of nations. "Comedy," in the sense that Gadafy is a full-time egomaniac with a dreadful taste in clothes—he often looks like a Bedouin drag queen—who doesn't realize how ridiculous his preening arrogance seems to others. But also "terrorist" because he really does kill people.

He's still killing them in Libya, where his secret police routinely torture and murder opponents of the regime, but he also used to kill foreigners. He shipped arms to the Irish Republican Army, he has acknowledged responsibility for the terrorist bomb that blew up Pan Am flight 103 over the Scottish village of Lockerbie in 1988, and as recently as 1998 he was implicated in the bombing of a French airliner over Chad.

Muammar Gadafy is not just an amusing head-case who happens to have run a major oil-producing country for thirty-five years. (He came to power in a military coup in 1969, when he was only twenty-seven years old). He is directly responsible for tens of thousands of deaths in Libya, and many hundreds of deaths in terrorist attacks abroad. He killed more Americans and Britons in the Pan Am attack than the total number of Spaniards killed in the recent bombings in Madrid.

But now, according to British Foreign Secretary Jack Straw, he is "statesmanlike and courageous." How has this miraculous transformation come to pass?

Gadafy started coming in from the cold in the later 1990s, as the United Nations trade and travel sanctions imposed in 1986 started to bite. The sanctions made it hard for the Libyans to import the equipment they needed to repair and update their oil production facilities, and the daily output gradually drifted down from the peak of 3.3 million barrels to only 1.4 million today. This cut deeply into the regime's income and caused dangerous resentment among the impoverished citizens of Libya, so Gadafy decided to make things up with the West.

His first step was to drop his support for the IRA, after which Britain restored diplomatic relations, but the real trick was to find a way around the Pan Am atrocity. Eventually Gadafy handed the Libyan intelligence agents accused of the bombing over to a special court sitting in the Netherlands but presided over by a British judge. One of the accused was found not guilty and the other is now serving a long term in a Scottish jail—but there was a curious aspect to the affair: the court never inquired about Gadafy's role in the atrocity.

Were we supposed to believe that Libya is the sort of place where the intelligence service would launch this sort of operation without mentioning it to the man at the top? No, we were just not encouraged to ask. The fix was in, and Gadafy was being shepherded back into the fold while a couple of junior agents were offered up as sacrificial lambs. His public renunciation of Libya's "nuclear weapons program" last December was just the last stage in this process.

That is the alleged triumph of Western diplomacy which Mr. Blair went to Libya to celebrate, but really—a Libyan nuclear weapons program? Gadafy did acquire some nuclear bits and pieces from the black-market operation run by Abdul Qadeer Khan, Pakistan's leading nuclear scientist. The US and British intelligence agencies now claim that Gadafy's program was "fairly advanced" because they want to show that their invasion of Iraq frightened him into giving up something really dangerous. But the International Atomic Energy Agency says tactfully that it was "in its early stages," and the truth is probably that it was never a serious enterprise at all.

Gadafy has spent a fortune over the years buying modern weaponry that now sits idle and useless on bases all over the country—hundreds of seized-up and rusted-out tanks, MiG-23s with their intakes full of sand that haven't flown since the day they were delivered, and quite probably old chemical shells that are now starting to leak poisonous fumes. They were all acquired not to be used, but just to boost Gadafy's self-esteem. The nuclear weapons program was almost certainly just as frivolous: he was buying toys to make himself feel good, but there was no coherent project that could ever have produced a usable weapon.

It's distasteful, but it's not necessarily wrong to make a deal with Gadafy: you give up the terrorism and rat on your Pakistani nuclear suppliers, and we'll end sanctions and help you boost your oil production. What is hard to take is the nonsense about how the invasion of Iraq made him give up his nuclear weapons.

Robin Cook, who quit as Britain's foreign secretary in protest against the Iraq war, put it best last December: "It is rich and comical that we should use an agreement with a country we did not invade—which did have weapons of mass destruction—as justification for invading a country that doesn't have weapons of mass destruction."

Then in April the Sunni city of Falluja, rebellious ever since sixteen local residents were shot while demonstrating in front of a school at the start of the occupation, rose in open revolt; the junior but influential Shia cleric Moqtada al-Sadr led his militia in defiance of American authority in the sacred cities of Najaf and Kerbala; the pictures of abused Arab prisoners at Abu Ghraib started leaking out—and it all went to Hell in a hurry.

IRAQ: IT'S ALL OVER NOW
May 2, 2004

The situation in Iraq is "disintegration verging on collapse," said Richard Holbrooke, former US ambassador to the

United Nations, on the last day of April. It was a month that saw more American troops killed than during last year's invasion, a decisive US defeat in the siege of Falluja, and horrific revelations about the torture and sexual abuse of Iraqi prisoners by both American and British soldiers. It may be years yet before the helicopters pluck the last Americans off the roof of the Baghdad embassy (or a post-Bush administration might still manage a more graceful exit), but basically the game is up.

One hundred and thirty-eight American soldiers were killed in Iraq in April, and over a thousand wounded. The ABC network's decision to devote its *Nightline* program on Friday to showing pictures and reading out the names of the 721 American soldiers who have died in Iraq was not driven by hostility to the Bush administration. The producers were just responding to what their audience was feeling—but it spoke volumes about the state of American public opinion.

Meanwhile, any hope of getting the consent of Iraqis to a permanent US military and political presence in the country has gone gurgling down the drain. It is still not clear who ordered the siege of Falluja in response to the killing and mutilation of four American "security contractors" (mercenaries) at the end of March, but it was a blunder that will be studied in military staff colleges for decades to come, the lesson being: when there is no way that you can succeed, it is wiser not to reveal your weakness by trying and failing.

There was no way that US Marines could occupy Falluja and destroy the local resistance forces without killing thousands of Iraqis, most of them civilians. There was no way that they could ever identify and capture the men who killed and mutilated the "contractors." Besieging the city was an emotional response that made no military or political sense, which they only realized about three weeks too late.

"They" may be Paul Bremer's occupation regime in Baghdad, or it may be the micro-managers back in the Pentagon who persistently usurp command functions in Iraq; the inquest that will finally lay the blame for this fatal move will only happen after US troops retreat from Iraq months or years from now. But in only one month, they have inadvertently succeeded in reviving Iraqi pride and national identity on the basis of a shared anti-Americanism and given the whole Arab and Muslim world nightly television lessons in how popular resistance can defeat US power.

After the first week's fighting killed the better part of a thousand people in Falluja (with Arab TV crews in the city making it clear that a high proportion of the victims were civilians killed by American snipers), somebody in the US occupation forces realized the extent of the disaster and insisted on the talks that eventually let the US forces walk away without launching their final assault. But the price, by then, was handing the city over to a brand-new "emergency force" consisting entirely of former Iraqi soldiers living in the city and commanded by a Saddam-era Iraqi general.

The first nominee for this job, General Jassim Mohammed Saleh, had to withdraw after protests about his role in killing Kurdish rebels in 1991, but his replacement, General Mohammed Latif, is operating under the same unwritten rules. Behind a face-saving pretense that he is operating under American command, Latif's Falluja brigade will include many of the resistance fighters who held the Marines off throughout April. There will be no "disarmament" of the resistance, no rounding up of the largely mythical "foreign fighters" and "Baathist remnants," and no hunting down of the men who killed and mutilated the "contractors."

Falluja has become a no-go zone for American troops, and that is also the likely outcome of the parallel showdown in the holy city of Najaf between American troops and the militia of radical Shia cleric Moqtada al-Sadr. Making these deals does less damage to the US position than plowing on with these unwinnable confrontations, but the damage has already been very great. The whole Arab world is absorbing the lesson that US military power has its limits—at the same time as it seethes in fury and humiliation at the brutal abuse of Iraqi prisoners by US and British forces.

One picture says it all: a twenty-one-year-old female American soldier grinning cockily at the camera, a cigarette dangling from her mouth, as she points in mockery at a naked male Iraqi prisoner who is being forced to masturbate by his captors. You could not come up with an image better calculated to enrage and alienate Muslim opinion if you hired all the ad agencies in the world.

So the entire US neoconservative adventure in the Middle East, never very plausible, is now doomed, though it will drag on in a broken-backed way for some time to come. Even the option of handing Iraq over to the United Nations and replacing American troops there with Muslim troops under UN command, still viable a month ago, will soon be foreclosed. It is going to get very messy.

The "emergency force" in Falluja disintegrated within two months—and the stuff coming out of Abu Ghraib just kept on getting worse.

ICONOGRAPHY
May 8, 2004

The defining image of the Vietnam War was the naked little girl running down the road crying, her clothes burned off by napalm. The defining image of the Iraq War will probably be Private Lynndie English in a corridor in Abu Ghraib prison, holding a leash attached to a naked Iraqi man lying on the floor. It is the picture that best conveys the contempt that ordinary American soldiers (and the government that sent them) feel for Arabs.

Maybe I'm wrong. US Defense Secretary Don Rumsfeld told the Senate armed services committee on Saturday that "the worst is yet to come. There are a lot more pictures and many investigations underway. . . . I looked at them last night, and they're hard to believe. . . . It's not a pretty picture." But the symbolism of this one will be hard to beat.

Iraqis "must understand that what took place in that prison does not represent the America that I know," said President Bush, and he was right. Americans do not generally do this to other Americans. But it did happen in Abu Ghraib prison in Iraq, and things very like it have probably happened in American prisons in Afghanistan and at Guantanamo too. Private England and her friends may have been enjoying it too much; however, the systematic humiliation of prisoners is probably policy.

"R2I" is short for "resistance to interrogation," and it's a course that most military people whose jobs put them at risk of being captured—pilots, special forces, etc.—have to take. They are exposed to the full battery of techniques that enemy interrogators might use against them—keeping them naked, sexual humiliation, anything that will "prolong the shock of capture" and weaken their will—but only in small and manageable doses. It's a kind of immunization against "torture lite" interrogation techniques.

But US and British interrogators also know these techniques, and so do the thousands of ex–special forces people who now work in Iraq. (One result of Rumsfeld's obsession with keeping US troop numbers down in Iraq, in order to prove that the US can invade countries like Iraq without incurring a big political cost at home, is the presence of twenty thousand "contractors" doing paramilitary jobs in the country.)

Do they employ these techniques in Iraq and elsewhere? Pierre Kraehenbuhl, director of operations for the International Committee of the Red Cross, said in Switzerland: "We are dealing here with a broad pattern, not individual acts. There was a pattern and a system." The ICRC has been warning the US of mistreatment of prisoners in Iraq for over a year.

Amnesty International concurs. "Our extensive research in Iraq suggests that this is not an isolated incident. . . . (We have) received frequent reports of torture or other ill-treatment by coalition forces during the past year. Detainees have reported being routinely subjected to cruel, inhuman or degrading treatment during arrest or detention. . . . Virtually none of the allegations of torture or ill-treatment has been adequately investigated by the authorities."

General Janis Karpinski, who commanded Abu Ghraib prison when those pictures were taken, is being set up to take the fall for all this. She was a reservist, reluctant to challenge regulars; so she didn't protest when military intelligence officers at Abu Ghraib discouraged her from visiting the cell block where they interrogated prisoners, or went to great lengths to try to keep the Red Cross from visiting their wing of the prison.

When General Geoffrey Miller, then the commandant at Guantanamo, flew into Iraq last September to offer "suggestions on how to make interrogations more efficient and effective," she didn't ask exactly what he meant—even when he talked of making the prison an "enabler for interrogation" and said that the guards should "set the conditions for successful exploitation of the internees." Now she has been relieved of her command and replaced—by the very same General Miller. This is a system, not an individual's aberrant behaviour.

It was all for naught, though, because most of the people detained at Abu Ghraib, at Bagram in Afghanistan, at Guantanamo and in the rest of the gulag are just innocent bystanders. "A unit goes out on a raid and . . . the target is not available; they just grab anybody because that was their job," Torin Nelson, a former military intelligence officer at Guantanamo who worked as a contractor at Abu Ghraib, told the *Guardian*. "They're not cultural experts. . . . I've read reports from capturing units where the capturing unit wrote, 'The target was not at home. The neighbour came out to see what was going on and we grabbed him.'" And then somebody else tortured him.

The American troops in Iraq are not cultural, political or historical experts. They are frightened and far from home, and a hundred Hollywood movies have taught them that Arabs are dirty, sly, cruel enemies of all that is good. The deliberately misleading propaganda of their own government has persuaded most of them that they are in Iraq as part of a "war on terror." (Even at home, according to a University of Maryland study, 57 percent "believe that before the war Iraq was providing substantial support to al-Qaida," and 65 percent believe that "experts" found weapons of mass destruction in Iraq.) So the US soldiers see Iraqis as inferior and hostile, and all the rest follows.

The pictures that have shocked the Arab and the wider Muslim world are not just about isolated instances of abuse. They are evidence of something bigger and uglier: a wilful ignorance and patronizing contempt that disfigure the entire US intervention in the Middle East. We will be paying for this for many years.

CHAPTER SIXTEEN

THE LOST CONTINENT

All right, Latin America is not exactly lost; we know where it is. But we don't hear very much from it, as a rule. It isn't rich or aggressive enough to compel our attention, nor is it so poor or war-torn that we are fascinated and appalled by it. But it is one-third of the West, in the broadest cultural sense of that word, and interesting things are happening there.

ZAPATISTAS: THE DICTATES OF FASHION
March 22, 2001

A ski-mask looks good on a revolutionary: a hint of the IRA, a whiff of Black September, but nothing that ties you to a particular agenda. And if you are a non-native intellectual leading an "indigenous rights" movement like the Zapatista National Liberation Army, which is the awkward position of "Subcomandante Marcos," then the mask also hides the fact that you are not actually "the colour of the earth," as he puts it.

A pipe is another excellent fashion accessory, because it suggests maturity, patience, even wisdom. Grey-bearded university professors smoke pipes. If you want to project an impression of authority and gravitas, a pipe is your natural prop.

But not the two together: a pipe sticking out of a ski-mask is like lipstick on a donkey. It is Trying Too Hard, which is the only real fashion crime. And herein may lie a clue to the sudden auto-deflation of the world's first designer revolutionary. He is beginning to look a little bit silly.

Marcos's problem is that he cannot afford to take "yes" for an answer. He did ten years as an apprentice revolutionary in the mountains of Chiapas, he has held the attention of Mexico and much of the rest of the world since he launched his revolt in 1994 (almost bloodless after the first two weeks), and now he has led a triumphant "march" to Mexico City. But where does he go from here?

President Vicente Fox Quesada, whose election last year ended the seventy-one-year stranglehold on power of the Institutional Revolutionary Party (PRI), pleads with Marcos to come and see him—"I reiterate my willingness to meet with you without any preconditions . . . Marcos, it's time to talk"—but after two weeks in Mexico City, Marcos continues to dodge. As a result, Fox is starting to win the propaganda war.

The Mexican Congress has now voted by a narrow margin to let Marcos speak before it in support of a constitutional amendment that would give special rights to the country's 10 million Indians. It will be great theatre, but neither Marcos nor Fox (who sent the legislation to Congress on the first day he took office) can guarantee the passage of the law, since the PRI holds more seats there than Fox's National Action Party (PAN).

Besides, Marcos isn't only interested in native rights. He is a post-Marxist revolutionary who is using the plight of Mexico's native peoples as a springboard for an assault on "globalization": he chose to start the revolt in Chiapas on January 1, 1994, the date that the North American Free Trade Area went into effect, for exactly that reason. If Mexico grants his demands for indigenous rights, he loses his pulpit.

That is why he responded to Fox's inauguration and offer of unconditional peace talks in December not with negotiations but with the media circus of a meandering two-week "march" on Mexico City (complete with 280 capering Italian anarchists in matching white jumpsuits doing homage to Fellini). That is why he deliberately notched up his nonnegotiable demands at almost every stop along the way. That is why he refuses to meet Fox.

Fox cannot make the Congress pass the constitutional amendment, and Marcos doesn't want the confrontation to end anyway. He *needs* a powerful, intransigent adversary in order to sustain his own carefully crafted image as the romantic defender of the underdog. But sustaining the image is getting harder, for Fox knows how to play the game too.

Up against another master at manipulating the media like Fox, Marcos is losing his sure touch. On arriving in Mexico City on March 11, he promised to stay until Congress passed the law on indigenous peoples. Then on March 19 he changed his mind and announced that the Zapatistas would all go home on the 23rd because they had been tricked and "insulted" by political leaders whom he called "cavemen." But on the 22nd he changed his mind again and said they would stay.

He will almost certainly change it again and go back to the forests of Chiapas. After a while, wearing a ski-mask in Mexico City begins to seem merely ridiculous, and Marcos wants to preserve his mythic status as a postmodern Che Guevara, an all-purpose symbol of protest.

As he modestly wrote: "Marcos is gay in San Francisco, black in South Africa . . . a Palestinian in Israel, a Mayan Indian in the street of San Cristobal, a Jew in Germany, a Gypsy in Poland, a Mohawk in Quebec, a pacifist in Bosnia, a single woman on the metro at 10 p.m., a peasant without land, a gang member in the slums, an unemployed worker, an unhappy student and, of course, a Zapatista in the hills." (One hopes that gang member Marcos never meets single woman Marcos on the metro at night.)

Marcos clearly enjoys what he is doing, and he can only do it from behind the ski-mask. If he stays in Mexico City and takes it off, he shrinks to a forty-three-year-old grey-bearded former professor, Rafael Sebastian Guillen Vicente, who had a little training in urban guerilla warfare in Cuba in 1982 and really likes the sound of his own voice.

So it will be back to the woods, soon enough, with or without a meeting with Fox. Even there, the myth will gradually erode. He will never seem so simple and so romantic again.

LATIN AMERICA: COLLAPSE OF THE CONSENSUS
August 6, 2002

After twenty years, the neoliberal consensus in Latin America is breaking up. It survived the Mexican financial crisis of 1995 and the Brazilian crisis of 1999, but it is not likely to survive the political and economic upheavals now sweeping South America. Mexico, safely ensconced in the North American Free Trade Area (NAFTA), may escape the coming changes, but almost nowhere else will.

The first sign that the good ship "Free Markets" had sprung a leak was former paratroop colonel Hugo Chavez's election as president of Venezuela in 1998 on a platform that denounced the local business "oligarchy" and the International Monetary Fund with equal enthusiasm. Chavez narrowly survived a coup in April that was tacitly backed by the United States, and elsewhere in the continent events are spinning out of control.

The ship began to list seriously when Argentina, long the darling of free-market ideologues, devalued its currency and defaulted on its debt last year. The Argentine peso is now down to a quarter of its former value, a large number of people have died in street riots, the country is running out of respectable politicians willing to accept the presidency and there is no light visible at the end of the tunnel. About three-quarters of the population are now living in desperate poverty.

The Argentine financial crisis has dragged in neighbouring countries such as Paraguay and Uruguay, both hit by riots and looting last week, and all of the Andean countries except Chile are being torn by intense confrontations between haves and have-nots. But Brazil, with almost half the continent's population, is the place that really counts, and the almost certain prospect of a socialist president being elected there in two months' time is panicking foreign investors and threatening to start a far bigger crisis. So where will it all end?

Latin American governments almost all bought into the "Chicago school" version of free-market economics during the 1980s. They didn't abandon their previous model of protectionism and state-led economic development voluntarily. What happened was that foreign loans became ludicrously easy to get in the 1970s, when Western banks were desperately eager to lend the "petrodollars" piling up in their vaults due to the huge jump in oil prices.

So Latin American governments borrowed as if there were no tomorrow—and then fell into crisis when interest rates soared in the early 1980s. The Mexican crash of 1982 was the beginning of a lost decade for Latin America, as one government after another fell into the hands of the International Monetary Fund (IMF) to avoid defaulting on its loans.

They all swallowed the medicine prescribed by the reigning First-World economic orthodoxy: drastic cuts to budgets and services, privatization, deregulation and free trade. In most cases, this package ("restructuring," as the IMF calls it) actually lowered people's living standards, but it seemed intellectually unassailable after the collapse of the opposite extreme model, Soviet-style state socialism, at the beginning of the 1990s. Until now, that is.

Over the past twenty years, Latin American economic growth has been markedly slower than in the bad old statist days of 1960 to 1980. The social welfare systems (such as they were) have been trashed and people have grown ever more desperate. They are responding by using the

273

democratic political systems they now possess to demand change.

True, the trigger for the current crisis has been not angry locals but foreign investors. They are often berated by the analysts for their ignorance and cowardice: too stupid to tell the difference between Argentina and Brazil, they tend to flee at the first sign of trouble anywhere in the region, taking their money with them. But at bottom the ignorant foreigners are right: the extreme free-market model they thought they were investing in is going belly up.

It doesn't necessarily mean that South American countries are heading back to dictatorship—democracy is compatible with all sorts of economic arrangements—but it does mean that they will probably bring back some of the protectionist measures that used to cushion local workers and employers from foreign competition. There is nothing fundamentally wrong with that: the rich countries preach free trade now, but when they were industrializing themselves they all hid behind high tariff walls.

The problem is that Latin America used to combine protectionism (often useful to developing countries) with heavy government regulation and state-owned industries (almost always bad). Then for twenty years it has combined deregulated internal markets and privatized industries (generally good) with wide-open financial markets and an American-style assault on all the social security systems that used to protect the poor (bad, bad, bad).

And the $64 million question now is whether they will have the wit, at the end of this crisis, to combine the good bits from both strategies—or whether they will simply flop back to the formula that failed them before.

Argentina did default, refusing the IMF's terms—and got away with it. The economy has begun to recover, unemployment is down and its creditors have been forced to accept a very close "haircut." Debt is a funny old business: if you owe the bank ten or twenty thousand dollars, you are under its thumb; if you owe it ten or twenty billion dollars, it is under yours.

LULA AND THE MARKETS
October 5, 2002

George Soros, the world's leading currency speculator, told a Brazilian newspaper in August that the 170 million Brazilians simply wouldn't be allowed to have Labour Party leader Luiz Inacio "Lula" da Silva as their president. The higher his standing rose in the opinion polls, the fiercer would be the speculative attacks on Brazil's currency, the real. If he actually won the presidency, the markets' reaction would be so negative that the country would have to declare a moratorium on its huge $260 billion foreign debt.

"In the Roman empire, only the Romans voted," Soros explained gently. "In modern global capitalism, only Americans vote. Not the Brazilians." Brazilians were so outraged that even outgoing president Fernando Henrique Cardoso was forced to defend Lula publicly—but since the former steelworker and trade union leader started climbing in the polls, the real has dropped in value by about one percentage point for every point that he has risen. Since April, it has lost more than a third of its value.

This has happened despite the fact that Lula is now closer to moderate socialists such as Britain's Tony Blair and Germany's Gerhard Schroeder than to Fidel Castro or

Salvador Allende. He has promised to service Brazil's international debt and to continue Cardoso's successful fight against inflation. Asked why he abandoned his old radicalism, he simply replies: "I changed. Brazil changed. Trade unionism changed. Everyone is now more organized, more mature." But the international money markets don't believe him.

In terms of his origins, Lula does have the classic left-wing activist's background. He never went to school and only started learning to read when he was ten. Eventually he found work in the steel mills of the industrial towns that surround Sao Paulo and became a union organizer. He founded the Labour Party in 1980 and led the strikes that brought down the military dictatorship in 1985. He is pure working class and proud of it—and that is precisely the problem.

A little story. Twenty-three years ago I spent some time in Brazil doing a radio series about the country—and on two successive days in Sao Paulo I interviewed the two most prominent figures of the Brazilian opposition to military rule: Fernando Henrique Cardoso, now completing eight years in the presidency, and Lula, who will have the job for at least the next four. They didn't get much foreign attention in those days, so they each gave me a full afternoon. Their goals were similar, but the differences in style were huge.

Cardoso, who had spent the harsh early years of the generals' rule in exile in Cambridge and Paris, was every inch the Marxist intellectual: a sociologist of middle-class origins who lived in a book-lined apartment overlooking the city. He didn't talk politics; he talked about "dependency theory" and other then-fashionable Marxist concepts. He was a pleasant man, but it occurred to me as I left that he lived somewhere along an axis that had Lenin at one end and Jean-Paul Sartre at the other.

The next day I went all the way out to Sao Bernardo do Campo to see Lula, the up-and-coming union leader. He was your classic horny-handed son of toil, but it soon became clear that while he had picked up some Marxist vocabulary, he would feel perfectly at home among American or British trade unionists. It was only the extreme repression and inequality of Brazil at that time that had pushed him into a more radical position.

If you had asked me then, I would have said that Cardoso was far the greater threat to the interests of international capital in Brazil. In fact, neither man is a radical anymore — but isn't it interesting that the markets didn't react when Cardoso became president, whereas now that Lula has won they're in a flat panic?

The answer is that Cardoso never *looked* threatening. Lula was a sweaty, gritty working-class hero who looked like a menace to the status quo, and frightened the impressionable, untravelled young men (and a few women) who make the market. After all, only two G8 countries (Germany and Canada) currently have working-class leaders, and a number of major countries — France, Japan, the United States — have never had one.

Cardoso did a good job as president — inflation is finally tamed, and important indices like infant mortality, education and housing are finally moving in the right direction despite sluggish growth — but he has used up his popularity. Lula could do good work too, if he is allowed, but he still scares the ignorant because he is an actual worker.

It makes no sense for currency speculators to bring down the world's seventh-largest economy and trigger an international financial crisis, but most of them are ignorant of the world beyond their trading rooms, and even the better-informed ones seek to anticipate the herd's instincts rather than to be right too soon and all alone. To punish Brazilians for electing Lula by destroying its currency and forcing Brazil into default serves nobody's interests, but it could still happen. The only people who still believe capitalists are rational are the Marxists.

Lula has done it differently, reassuring the markets through the most rigorous fiscal orthodoxy (at some cost to the Brazilian poor and to his own political popularity). This is very unfair, since right-wing politicians can run up vast deficits without panicking the markets—consider Ronald Reagan's "voodoo economics" in the 1980s, or George W. Bush's astounding fiscal indiscipline today. But now the Brazilian currency has stabilized, the markets have calmed and Lula is free to begin acting on his election promises. "We've cleared the iceberg from the Titanic *and welded the holes where she was taking water," he said in late 2003.*

Lula probably won't have time before the next election to deliver fully on promises like 8 million new jobs and programs like Zero Hunger ("If every citizen is able to eat three times a day, I will have fulfilled my life's mission"), but he has already established something of great long-term importance. The normal democratic alternation in power between parties of the left and right will not again be a reason for panic in Brazil.

WHY IS HAITI CURSED?
February 19, 2004

Haiti's trip to the brink of civil war began last September, when Amiot Metayer, the leader of a gang of street thugs called the Cannibal Army that enforced President Jean-Bertrand Aristide's will in the northern city of Gonaives, threatened to reveal details of the murder of opposition figures. It was presumably in connection with some quarrel over the division of the spoils, but Metayer was promptly murdered. His widow then conducted a voodoo seance in which his soul appeared and identified his killers: local supporters of President Aristide.

Thereupon, the Cannibal Army switched sides, changed its name to the Gonaives Resistance Front, and started killing Aristide's prominent backers in the city. Meanwhile in the capital, Port-au-Prince, nonviolent demonstrators protesting Aristide's rigging of the 2000 elections were being murdered by government-backed vigilantes known as *chimères* (monsters): forty-five were killed between September and January. Then on February 5th the former Cannibals seized control of the whole city of Gonaives, killing and mutilating more than a dozen policemen.

Since then they have seized more towns in the north and been joined by various unsavoury figures from former regimes, such as former police chief Guy Philippe and former paramilitary death-squad leader Louis-Jodel Chamblain. Aristide denounces them as "terrorists" while his own thugs continue to attack the nonviolent protests of the civilian opposition in the capital.

Just change the names, and Haitians have been here countless times before: there has been only one peaceful and more or less democratic change of president in the country's two hundred years of independence. Nowhere else in Latin America comes close to matching Haiti's dismal record of violence, poverty, corruption and oppression—and yet Aristide was supposed to be the man who finally changed all that.

A former priest who commands a devoted following among the poorest of the country's poor, Aristide was elected president in 1990 after the overthrow of the Duvalier family's twenty-nine-year dictatorship. He was overthrown himself by the army only seven months later, was returned to power by twenty thousand US troops in 1994—and proceeded to go bad. Foreign aid was squandered, democratic rules were abused, vocal opponents were harassed, silenced or killed, and street gangs loyal to Aristide were granted a monopoly on local crime in return for defending his rule.

It's awful, but it's also perfectly normal. Eighty percent of Haiti's 10 million people are unemployed and the average income is three dollars a day. The trees are long gone and the rich soil is eroding away into the sea at a frightening rate: much of the population survives only because of food aid. Average life expectancy is fifty-three, the rate of HIV/AIDS infection is the highest outside Africa, and most Haitians would like nothing better than to leave their country and live elsewhere. They know—or at least they believe—that it never gets better for long in Haiti.

But why is Haiti so much worse than anywhere else in the Americas? Other countries in Latin America have had terrible dictatorships and serial coups in their pasts, but have managed to move beyond them. Other countries in the region have lived through lengthy US military occupations and emerged without fatal damage to their national pride and culture. Other Caribbean islands also have populations of predominantly African origin, but they are peaceful, democratic, relatively prosperous places.

Haiti's crime, for which it is still being punished, was to be the location of the one great and successful revolt by

African slaves. It was France's richest colony when the slaves who grew the sugar, inspired by the egalitarian principles of the democratic revolution that had just toppled the monarchy in France, rose in rebellion in 1791 and killed a thousand white planters in a single night. British, Spanish and French armies failed to suppress the twelve-year revolt, and in 1804 Haiti became the world's first black-ruled republic.

But practically everyone who had not been born a slave had been fled or been killed by then, and Haiti was shunned by the rest of the world, where slavery was still legal. (The United States didn't recognize Haiti until 1862.) People whose parents or grandparents had been taken as slaves from Africa and whose only common language was that of their former slave-masters, who had been denied any education and who had no social structure beyond that of the slave barracks, were left to create and run a country without resources or friends. They made a hash of it, and that burden still weighs on their descendants today.

When slavery was abolished throughout the British Empire by law in 1832, or by war in the United States a generation later, there was at least some help available for the former slaves. More importantly, they were still living in complex, modern societies that gave them models of how things are done as they tried to rebuild their lives as free men and women. Haitians had none of that, and they are still paying the price two centuries later. It doesn't excuse how Aristide has misused the opportunity that he was given, but no matter how or when he goes, the prognosis is still not good.

THE NICER PERÓN: CHAVEZ AND VENEZUELA

August 8, 2004

It is Hugo Chavez's own fault that he faces a referendum on his rule next Sunday (August 15), because he wrote the clause about a recall vote into the Venezuelan constitution himself. His enemies, who include practically everybody with money in Venezuela, are hoping to use it to eject him from the presidency two years early. The opinion polls differ wildly, but here's a prediction: Chavez will be in power for a long time—and as time passes, he will become as great a curse for Venezuela as Juan Perón was for Argentina.

Hugo Chavez is a much nicer man than Juan Perón: he has all Perón's skill in the art of populist rabble-rousing, but he is a sincere social democrat where Perón was a cynical fascist. Unfortunately, Chavez has also polarized Venezuela as Perón polarized Argentina—maybe even more so, for his obvious Amerindian and African ancestry adds a racial dimension to the class conflict in Venezuela (where most of the rich are white and many of the poor are mixed race) that was largely absent in Argentina.

He has an uncompromising line in rhetoric, too: "The real rivals we are facing [in this referendum] are the imperialist forces. . . . They will not take our oil!" Venezuela is the fifth-largest oil producer in the world, and most of its exports go to the United States, so it is no secret that the Bush administration would like to see Chavez gone. But the real problem is that he has divided Venezuelan society so deeply that almost any extreme outcome—even a military coup or a civil war—has become imaginable.

Venezuelan society was already divided before Chavez. The country preserved the forms of democracy through the

'60s, '70s and '80s, when most South American countries fell to right-wing military coups, but in practice power just passed back and forth between two deeply corrupt traditional parties that might as well have been called Tweedledum and Tweedledee. The oil wealth circulated among a few million privileged Venezuelans while the excluded majority lived in poverty, and the political system was rigged to keep it that way.

Chavez's parents were teachers who got one foot on the ladder through education, and he climbed higher by becoming an army officer, but he always burned with resentment at how Venezuela was run. As a young colonel in 1992 he launched a military coup that ended in bloody defeat, but made his name among the poor. When he emerged from jail, he founded the Movement for the Fifth Republic, and began his campaign for the presidency. He won it in 1998, and after rewriting the constitution won it again in 2000.

Unfortunately, his reckless rhetoric terrified the rich: he talked about the senior executives of the national oil company "living in luxury chalets where they perform orgies, drinking whisky," and declared that the Catholic bishops of Venezuela "do not walk in the path of Christ." He alienated the US government with high-profile visits to Fidel Castro in Cuba and Saddam Hussein in Iraq. He imported ten thousand Cuban doctors to extend free medical service to the poor in urban slums and the countryside. And so the attempts to unseat him began.

The first was a military coup in April 2002, reversed after twenty-four hours when masses of Chavez's supporters flooded the streets of Caracas. (The Bush administration officially denied involvement, but it recognized the "new government" with unseemly speed, and then had to accept

Chavez's return.) In December 2002 the pampered employees of the state oil company walked out in an attempt to cut the flow of oil revenues and bring Chavez down, but he won the confrontation, fired many of the strikers, and started diverting much of the oil income into "missions" to combat illiteracy, provide employment and distribute cheap food to the poor.

That was when the opposition parties (which control most of the mass media) began to demand a recall referendum. After a year-long legal struggle over whether they had gathered enough valid signatures, the electoral authorities declared in May that the requisite 20 percent of registered voters had signed the petition, and the referendum was scheduled for August 15. If Chavez loses, a new presidential election will be held next month.

But he almost certainly won't lose. Only 2.4 million signatures were needed for the referendum, but at least 3.7 million people must now vote against him for the recall to succeed. Besides, he would then run for president again next month — the constitution does not explicitly forbid it—and he would probably win again. And again. He is still young enough to blight Venezuelan politics for decades to come.

Chavez is a man of passionate conviction who is loved and hated to extremes. Emphasizing the gulf between the privileged and the poor in Venezuela is no crime if it is a step on the road to closing it, but his impulsiveness and poor follow-through offer little hope that he will achieve that goal. Instead, he has become the intensely romantic incarnation of the class war in Venezuela.

The parallel with Juan Perón is not perfect: Chavez is neither a cynic nor a scoundrel. But like Perón, his charismatic presence prevents the emergence of a more practical and

moderate reform movement and drives establishment conservatives into furious resistance. The result, as in Argentina
from the mid-forties to the mid-seventies, may be a prolonged period of political paralysis punctuated by outbreaks
of violence.

*Maybe I'm wrong about Venezuela's future. I hope so. But the
best hope for South American countries, as it probably is for
African ones and has already proved to be for European ones,
is to create a continent-wide organization that goes beyond a
mere common market and sets democratic and legal standards
for all the members. Something like the European Union.
They could call it . . .*

THE SOUTH AMERICAN UNION
December 6, 2004

It's not even a free trade area yet, but when it grows up it
wants to be just like the European Union. The whole history
of the continent is against it, of course, but then Europe's
previous history didn't leave much room for optimism
either.

On Thursday, December 9, the leaders of every South
American country will gather in Ayacucho, Peru, to sign the
preamble to the Foundation Act of the South American
Union (SAU). They chose Ayacucho because that was where
South American patriots defeated the last Spanish royal
troops and ensured the independence of the Spanish-
speaking half of the continent exactly 180 years ago this
month — but the single, united republic that Simon Bolivar
dreamed of was swiftly defeated by the realities of geography.

The Portuguese-speaking half of the continent has always been a single country, because communications are relatively easy in Brazil, but the mountains and rivers that divide up the rest of the region ensured that there would be nine separate Spanish-speaking republics (with about the same total population) in the other half. It has truly been "180 years of solitude," to adapt Gabriel García Márquez's famous phrase, with land travel between the various South American countries generally more difficult than in any other continent except Africa. Now they want to change all that.

The original concept of the SAU came from Brazil's last president, Fernando Henrique Cardoso, who invited the other South American presidents to Brasilia in 2000 for a first-ever continental summit, but the idea has been vigorously backed by his successor, President Luis Inacio "Lula" da Silva, and by Venezuelan President Hugo Chavez. Both men, unsurprisingly, are on the left: South American solidarity has grown more attractive as the United States has moved right and many South American governments have moved left. But there is more to it than that.

South Americans were acutely conscious that as the rest of the world moved into trading blocs, their continent was being left behind once again. The European Union, the North American Free Trade Area (NAFTA) and the Association of South-East Asian Nations (ASEAN) were old news, but Washington's proposal for a hemisphere-wide, US-led Free Trade Area of the Americas (FTAA) threatened to extinguish any prospect of a common South American future and goaded many local patriots into action.

Last month's announcement that the ASEAN leaders and China, Japan and South Korea were contemplating a broader

East Asia Free Trade Area raised the stakes considerably, for such a trading bloc, especially if it also included India, would embrace about half the human population and a good third of the world's economy—the fastest-growing part, at that. If the FTAA were anywhere near ready, the lure of belonging to such a large trading bloc might trump the attraction of a mere South American Union, but it is not.

The Bush administration has been totally distracted by Iraq, and there have not even been substantive negotiations on the FTAA for two years. The Central American Free Trade Area (CAFTA), lowering tariff barriers between the US and six smallish Central American and Caribbean countries, was supposed to be a stepping stone towards the FTAA, but even that deal now faces probable defeat in the US Congress over a piddling question of sugar quotas. So the runway was clear for the SAU.

The South American Union is not meant to be just a free trade area, either, although that will be the first major step in the process. Its founders are talking about a parliament for the whole continent, and even about a common currency in the end. Their model is explicitly the European Union, which grew to its present scope of 450 million people in twenty-five countries speaking eighteen languages by similar stages over five decades. They believe that South America, with 400 million people in twelve countries, all of them except little Guyana and Surinam speaking either Spanish or Portuguese, can do it even faster. They may be right.

The ceremony at Ayacucho is a modest start: the ten presidents are signing a two-page preamble to a constitution whose contents will only be discussed in detail at a conference that is still six months away. However, this month should see the signature of a free trade deal between the two existing trading blocks in South America, Mercosur and the Community of Andean Nations, which together include all the SAU members except Chile. That is a real signal of intent.

It will obviously be years before anything resembling a true South American common market, let alone a unified political space, begins to emerge from the negotiations, and at least two countries, Chile and Uruguay, are openly skeptical about the prospects for success. In fact, if the United States could drag its attention away from the Middle East and re-focus on its ambitions for its own hemisphere right now, it would probably be able to seduce some potential SAU members away with special one-to-one free trade deals with the US and wreck the whole plan.

But there is little sign of that happening soon, and after a couple of years the momentum towards the South American Union will start to build up. After centuries off in the corner, South America may be joining the world at last.

CHAPTER SEVENTEEN

EAST ASIAN GAMES

There is a large element of bluff in politics everywhere, but in the East Asian region it dominates. More often than not, things are not what they seem, and most of the panics about North Korea or the China–Taiwan relationship that periodically sweep through the world's media are simply false. This is not because of some particularly oriental inscrutability; it is because two of the major players, China and North Korea, are Communist states where real politics happens in secret and the systematic misrepresentation of reality is a national industry.

A SECOND KOREAN WAR?

July 3, 2003

Fifty years after the end of the Korean War in July 1953, could there be another one?

President George W. Bush said two months ago that North Korean nuclear weapons "will not be tolerated." Last week North Korean officials at the United Nations defiantly informed their American counterparts that their country has finished reprocessing enough plutonium to create half a dozen nuclear bombs, and will move ahead quickly to produce the actual weapons. This moved former US Defense Secretary William Perry to worry aloud in a *Washington Post* interview that the Bush administration is "losing control" of the situation. "I have thought for some months that if the North Koreans moved toward [reprocessing], then we are on a path toward war."

How bad would such a war be? If "regime change" in Pyongyang and an Iraq-style conquest of North Korea were the American war aims, very bad indeed. That was the US war aim for a good deal of the time during the first Korean War, and in three years that war killed 3 million Koreans and levelled every city in both North and South Korea. Half a century later, the Korean peninsula is at the heart of industrialized Asia, with Japan to the east and China to the west. According to US military estimates, 1 million people, including fifty thousand American troops, would be killed in the first month of a second Korean war.

It is not, however, a high probability. To believe in a second Korean war, you must believe that North Korea already has or soon will have usable nuclear weapons, and that North Korea's "Dear Leader" Kim Jong-il is crazy enough to use them knowing he would die in a nuclear fireball himself twenty minutes later. Or else you must believe that the Bush administration is crazy enough to launch a full Iraq-style invasion of North Korea with the objective of regime change, and that South Korea would let the United States do that.

Otherwise, the worst thing that can happen in the Korean peninsula is unilateral American air strikes against North Korean facilities that somebody in the US intelligence community thinks are nuclear weapons production sites. That would not be a happy development, but it would not be anything as bad as another Korean war.

Are there nuclear weapons in North Korea? "If you combine known facts with circumstantial evidence, we can be more confident that weapons of mass destruction exist in North Korea than in Iraq," says Ahn Young-sop, professor of North Korean Studies at Myongji University in Seoul. Yes, but most of those "facts" and evidence come from the same US intelligence agencies that brought us the fabulous vanishing WMD of Iraq, so how confident is that?

North Korea had a nuclear weapons program before 1994, and continued with some clandestine work on uranium enrichment even after its deal with the United States, China, Japan and South Korea in that year supposedly halted it. The program has doubtless gone back into high gear since January 2002, when Mr. Bush's speech writers added North Korea to the "axis of evil" almost at random (they needed some non-Muslim state for balance, according to former White House speech writer David Frum), because Bush's speech scared Kim Jong-il half to death. But is it now on the brink of producing actual weapons? Nobody outside North Korea knows.

Getting nuclear weapons as fast as possible is a rational response by Kim Jong-il to finding himself on a US hit-list: the best deterrent to an American attack is the ability to strike at South Korean and Japanese cities with nuclear weapons. (Pyongyang has no rockets capable of reaching the US.) And if "as fast as possible" isn't really very fast, then it makes sense for North Korea to bluff and say it already has nukes.

But the only situation in which it might plausibly use them (if it has them) is against a full-scale American invasion that threatens the regime's survival. That could not happen without a huge US military build-up in South Korea, but the existing US troop commitment in Iraq simply doesn't leave enough troops available for another ground war. In any case, the South Korean government probably wouldn't allow it: as President Roh Moo-hyun said during the election campaign last December (before his handlers hushed him up), "If the US and North Korea start a fight, we should dissuade them."

North Korea, which is hopelessly outgunned, is certainly not going to start a fight, and the only attack the US can make without South Korean support is conventional air and missile strikes against North Korean nuclear facilities. That would unleash a major diplomatic crisis in East Asia but it would not threaten the survival of the North Korean regime, so it would probably not lead to ground war in Korea. And it would still make no sense for Pyongyang to launch a nuke either at Seoul or at US forces in South Korea, since American retaliation would be instant and terrible.

The only problem with this argument is that it depends on the North Korean regime remaining rational no matter what Washington does.

HONG KONG: A VERY INSTRUCTIVE COCK-UP

July 10, 2003

Historians generally divide into two schools: the paranoids, who believe that there is a secret plot behind everything that happens, and the realists, who think that most large events are the result of a cock-up somewhere. The remarkable events in Hong Kong over the past two weeks are a powerful argument for the Cock-Up Theory of History. They are also very encouraging.

It is not clear why Hong Kong's Chief Executive, Tung Chee-hwa, chose this July to enact a draconian new law on sedition. The Basic Law that has served as a kind of constitution since Hong Kong reverted to Chinese rule in 1997 requires the passage of a security law covering issues like subversion and spying eventually, but under the "One Country, Two Systems" deal that guaranteed civil rights and limited democracy in the former British colony, the Communist authorities in Beijing left both the details and the timing of those laws to local lawmakers.

Maybe some people in Beijing suggested that Tung should get a move on with an antisubversion law, but there is no evidence that the orders came from the top, or that Beijing wrote the harsh clauses that horrified most people in Hong Kong. It's more likely to be the old story of the overzealous subordinate trying too hard to please the master, and making a major mess in the process. Anyway, Tung brought in the law, and the people of Hong Kong basically threw it out.

Hong Kongers have traditionally been seen as people who don't care about politics so long as they can go on making money, but on the 1st of July, in the stifling heat of midsummer, half a million of them came out on the streets in a good-humoured but massive demonstration against the new law. The sheer number of people astonished everybody, including the organizers. It was the biggest demo anywhere in China since the Communist regime nearly lost power during the pro-democracy demonstrations on Tiananmen Square in Beijing in 1989, and it changed everything.

The opposition leaders were not impressed by the token concessions that Tung offered, but he insisted that his antisubversion bill would still go before the Legislative Council on Wednesday the 9th. So the pro-democracy movement in Hong Kong promised more and bigger demonstrations—and meanwhile, up in Beijing, surprise and confusion were rapidly turning to worry.

What if the demos get out of hand in Hong Kong, which still earns much of China's foreign exchange? What if they spread to China itself, where popular grievances are far bigger and the government has even less legitimacy in the public's eyes? What has that fool Tung set loose? Soon Hong Kong businessman James Tien, an ally of Tung's, was flying back from a visit to Beijing with some important news.

Two senior Chinese officials had told him, Tien said, that Hong Kong was free to decide both the timing and the content of the security legislation on its own. In these circumstances his Liberal Party could not support Tung's law now. Without the votes of the Liberals (not elected politicians, but a group chosen by the business community who normally put "stability" and good relations with Beijing first), Tung had no chance of getting his law through the Legislative Council, so late last Sunday he deferred it indefinitely.

Beijing will probably replace the badly damaged Tung in a few months' time, and no new attack on civil rights in Hong Kong is likely to happen soon. Good. But what does Beijing's placatory response to this crisis tell us about the state of affairs in China itself?

It tells us that the new "fourth generation" of leaders who took over most of the senior positions last November understand what thin ice they are skating on. This is good news, as it is in nobody's interest that they fall in. What China and the rest of the world need is not another Tiananmen Square, but a recognition by the "Communist" leadership that the country must have gradual democratization if it is not to have a political explosion whenever a serious economic downturn comes along.

China has not been Communist economically for many years: it already has lower taxes, less social welfare and a bigger proportion of the economy in private hands than many European countries. In terms of the gap between rich and poor, it is less egalitarian than the United States, probably even less than Russia. Yet it has no free press, no independent democratic institutions, nothing that could act as a safety valve and an early warning system for the "Communists" who still rule it with an iron hand.

President Hu Jintao and the men around him, having just attained supreme power, are not going to hand it over any time soon, but their response to the recent events in Hong Kong shows that they understand enough not to pour fuel on the flames. They will back up, compromise, make deals, anything that keeps the show on the road a little longer—and maybe that will win enough time for real political changes to start happening.

After a decent interval to save Beijing's face, Tung Chee-hwa
"resigned" in March 2005.

TAIWAN: THE BEST POSSIBLE OUTCOME
March 21, 2004

"If Chen loses, the chances of war are about 20 percent,"
said Arthur Ting of Cheng Kung University in Taiwan, only
days before the vote on March 20 in which President Chen
Shui-bian was seeking re-election. "If he wins, the risk rises
to 40 percent." He won.

Communist China's official statements have gotten
steadily angrier as Chen's Democratic People's Party (DPP)
edged closer to declaring independence. Last December
Colonel Luo Yuan of the Chinese Academy of Military
Sciences warned, "Chen has reached the mainland's bottom line on the Taiwan question. . . . If they refuse to come
to their senses and continue . . . they will push Taiwan com-
patriots into the abyss of war."

Yet Chen said in his acceptance speech that his victory
marks "a new era for peace across the Taiwan Strait," the
160-kilometre body of water that separates Taiwan from
the People's Republic of China. Does he really believe that
Beijing, which fired missiles over Taiwan during its first
presidential elections in 1996 and broke off talks with Taipei
entirely after the DPP won in 2000, will talk to him now that
he has won again?

Not right away, but he probably thinks that it will in the
end. The thing about Chen is that he is used to dealing
with totalitarian regimes. He knows that no matter how
fearsome they seem, no matter how loudly they swear that

they will kill everybody before budging from their current position, in the end they generally do have to talk, because they really do live on the same planet as everybody else.

Chen grew up fighting against Taiwan's own totalitarians, the Kuomintang (KMT), who had retreated to the island in 1949 after losing the civil war with the Communists on the mainland. The KMT were totalitarians of the right who ruled Taiwan with an iron fist for forty years, and they were just as brutal as their rivals on the mainland: Chen's wife Wu Shu-chen is still in a wheelchair after a 1985 murder attempt in which she was hit by a truck and then run over three times. Every leading member of the DPP has spent years in jail for opposing the KMT.

Now Taiwan is a democracy, and the KMT is the opposition party. It is no longer dedicated to re-conquering mainland China, and doesn't even give lip service to reunification anymore: KMT presidential candidate Lien Chan promised that Taiwan "would never merge, be taken over, or united with the People's Republic of China." The lesson is clear: don't listen to what they say; figure out what they are going to do in the end. Generally, that is much less fearsome.

Chen and his opponents in Beijing are both just making the usual politician's calculations about what will play well in the domestic political marketplace, and balancing that against what will work in the wider economic and international arena. For Beijing, talking loudly about Taiwan's indissoluble bonds with the motherland plays well with a local public that no longer responds to Communist rhetoric but is strongly nationalistic. For Chen in Taiwan, it works the other way around: most Taiwanese would like to be independent from China, so he plays that card domestically.

China would be hugely reluctant to invade Taiwan even if it were militarily feasible, because the resulting crisis would kill economic growth at home and might eventually bring the Communist regime down. Chen knows that, and he never goes far enough to goad Beijing into attacking anyway. He was running ten points behind the KMT only two weeks ago, mainly because Taiwan's economy is stagnant and unemployment is almost 5 percent, so he needed the independence issue to close the gap—and he counted on Beijing to understand. It almost certainly does.

Was the assassination attempt the day before the election another political stunt? Certainly not. No hired gun on earth could fire a handgun at a man in a moving car and be sure of grazing his stomach (Chen needed fourteen stitches) but be equally sure of not killing him. The attempt was real, and Chen was doubly lucky, because he survived and then he got the sympathy vote.

Now he's back in office for another four years (barring a recount that reverses the outcome, which is unlikely). Will he vigorously pursue Taiwan's independence? Of course not. As he fully expected, he lost a referendum that was supposed to set the precedent for Taiwan holding a real referendum on independence later on: for the outcome to be valid, 50 percent of the voters in the presidential election had to ask for a referendum ballot, and since the KMT told its supporters to boycott the referendum, there was no risk of that happening.

The referendum failed, and Chen is free to carry on as before. Just maintaining Taiwan's de facto independence has produced ample rewards for most people, and they are not thirsting after martyrdom in the name of some political ideal. Neither is Chen: the crisis was never real.

The great question in East Asia, of course, is: what becomes of China? Can the Communists really hold on there for decades, or are they destined to go the way of their European colleagues?

CHINA: DISSENT AT THE TOP
August 19, 2004

It would be misleading to say that there is a hidden war going on at the top of the Chinese Communist Party, because there is *always* a secret war going on there. But the struggle in Beijing at the moment seems much fiercer than usual. It could even be the one that finally cracks the system open.

As usual, only fragments of evidence about what is really going on in the party's upper ranks reach the outside world, but in the past few months they have hinted that fundamental issues are being debated. The most recent hint was an article by ex-premier Li Peng in the party magazine *Seeking Truth* in which he defended his decision to send in the army to clear Tiananmen Square in June 1989, killing hundreds of student demonstrators.

Most Chinese old enough to recall those terrible events see Li, now seventy-five, as the man chiefly responsible for the massacre, which permanently undermined the legitimacy of Communist rule. However, his article gives the main responsibility to the late leader Deng Xiaoping, who is virtually above criticism: "With the boldness of vision of a great revolutionary and politician, comrade Deng Xiaoping, along with other party elders, gave the leadership their firm and full support to put down the political disturbance using forceful measures." But why is he mentioning it at all?

You can see why Li, probably the most hated man in China, might want to shift the blame, but normal party policy is to suppress all public discussion of the slaughter on Tiananmen Square. It is still highly controversial even within the party: a video has been made, for viewing by cadres only, pushing the official line that the pro-democracy demonstrations were a "counterrevolutionary riot" that had to be crushed to preserve China's stability. It is most unusual for these events to be raised in public—but it's not the first time recently.

In February Dr. Jiang Yanyong, famous throughout China as the whistle-blower who revealed the official cover-up of the extent of the SARS epidemic last year, released a letter he had written to the Communist Party in which he recalled treating dying students on the square and asked it to accept that they had been patriots who were just trying to improve their country. The Beijing rumour mill claimed that he had the support of some party leaders, but in the end his letter was not reported in the Chinese media—and Jiang was arrested and whisked out of Beijing for a few days on the fifteenth anniversary of the tragedy in June.

Another sign that the hidden war in the party is heating up was Beijing University journalism professor Jiao Guobiao's tirade against the state propaganda department in May. "Where can you find propaganda departments? Not in the US, the UK or Europe. But you did find them in Nazi Germany, where Goebbels said 'a lie that is repeated a thousand times becomes the truth' . . . [The state propaganda department's] censorship orders are totally groundless, absolutely arbitrary, at odds with the basic standards of civilization, and as counter to scientific common-sense as witches and wizardry."

This was not the normal nuanced criticism that loyal Communists allow themselves in public. "I cannot stand seeing the Communist party develop in this way," Jiao explained. "We must take responsibility for China." And although his protest was kept out of the mainstream media, he said that he had been "encouraged by (party) elders" to write the essay—and it could readily be seen on the Internet.

It's easy to guess what the struggle in the party is about because it has been the same war for fifteen years now. Should the party take the lead in liberalizing China, before rising educational and living standards create a demand for freedom and democracy that will simply sweep it away? Or is gradual reform impossible, and must the party therefore struggle to hold the line forever, knowing that even one step backwards could be fatal?

That was already the argument in 1989. The secretary-general of the Communist Party at the time, Zhao Ziyang, was a moderate who wanted to negotiate with the students on Tiananmen Square, but he was overruled and removed by the hard men around Jiang Zemin (later president) and Li Peng. Zhao remains under house arrest to this day, and even senior party members cannot visit or communicate with him without permission from the central committee of the party.

It was widely hoped that Jiang Zemin's retirement from the presidency last year and the choice of Wen Jiabao as premier would lead to a gradual loosening of totalitarian controls—Wen was one of the few senior leaders to visit the students on Tiananmen Square—but it has not happened. The frustration must be intense among senior Communists who believe that the party will only survive if it takes the lead in opening the system up, and so battle has been joined.

The champion of the hard-liners is still Jiang Zemin, semiretired but still in charge of the military, and it is the parts of the apparatus that his partisans still control (like the state propaganda department) that the advocates of change focus their attacks on. The conservatives fight back (as Li did) with strong defences of their actions at the time of Tiananmen Square, but the public sees only a hundredth of what is really going on. It may go on for years without a decisive victory, but it really is a battle for the future of China.

Jiang surrendered his last major office in late 2004. Zhao died at last, still under house arrest, in January 2005.

MEMORIAL FOR THE LAST COMMUNIST
January 29, 2005

After two weeks of dithering and delay, the Chinese Communist Party permitted a low-key memorial ceremony for disgraced former premier Zhao Ziyang at Beijing's Babaoshan cemetery for Communist heroes on Saturday (January 30). He was often portrayed as China's lost Gorbachev, the reformer who might have democratized China if he had not been ousted from power at the time of the Tiananmen Square crisis in 1989.

That was why the country's current rulers were so nervous about publicly acknowledging Zhao's death, and why even now the regime's police are beating up citizens who appear in public wearing white mourning flowers in his memory. But he was actually one of the last of the ancient breed of Communist true believers. They will not be missed.

Zhao's passing, almost sixteen years after he was fired from all his posts and placed under permanent house arrest for his alleged support for the students on Tiananmen Square, raises two questions. One is whether the pro-democracy demonstrators could ever have succeeded in the face of a Communist Party that was then still run by true believers. The other is whether China would have been better off if the Communists had never gained power at all.

Zhao was born at a time when fanatical ideologies were sweeping Europe and Asia, and he never deviated from his loyalty to the Communist Party whose youth wing he joined at thirteen. He did not even object when his own father was murdered by Communists as a "rich peasant" in 1948.

When collectivization led to famine in Guangdong province in 1958–61, he enthusiastically led the campaign to torture peasants whom Mao accused of causing the famine by hiding their (imaginary) grain reserves. His subservience to the party was not even shaken when his elderly mother died after being denounced by Red Guards during the Cultural Revolution.

By the late '70s Zhao had become one of Deng Xiaoping's allies in opening up the Chinese economy to capitalist ideas, and by the late '80s he was even dabbling in notions of political reform. When university students occupied Tiananmen Square in 1989 and demanded political change, he sympathized with them—but when the party elders insisted that the protests must be suppressed, he submitted to party discipline yet again.

Much has been made of Zhao's tearful visit to the students on the square the night before martial law was declared—"I'm sorry; I have come too late," he said—but he didn't actually stay with them. Nor did he protest aloud when the army massacred them two weeks later on June 4, 1989: he lived and died a loyal son of the party.

Zhao spent the last sixteen years of his life in a comfortable courtyard house in central Beijing, emerging only to play golf and writing occasional letters containing mild requests that the party "reverse the verdict of Tiananmen Square." If this was a hero of democracy, Heaven preserve China from its enemies.

But the last of the Communist true believers are dying off in China now. What has taken their place, in a party as riddled with cynicism and corruption as the Soviet Communist Party was in Gorbachev's time, is a band of careerists whose mutual loyalty mainly depends on the fact that they must hang together lest they hang separately.

Their only claim to popular support is the economic miracle that they have allegedly wrought in modern China—but the real question is whether China would be better off if their genuinely Communist predecessors had never seized power at all.

In the dying days of the old Soviet Union it became popular to calculate how much better off Russia would have been if the Communists had not seized power in late 1917. At the start of the First World War in 1914, Russia had reached about the same level of urbanization and industrialization as Italy, and was growing about as fast. Despite two world wars and the Great Depression, by 1989 Italians were about three times richer than Russians, and the gap remains as wide even today.

It is harder to make the same argument for China, which was still scarcely industrialized at all when the Communists seized power in 1949. But Communist rule merely redistributed misery and produced very little net growth during their first thirty years in power—and they caused the deaths of about 40 million Chinese through murder and starvation.

The subsequent twenty-five years have seen rapid economic growth, but it's hard to believe that even the most corrupt and incompetent Nationalist regime would have delivered less net growth since 1949. In fact, if you consider Taiwan, which started out under exactly that sort of regime in 1949 and today enjoys three or four times China's per capita income, it is quite impossible to believe.

Zhao changed as he aged, becoming less fanatical and abandoning his old enthusiasm for murder and torture as useful political tools, and he always meant to do good for China. But if he is the last of the ancient breed, good riddance.

CHAPTER EIGHTEEN

IRAQ AND TERRORISM: A SENSE OF PROPORTION

Iraq is not the most important country in the Middle East, and the Middle East is not the most important region in the world. Far from it: even counting all its oil exports, the GDP of the entire Arab world is about the same as the GDP of Spain. So it doesn't matter all that much what happens to Iraq (except to Iraqis), and it doesn't even matter all that much what happens to the whole region, politically speaking: whatever happens, they have to go on selling their oil in order to eat. As for terrorism, it is marginal by definition.

The only thing that really worries me is the way that the other great powers may interpret and respond to the behaviour of the United States. Because the reason they are called great powers is that what they do really matters.

IRAQ: A THOUGHT EXPERIMENT

August 1, 2004

Let us conduct a little thought experiment. The year 2014 will arrive in only ten years' time, and the US occupation of Iraq will be long over by then. Let's imagine that Iraq does not break up in the civil war that the US government keeps telling us is the only alternative to a continued American military presence. What is the best-case outcome for Iraq a decade from now?

Iraq was the most developed of the bigger Arab countries before Saddam Hussein dragged it into the war with Iran in 1980, and it could easily recover that status given just one decade of good luck and good management. Only three things have to happen right. One, the occupation ends quickly. Two, the country does not tear itself apart in an orgy of ethnic and religious violence. Three, the cash flow turns positive.

The occupation will end relatively soon — maybe as soon as next year, but certainly before the next US presidential election in 2008 — because the American public simply won't stand for the cost and the casualties. Neither President George W. Bush nor Democratic challenger John Kerry will talk about a US pullout now, but the flimsy link that Mr. Bush made between the "war on terror" and the invasion of Iraq was destroyed by the report of the 9/11 Commission. When the going gets really rough for the US in Iraq, that will be what tips the scale.

One year or four years from now matters a lot in terms of what the international scene looks like by 2014—we could be back in a global confrontation between rival alliances if Iraq goes on too long—but strangely, it matters less in terms of Iraq itself. Either the country breaks up when the US pulls out, or it does not. Whenever it happens, the choice for Iraqi Kurds, Arabs and Turcomans, for Sunnis, Shias and Christians, will be to bury their rivalries and prosper together, or to live apart in misery.

Choose wrongly, and Iraq ends up as a super-Lebanon, immersed in a civil war of all against all at ten times the scale of the 1975–90 Lebanese civil war. But Iraqis have always avoided civil war in the past, though sometimes at the price of tyranny.

The Baathist regime that came to power in the 1960s was a horror politically, but it knew how to use its oil wealth. The country was the second-largest oil producer after Saudi Arabia, and on the eve of Saddam Hussein's invasion of Iran in 1980 its GDP was about $200 billion in today's dollars.

That provided for free education for everybody (including university, if you qualified), a growing middle class, a diversified economy that did not depend solely on oil, and the most liberated female population in the whole Arab world. Saddam Hussein was not yet at war, so Iraq's abundant natural and human resources produced the prosperity you would expect.

Then came the criminally foolish invasion of Iran and an eight-year war that should have spelled the end of Saddam Hussein—but did not, mainly because the Reagan administration decided that saving Saddam was a lesser evil than letting Iran win. US support for Saddam ended with his invasion of Kuwait and the Gulf War of 1991, but Iraq had to endure twelve years of United Nations sanctions before he was finally overthrown in the US invasion of 2003.

By now, after almost a year and a half of further damage from looting, foreign occupation and guerrilla war, the Iraqi economy is about a quarter of what it was in 1980. But the natural resources and the people are the same as they always were.

Countries with deep ethnic, linguistic and religious divisions *that can see the promise of prosperity as the reward for cooperation* can often surprise the pundits by burying their rivalries and pulling together. Think of Malaysia, of South Africa, of India. The Iraqis could confound the pessimists and do the same—and then, provided they sorted the cash-flow issues, they could be seeing prosperity again by 2014.

Iraq's foreign debt, largely incurred during the war with Iran, now amounts to about $120 billion, which is a crippling burden. If the debt could be written down to one-third of its present amount, then Iraq would have a chance. If Iraqi oil exports could be boosted to 7 or 8 million barrels a day, which could be achieved with five years of serious investment, and if oil prices stay high—which seems practically guaranteed—then it would have a very good chance.

Would this newly prosperous and powerful Iraq be a democracy of sorts? Maybe, though it would be more likely to resemble Malaysia than South Africa. But it could just as easily be a regime that resembles the old Baathist secular dictatorship or the theocratic tyranny of neighbouring Iran: neither prosperity nor power is necessarily linked to democracy.

Would any members of the US-appointed "sovereign government" of Iraq still be in power? Quite possibly: politicians are born acrobats. But they won't be talking much about their past: any Iraq that has really recovered its independence will see the US invasion as a national humiliation and regard America as its enemy for at least a generation to come. Even if the Bush administration's motives for invading Iraq were pure and selfless, it would still be the same. Ingratitude is not just the norm in politics. It is an iron law.

TANGERINE ALERT
August 5, 2004

Here's a game the whole family can play. Pick any warning of a domestic terrorist attack issued by the US Homeland Security Department, and replace the word *terrorist* throughout with some other frightening word. It greatly enhances the entertainment value of the statement without substantially changing its credibility.

Take, for example, Secretary Tom Ridge's recent warning that various "iconic" financial institutions on the US east coast would be on Orange Alert until—oh, probably well into November. Now do the substitution: "Let me be clear: while we have raised the threat level for the financial services sector in the affected communities, the rest of the nation remains at an elevated, or Code Yellow, risk of vampire attack. . . . The vampires should know [that] in this country, this kind of information, while startling, is not stifling. It will not weaken the American spirit, etc., etc."

It works just as well if you substitute the words *werewolves* or *zombies* or even *aliens with anal probes*. And the reason it works so well is because the "terrorists" being promoted by Tom Ridge and his friends are not flesh-and-blood enemies with clear political goals and coherent (though violent) strategies for achieving them. Acknowledge that reality, and you could end up having to admit that there is some connection between US policies, especially in the Middle East, and the rage of the Islamist terrorists.

It's much more effective politically to portray them as faceless demons driven by a love of evil and an unmotivated hatred of Americans. When Basque ETA terrorists blow things up in Spain or Tamil Tiger suicide bombers do the same in Sri Lanka, the target population knows that its attackers are real people with specific and limited political objectives. The terrorists that the Department of Homeland Security purports to be defending Americans against could easily be the baddies in an episode of *Buffy the Vampire Slayer*.

So the Homeland Security people run the threat levels up and down, keeping ordinary Americans in a permanent state of anxiety, and most of the US media disseminate this nonsense as though it had some connection to reality. You would never know from the media coverage that the United States is a country of almost 300 million people where not a single individual has been killed by Islamist terrorists in the past thirty-five months.

You can, if you like, put this down to the vigilance of the various US intelligence and security forces (though they have not actually caught any terrorists who were in the United States and actively planning attacks). You could equally well conclude that al-Qaeda and its friends don't have sleepers in the US who are able to carry out further attacks, or that the Bush administration's response to 9/11 so perfectly suited their plans that no further attacks have been necessary.

Terrorism is a *small* threat that has been inflated for political purposes, and the clearest evidence that this is conscious policy is the irrational but politically astute way that spending has been allocated between competing security threats since 2001. The weapon that caused the carnage on 9/11 was hijacked civilian airliners, and the public's understandable response was to demand greater airport and airline security. And that is where the great bulk of the administration's new security spending actually went—even though it made no sense strategically.

The threat, small but real, is from clever, ruthless and versatile terrorists, not from habitual airplane hijackers. Improving aerial security is popular, but it is preparing to fight the last war all over again: not a task the security people can completely neglect, but certainly not one that deserves most of their attention. Meanwhile, only 3 percent of containers entering the United States by sea are subject to random checks, and there are no plans for moving the terminals for the giant floating bombs called liquid natural gas carriers away from the harbours of large cities.

If I were a senior al-Qaeda planner, I would not be in any hurry to attack targets in the American "homeland" again. Even if I did want to destroy America's freedoms, I wouldn't feel the need for another attack: when that loaded *homeland* word starts being used by official circles in any language— *patrie, Heimat, watan, rodina*—you can already hear the symbolic jackboots marching in the distance.

Since we senior al-Qaeda planners don't actually give a damn about how the Americans run their domestic affairs, I would instead wait until after the November election to see if Bush continues, or Kerry adopts, the current, highly satisfactory US foreign policy of invading Muslim countries and driving their populations into the arms of our Islamist allies. We certainly don't need to devote scarce resources to the task of scaring the American public when the Homeland Security Department does it for us for free.

Most people don't even understand their own country's politics. Trying to understand the way the game is played, or even the stakes, in an unfamiliar culture is uphill work, and most of the time the Western media don't even try with Iraq: they assume, perhaps correctly, that a few broad-brush categories like "fundamentalists" and "moderates" are as much as their audience will stand for. Complexity is never popular.

SHIA SHOWDOWN

August 15, 2004

The claims and counterclaims make it hard to discern the strategies behind the showdown in Najaf, and the language that is used blurs the situation even more. US military spokesmen, for example, always call the young men who are defending the rebel Shia cleric Moqtada al-Sadr "anti-Iraqi forces," although not one in a hundred of them has ever been outside Iraq. But you can guess why the US authorities in Iraq chose this moment to try to eliminate al-Sadr and his al-Mahdi militia.

From the start, the biggest obstacle to the creation of a compliant, pro-American regime in Iraq has been the fact that the Shias, who make up about 60 percent of the population of Iraq, could elect a majority government that could and probably would defy US wishes if they voted as a bloc. Moreover, senior Shia clerics command great respect in the community, making it much likelier that the Shia would indeed vote en bloc. So elections were too risky.

Retired general Jay Garner, the original choice as US pro-consul in Iraq, was dismissed after a month because he called for early elections in Iraq: "The night after I got to Baghdad, [Defense Secretary Donald] Rumsfeld called me and told me he was appointing Paul Bremer as the presidential envoy. . . . The announcement . . . was somewhat abrupt." Garner said that Rumsfeld was worried that an elected Iraqi government would resist mass privatization of the economy, but he was equally worried that such a government would be Shia-dominated and insist on an Islamic state.

The problem was compounded by the fact that Washington's favourite ayatollah, Abdul Majid al-Khoei, was killed the day after Baghdad fell. Khoei had become a personal friend of British Prime Minister Tony Blair during his long exile in London, and had strong US backing. But a mob hacked him to death in the Imam Ali mosque in Najaf on April 10, 2003, the day after he arrived, leaving the field open to less pro-American rivals.

One was Iraq's current senior ayatollah, Ali al-Sistani, an Iranian-born scholar who issued a fatwa early in last year's US invasion calling on all Muslims to fight the invading infidel forces. His principal rival for the loyalty of Iraqi Shias was Ayatollah Muhammad Baqr al-Hakim, an Iraqi-born cleric who had spent more than twenty years in exile in Iran after backing that country's Islamic regime against Iraq in the 1980–88 war.

Hakim was willing to cooperate with the US occupiers in the hope that an election would ultimately give the Shias power—but he was killed by a huge car bomb outside the Imam Ali shrine on August 29, 2003. That left only the recalcitrant Sistani—and the young firebrand Moqtada al-Sadr. At thirty, al-Sadr is less than half the age of his rival, and he lacks a rigorous education in Islamic law; but he is the son of a revered former grand ayatollah who was murdered by Saddam Hussein's regime in 1999, and he has a strong following among the urban poor.

Last March Paul Bremer made a deal with Sistani: the ayatollah guaranteed that the Shia would remain quiet this year (until George W. Bush's re-election bid in the US is safely past, in other words), in return for free elections in Iraq early next year. And then, seeking to insure against the risk that al-Sadr would try to spoil the deal, Bremer did something foolish: he attacked al-Sadr directly.

In early April the US occupation authorities closed down al-Sadr's newspaper, a weekly with a circulation of ten thousand, that stridently condemned the occupation but had little influence, and issued an arrest warrant charging al-Sadr with Khoei's murder. Al-Sadr took his militia to the sacred city of Najaf and defied the Americans to come and get him. Impoverished young Shias rose in revolt in east Baghdad and the cities of the south, and hundreds died before the US command negotiated a truce. By then, Moqtada al-Sadr was famous across Iraq and the whole Muslim world.

US troops could have fought their way into Najaf, violated the Imam Ali mosque and killed al-Sadr if they were willing to pay the price, and the price in American lives would not even be great: American firepower, equipment and training mean that a hundred young Shia men die in the fighting for every American who is killed. But the *political* price would have been huge, so the US forces were called off in May. Why are they attacking again now?

Whatever the truth about the incident that re-started the fighting, it's clearly an American choice to go for broke against al-Sadr. US forces were under no compulsion to escalate as they have done, and the newly appointed Iraqi "transitional government" could not have forced them to. The likely answer is that the sudden removal of Sistani from the scene (he flew to London for heart treatment two weeks ago) has made al-Sadr too powerful, and too dangerous to the "transitional government," to be left alive.

There are to be no witnesses this time: the few journalists in Najaf have been ordered to leave on pain of arrest. But if this ends in a last stand and a massacre of the al-Mahdi militia in the most sacred site in the Shia world, possibly doing serious damage to the Imam Ali mosque itself, the long-term cost to the United States will far outweigh any possible gains. The logic of the strategy is still very hard to follow.

Sistani flew back from London and his people mediated another deal under which Moqtada al-Sadr walked free. The American policy of trying to arrest or kill him did not make sense, especially if it required the destruction of the Imam Ali mosque by American artillery, so once again they walked away from the fight. Once again, too late to win any credit for it.

BIN LADEN SPEAKS (BUT NOT THE TRUTH)
October 31, 2004

Osama bin Laden is a master of the art of public relations, and his videotaped message on Friday, October 29 was a little masterpiece of spin and misdirection. All that nonsense about how he decided to attack the "towers" of New York when he saw the "towers" of Beirut under attack by the Israelis and the US Sixth Fleet in 1982, for example.

When Israel invaded Lebanon and the US sent troops to

help, Osama probably didn't like what he saw, but he hadn't even gone to Afghanistan and become a mujahedin yet. He didn't spend nineteen years planning the 9/11 attacks. And as for telling Americans that they will be safe if only they stop attacking Arab and Muslim countries—"Your security does not lie in the hands of Kerry, Bush or al-Qaeda. Your security is in your own hands. Each and every state that does not tamper with our security will have automatically assured its own security"—it is a cynical lie.

True, it was America's deep military involvement in the Arab world and its support for tyrannical Arab regimes that made it a target for the extremists in the first place, but that is thirty years of history that cannot be undone. The United States has become a tool in the Islamists' struggle to overthrow those regimes, and there is little it can now do to escape that role.

The vast majority of the Islamists live in the Arab countries, but their attempted revolutions against regimes they condemn as secular and/or sold out to the West—in Egypt, Syria, Saudi Arabia, Algeria—have been stalled for twenty-five years because they were unable to win enough popular support. Their main weapon was terrorism—and mere terrorism never overthrows governments.

Terrorism is a useful device for getting your name and program before the public in a dictatorship where you cannot openly advocate your political ideas, but the end-game of revolution usually requires a million people in the street willing to risk their lives to bring the target regime down and put you in its place. For the Islamists, the million people just won't come out.

Relatively few Arabs are willing to risk death to overthrow the corrupt, worn-out, sold-out regimes they live under, if what they are going to get instead is rule by a band of violent religious fanatics who will just ruin their lives and their economies in a different way. Support for the Islamists is higher in the Arab world than in other Muslim countries because the Arabs have had a hard time at the hands of the West (including Israel) in recent decades, but it probably doesn't get above 5 or 10 percent even in Egypt and Saudi Arabia.

For a quarter-century, the Islamists have been stuck in a bloody stalemate with the various regimes they seek to over-throw. Osama bin Laden's claim to fame was his insight that popular support for the Islamists might finally be boosted up to the level needed for successful revolutions if they could lure the United States into even deeper military involvement in the Muslim world—full-scale invasions, if possible—that would drive millions of Arabs into the Islamists' arms.

That was what 9/11 was about, and it failed. The United States immediately invaded Afghanistan, as bin Laden doubtless intended—but without the consequences he hoped for. The US invasion was swift, efficient and cost rela-tively few lives: probably under four thousand Afghans killed, and only a dozen Americans. Nothing like the ten-year guerilla war generating thousands of images of inno-cent Muslims suffering under American firepower that he had hoped for, working from the precedent of the long guerilla struggle against the Soviet occupation of Afghanistan in 1979–89 where he had made his reputation.

If the United States had not invaded Iraq last year (which bin Laden could not have foreseen), 9/11 would have been a complete failure. Even with the horrifying images that Iraq generates and the fury and hatred that they engender among Muslims elsewhere, there has still not been a single revolution anywhere in the Arab world: the Islamists still cannot get the masses out in the streets to overthrow Arab regimes.

That speaks volumes for the moderation and basic common-sense of the Arab people, and it argues that the Islamists are doomed to remain a marginal force in Arab politics no matter how many people (local and foreign) they manage to kill. But they have not given up on their strategy, which means that bin Laden's promise was a lie. He *needs* America to remain militarily entangled in Muslim countries, so he will go on ordering the attacks that he thinks will produce that result—insofar as he is capable of ordering anything at all.

He is probably not able to order very much. Al-Qaeda was never a real organization in the traditional sense, more an idea and a blueprint, and now it scarcely exists at all (though its clones and emulators have proliferated). All bin Laden can do is go on making his videos and hope that his ideas and his example will take root in many parts of the Muslim world. So far, it isn't working.

The dirty little secret at the heart of international politics at the moment is that almost all the other great powers are hoping that America will fail in Iraq, and fail dramatically and soon. They can never admit this in public because it means wishing the deaths of many American soldiers and far larger numbers of Iraqis—and of course they feel pity and guilt for those whose deaths they are willing. But they continue to will them, because they believe that the stakes are so high.

WAITING FOR IRAQ
November 7, 2004

Most Americans don't realize how much the rest of the world opposed their country's invasion of Iraq, because most US mass media shield them from the knowledge. Watching the domestic service of CNN just after the election, I heard three different newsreaders in the same day explain to their American audience that France and Germany had been "cool" to the American attack on Iraq.

They weren't "cool" to it; they opposed it utterly. They saw it as an illegal act intended to undermine the entire multi-lateral system and replace it with a unilateral system in which America is the global policeman—indeed, the global judge, jury and executioner. They refused to support it at the United Nations, and in that refusal they had the support of every other great power except Britain. So what do all these great powers—France, Germany, Russia, China and India—do now?

They were never that confident that President George W. Bush would lose the election, or that Senator John Kerry would make much difference if he won. They know that there is now a broad consensus in the United States on the desirability of imposing a *Pax Americana* on the world through the unilateral exercise of overwhelming US military power. They will never accept that, but they still want to avoid a direct confrontation with the United States, as that would also destroy the multilateral system. So they are hoping that the war in Iraq will erode US popular support for the whole unilateralist adventure.

To be specific, they are hoping for the rise of an anti–Iraq-war movement in the United States like the one that ultimately destroyed popular support for the US war in Vietnam a generation ago. And they need it to happen soon, because their no-confrontation policy has a limited shelf life. It must succeed before popular pressures at home push them into open confrontation with the US.

So how fast can Iraq go bad in the eyes of the American public? In Iraqi eyes, of course, it has already gone bad, with every opinion poll since last spring showing massive support among Arab Iraqis for the resistance forces and a huge majority in favour of immediate US withdrawal. But it is Americans who must be convinced that the whole neocon-servative project for re-ordering the Middle East and estab-lishing US global hegemony is foolish and doomed.

That may take more time than is available, for what US public opinion responds to is American casualties. If too many American soldiers get killed in Iraq, then the public will eventually pull the plug on the war, just as they did on Korea in the 1950s, on Vietnam in the 1960s and 1970s, on the US military intervention in Lebanon in the 1980s, and on Somalia in the 1990s. But how many is too many? That depends.

American military deaths in Iraq are now nearing eleven hundred, but there is little likelihood that the total will rise as fast as it did in the Vietnam War. American soldiers are basically fighting lightly armed guerillas in Iraq, not a regu-lar army like North Vietnam's, and US tactics are deliber-ately designed to minimize American casualties by a massive use of firepower, especially air power.

This does have the side effect of killing large numbers of Iraqi civilians. A survey of thirty-three randomly selected Iraqi neighbourhoods conducted in September by the Bloomberg School of Public Health at Johns Hopkins

University in Baltimore and published online by the British medical journal the *Lancet* late last month concluded that there have been between one hundred thousand and two hundred thousand "excess deaths" among Iraqi civilians since the March 2003 invasion, and that most of these deaths were due to American air strikes in civilian areas. But Iraqi deaths have little impact on American public opinion.

The number of American military casualties that the US public will tolerate fluctuates over time, and is now much higher than it was before 9/11. Nobody knows what the critical number actually is now, but it is probably well above a thousand American dead a year. It remains to be seen if Iraq will cause American casualties on a much larger scale than that.

Iraq is already a quagmire for the US armed forces: even as thousands of American troops prepare to level the defiant city of Falluja, the city of Samarra, which US forces allegedly "pacified" in September, is slipping out of their control again. But it is a relatively small quagmire, and it may not produce a powerful antiwar movement in the United States as quickly as the other great powers hope. Especially if al-Qaeda, freed from the need to abstain from terrorist attacks on the US for fear of sabotaging President Bush's re-election, manages to carry out an attack or two, however small, on US soil.

If the US does not change course, the other great powers will eventually give up on the waiting game and move to counterbalance and contain American power. That would mean alliances, arms build-ups, all the lethal nonsense we thought that we had left behind us. Nobody wants to go down that road, but they inevitably will if US policy doesn't change. We probably have a few years before that starts, but we don't have a long time.

DEMOCRACY AND RHETORIC

January 24, 2005

"We have declared a fierce war on this evil principle of democracy," said Jordanian-born terrorist Abu Musab al-Zarqawi, leader of of the organization that calls itself "Al-Qaeda in Iraq." Al-Zarqawi is the bogeyman that the US government currently blames for almost everything that has gone wrong in Iraq, but he does speak essentially the same language as President George W. Bush.

For Bush, as for al-Zarqawi, political principles come from God. In his "God-drenched" inauguration speech (as Ronald Reagan's former speech writer, Peggy Noonan, described it), President Bush explained that people have inalienable rights because they "bear the image of the Maker of heaven and earth," and that America's mission to spread democracy around the globe comes directly from "the Author of liberty."

Bush recently remarked that he did not see "how you can be president without a relationship with the Lord"—so it is America's duty and right to bring "freedom" to those who still live in darkness, both in order to make itself safe and as a public service: "By our efforts, we have lit . . . a fire in the hearts of men. It warms those who feel its power, it burns those who fight its progress, and one day this untamed fire of freedom will reach the darkest corners of our world."

Bush speeches are a treasure-trove of innocent fun. His speech writers took the quote about having "lit a fire in the hearts of men" from Fyodor Dostoevsky, presumably not realizing that they were quoting a bunch of terrorists who featured in his novel *The Devils*, and the "dark corners of the world" phrase pops up in every second Bush speech.

The problem is that George W. Bush's belief that Americans basically own the copyright on democracy is widely shared even by Americans who deplore his actions. "Americans, of all people, should never be surprised by the power of our ideals," he said in his inauguration speech, and most Americans would probably agree that the United States is not just the "home of the free"—it is the main source of freedom in the world. The US crusade for freedom (aka democracy) is justified, even if it requires cluster-bombs and Guantanamo Bays, because otherwise there will be no freedom.

That is their fundamental mistake. The United States was the first mass democracy in history, but the "Founding Fathers" who carried out that revolution were the heirs of the European enlightenment and of over a hundred years of radical egalitarian thought in England: it was the English Levellers who first declared in 1647 that "all government is in the free consent of the people." And only twelve years after the American Revolution, a far more radical revolution broke out in what was then the biggest nation of the West, France.

America's democratic revolution had a huge impact on the world, but it was both less, and less indispensable, than most Americans suppose. Democracy was on its way any-way: to European countries first of all (maybe because practically everywhere else was under European imperial rule), but in due course even to the "dark corners of the world." We are living through the final wave of that process in this generation, with nonviolent democratic revolutions from Bangkok, Dhaka and Seoul to Berlin, Moscow and Johannesburg, and on to Jakarta, Tbilisi and Kiev. Few of them had American help.

This notion that the United States should "seek and support the growth of democratic movements and institutions in every nation and culture, with the ultimate goal of ending tyranny in our world," as President Bush put it in his inaugural speech, is profoundly misleading, because it suggests that American support for such transformations is essential. It isn't even relevant, in most cases. People have to do it for themselves, and the most helpful thing that Washington could do would be to stop supporting the oppressors.

Most of the world's countries already are democratic, and the exceptions are mainly in the Middle East and Africa, the two world regions where Western military interventions have been most frequent since the end of the colonial era. Indeed, it's striking that within the Middle East, the primary focus of American anxieties about terrorism, the Islamist terrorists come overwhelmingly from countries that have close links with Washington—Egypt, Saudi Arabia, Algeria, and now Iraq—and not from places like Syria, Libya and Sudan. This is hardly an argument for further US military interventions.

Liberty and *freedom* (words President Bush used forty-two times in his speech), are American catch-phrases for what other people call democracy: freedom under the law, and under the presumption that we are all equal before the law. That is the great revolution that has swept over the world in the past couple of centuries, and it is not an American gift to mankind. It's not necessarily God's gift either, unless you are religious. It's just who we are.

Which is why, in an opinion poll carried out in fifteen of the biggest democratic countries in the week of Bush's inauguration, 58 percent of the twenty-two thousand people polled said that they expected his re-election to have a negative impact on peace and security, as compared to only 26 percent who thought it would be positive. In Canada, Britain, Australia and South Africa, France, Germany, Italy and Russia, Mexico, Brazil, Indonesia and Japan, the story was the same: deep distrust for the Bush administration's policies and motives.

Mind you, 47 percent of Americans have the same response.

CHAPTER NINETEEN

THE FATE OF ISRAEL

Israel is not unique. It is just a country: a very powerful, extremely complicated country that lives in a dangerous part of the world. That, at any rate, should be the point of departure for any non-Zionist who presumes to write about Israel. It is not anti-Israeli, let alone anti-Semitic, to suggest that sometimes the Israeli government lies, or that some Israeli policies are not just wrong but wicked. Israelis themselves regularly say such things in public; it's just in the rest of the world that the situation becomes a bit trickier.

THE STRATEGY OF SUICIDE BOMBS

January 6, 2003

On Sunday, for the first time since November, a couple of Palestinian suicide-bombers got through and blew themselves up in central Tel Aviv. At least twenty-three people were killed, most of them foreign workers from Africa and Asia who came to Israel to do the low-wage jobs that were once filled by Palestinians. With wearisome predictability, Prime Minister Ariel Sharon's spokesman blamed Yasser Arafat: "This terrorist attack has earned the Palestinian Authority's stamp of approval. It is a direct result of persistent incitement coming out of the Palestinian Authority and its refusal to rein in the terrorists in its midst."

Sorry, could you run that by me again? You're talking about Yasser Arafat, the man whose whole career was dedicated to the goal of getting his people recognized as Palestinians (with rights to at least some of the land of what used to be called Palestine), rather than mere refugees with a right only to a tent and daily rations? The man who then risked assassination by his own hard-liners by renouncing terrorism, signing the Oslo accords with Yitzhak Rabin, and then, after Rabin was assassinated, waiting patiently while Binyamin Netanyahu stalled for three years on fulfilling the terms of the accords? You reckon he sent the bombers?

Sharon's spokesman doesn't really believe that Arafat sent the bombers. He's just "on message"—the message being that we must discredit Arafat because he's still the really dangerous Palestinian, the one who wants to make a deal. Sharon isn't interested in making any deal that gives the Palestinians a viable country in what remains of their original territory, because that would block his purpose of incorporating much of that land into Israel. So his goal is to paint all Palestinians who want to make a deal as unreasonable terrorists who have no interest in a deal.

Yasser Arafat is his own worst enemy, of course. He was a brilliant guerilla/terrorist leader, cunning, long-sighted and staunch in adversity, but he is an inept negotiator and a dreadful administrator.

The reason everybody has all but given up on the Palestinian Authority is that Arafat never graduated from being a guerilla leader: he maintains control over his administration by appointing three, or four, or five men to do the same job, setting them against one another so that only he can adjudicate the disputes. When you finally get in to see him, five or six hours after the agreed time, you are likely to find him personally signing cheques for only a few hundred dollars: Arafat is a bandit chieftain who never managed the transition to real power.

The last and greatest service he could have done for the Palestinian people would have been to die in the siege of Beirut twenty years ago, leaving it to a younger, better-educated generation of Palestinians to negotiate a land-and-peace agreement with a triumphant but still vulnerable Israel. Alas, he didn't.

So there he sits still, a trembling, superannuated relic who now serves mainly as an Israeli bogeyman. But did he really send the bombers to the Tel Aviv bus station to kill all those foreigners? Don't be silly.

Comfortable people in safe places see the phrase *enemies of peace* as mere rhetoric. I mean, nobody could really be the enemy of peace, could they? But there are people on both sides of the Israeli–Palestinian conflict who are genuinely the enemies of peace—or at least, of peace on any terms that would be acceptable to the other side. They are the whole-hoggers, who don't ever want to compromise on the territory they believe is theirs, and many of them are quite willing to kill in order to prevent the wrong kind of peace. On the Palestinian side, most of them are Islamists, but some are not.

The al-Aqsa Brigades who claimed responsibility for Sunday's Tel Aviv bombings are not Islamists. They are a faction that still has a formal connection to Arafat's Fatah organization (unlike Hamas and Islamic Jihad, who do not). But either al-Aqsa are a very stupid group of people who have let their anger lead them astray, or they have consciously gone over to the side of the Islamists who dream of a total victory over Israel in the long run, and fight to prevent a negotiated peace in the short run.

The effect of these attacks, obviously, is to improve Ariel Sharon's chances of being re-elected at the end of this month, which would guarantee that there is no risk of a negotiated peace that gives Palestinians only part of Palestine for the indefinite future. It was never likely that the peace candidate, Amram Mitzna, would win, but you can't be too careful. So the bombers are out in force, just as they were in 1996 when there was a risk that the peace candidate, Shimon Peres, would win against Netanyahu. Terrorism is never "blind"; it is politics by other means.

THE FATE OF ISRAEL

January 11, 2004

Jerusalem fell to the Crusaders in 1099. The subsequent battles swayed to and fro, but the Crusaders held most of the eastern Mediterranean coast (what is now Israel, Lebanon and Syria) for almost two centuries. Then the local people, overwhelmingly superior in numbers then as now, expelled them. It is an open question whether Israel will last that long.

Listen to Avraham Burg, speaker of Israel's Knesset (parliament) in 1999–2003. "It turns out that the two-thousand-year struggle for Jewish survival comes down to a state of settlements, run by an amoral clique of corrupt lawbreakers. . . . A state lacking justice cannot survive. More and more Israelis are coming to understand this as they ask their children where they expect to live in twenty-five years. Children who are honest admit, to their parents' shock, that they do not know. The countdown to the end of Israeli society has begun."

Burg's sense of panic is not misplaced. Seven hundred and sixty thousand Israeli citizens now live abroad (in a country with only about 5 million resident Jews), and that total has increased by two hundred and ten thousand in just the past three years. The embassies of eastern European countries whose citizenship will soon confer the right to live anywhere within the European Union now have long queues of second- and third-generation Israelis seeking to recover their ancestral passports just in case.

In November, four former directors of Shin Bet, Israel's security service, condemned the government's refusal to negotiate with the Palestinians: "It is clear to me that we are heading toward a crash," said ex-director Carmi Gilon. But intelligence people deal in short-term risks like a full-scale Palestinian uprising or a Middle East war—nasty enough, but nothing that would actually endanger the survival of Israel right now. Israel also has a long-term problem, and that is much more serious.

Israel's problem is not as acute as the one that faced the Crusader states, for at the moment it enjoys a huge technological and economic lead over the rest of the region. If there is still to be an Israel even two hundred years from now, however, then it must make its peace with its neighbours in the next few decades, while it still holds all the cards.

None of Israel's current advantages—a monopoly on nuclear weapons, conventional military superiority over all its neighbours combined, and an unconditional US guarantee of its security—is likely to exist a hundred years from now. Some may be gone in twenty years. If Israel makes a deal with the Arabs while it still has the upper hand and creates trade and personal ties throughout the region, then it could become an established part of the neighbourhood and last a very long time. If not, then sooner or later it faces the fate of the Crusader states.

Palestinians are crucial in this context because there can be no lasting peace with the Arab world that does not reconcile the Palestinians. After thirty years when no Arab country would consider making peace with Israel (1948–1978), we have just passed through a quarter-century when several Arab countries did make peace and even the Palestinians were willing to recognize Israel's right to exist in return for an independent homeland in what remained of their territory. That era may now be coming to an end.

Never mind who's to blame. There were people among both the Israelis and the Palestinians who were willing to settle for a compromise peace based on the division of former colonial Palestine into two states, one Israeli and the other Palestinian, and there were others who were not. The rejectionists on both sides have won, and the compromise deal, packaged in half a dozen different ways from the 1992 Oslo accords to the recent "roadmap," is fading away.

In Israel, Prime Minister Ariel Sharon is building a wall that will leave the Palestinians with only 9 percent of colonial Palestine and no peace treaty. In the occupied territories Palestinians are abandoning the "two-state solution" and adopting the goal of a single nonethnic state within the borders of old Palestine that includes both Jews and Arabs. It means another generation of waiting, of course, but what attracts them to that one-state solution is that within fifteen years Palestinian Arabs will again outnumber Israeli Jews within the lands between Jordan and the sea.

Professor Ali Jirbawi of Bir Zeit University in the West Bank put the new position very clearly in November: "We should say we accept a two-state solution, but that it means going back to the 1967 borders (before Israel conquered the West Bank, East Jerusalem and the Gaza Strip) and a fully independent and sovereign Palestinian state. We should give them six months. If there is no decision we should say that Israel, by its own choice, doesn't want a two-state solution. If Israel wants a one-state solution, we accept. But twenty years from now, we're going to ask for one person, one vote."

People like Palestinian Authority Chairman Yasser Arafat still cling to the two-state goal, and Sharon pursues his one-and-a-quarter-state solution (which merely drives the Palestinians deeper into rejectionism), but the caravan is moving on. The notion of a second partition of Palestine that produces ethnically defined Israel and Palestinian states living side by side is sliding off the table, and that is not good news for Zionists. A united, democratic Palestine would not be a Jewish-majority country, so it will not happen. But if that is the only alternative to continued occupation and confrontation, then Israel is in big trouble in the longer term.

THE COURAGE OF THE CLERK
April 18, 2004

> I am the clerk, the technician, the mechanic, the driver.
> They said, Do this, do that, don't look left or right.
> Don't read the text. Don't look at the whole machine.
> You are only responsible for this one bolt, this one rubber stamp.

Mordechai Vanunu wrote that about halfway through his eighteen-year jail sentence (twelve years of it in solitary confinement), which was imposed because he told the world about Israel's nuclear weapons. On Wednesday he comes out of jail at last, having refused early parole in return for a promise never to speak about his kidnapping, his prison ordeal or Israeli nuclear weapons. "He is the most stubborn, disciplined and tough person I have ever met," said his former lawyer Avigdor Feldman. But his ordeal is not over.

In January, knowing that Mr. Vanunu was scheduled for release on April 21st, Israeli Prime Minister Ariel Sharon called a meeting attended by the defence minister, Shaul Mofaz, the attorney-general, Menachem Mazuz, Yehiel Horev, who has final responsibility for both Shin Beth and Mossad, the country's internal and external intelligence services and a representative of the Israeli Atomic Energy Committee. They decided that Vanunu will only be a little bit free.

He cannot leave the country, nor can he even leave the town he settles in without permission—and he is not allowed to approach any port, airport or border crossing. He cannot have a passport, and he is banned from contact with foreigners or with foreign embassies in Israel. He is not allowed to tell anybody, including Israelis, anything about his work at Israel's nuclear weapons production facility at Dimona (even though it is now nineteen years since he worked there) or about the circumstances surrounding his kidnapping by the Israeli secret services.

"They say I have additional secrets," said Vanunu, who is appealing the restrictions, "but that is a lie, an excuse, a cover-up. All that was known to me has been published. Anything I can say will be a repetition." And a senior Israeli security official more or less confirmed that to the *Independent* newspaper in Britain, admitting, "He may have no new secrets, but it is sufficient that he will mount a campaign. People around the world will use him as a banner. There is no reason for us to allow this kind of provocation when we can stop it."

No reason except that Israel used to be a country under the rule of law, where a citizen who had discharged his prison sentence, justifiable or not, was once again a free person. If he opens his mouth and you think he has spilled new secrets, take him to court and prove it. And by the way, what right have you to forbid an Israeli citizen to leave the country?

Mordechai Vanunu was "the clerk, the technician, the mechanic" who got mixed up in nuclear weapons. He was one of eight children of a poor family of orthodox Jews who immigrated from Morocco to Israel in 1961, and after doing his army service he got a job as a technician at the Dimona nuclear plant in the Negev desert, where Israel manufactures

its nuclear weapons. After working quietly away in a relatively low-level job for nine years, he was laid off in 1985,
probably because his friendly contacts with Palestinians and
his links with a group called the Movement for the
Advancement of Peace had alarmed Shin Beth.

He travelled across Asia and ended up in Sydney,
Australia, where he converted to Christianity. He was already
much troubled about his role in helping to make nuclear
weapons, and a journalist he met in Sydney put him in contact with the *Sunday Times* in London. He told reporter
Peter Hounam the whole story, flew to London to meet
nuclear scientists there for further debriefings—and then,
catastrophically, got frustrated by delays in publication at
the *Sunday Times* and dropped some pictures off at the
Daily Mirror as well.

He did not know that the *Mirror*'s publisher, Robert
Maxwell, was a dedicated Zionist with close links to the
Israeli government. Maxwell sent Vanunu's pictures of
the Dimona plant to the Israeli embassy, which immediately
put a female agent called "Cindy" posing as an American
tourist in Vanunu's way. Cindy persuaded him to fly to Rome
with her on holiday, and Israeli agents at Fiumicino International Airport kidnapped him (perhaps with the Italian
government's cooperation) and flew him back to Israel even
as the *Sunday Times* was finally publishing his story.

Eighteen years later, he's coming out of jail. The two
hundred fission-based nuclear weapons that Israel was
estimated to possess then may have doubled or tripled in
number in the meantime. The thermonuclear weapons
that it had just developed then are probably now quite
commonplace. And the 1,600-kilometre-range (1,000-mile)
Jericho missiles that can deliver those weapons as far as

Rome and Tehran will soon be supplemented by submarine-launched cruise missiles that will let Israel strike almost anywhere.

Everybody who matters knows this, including all the Arab governments, but Israel maintains a policy of "nuclear ambiguity" in the hope that if it doesn't openly admit to having nukes, Arab governments will be under less public pressure to match that accomplishment. It was the challenge to that ambiguity, not the betrayal of nuclear secrets, that Mr. Vanunu was really sent to jail for eighteen years ago, and that is why they are still trying to shut him up now. They are unlikely to succeed.

They didn't succeed, but as a result Vanunu is now (June 2005) facing further charges in Israel for the crime of speaking to foreigners.

PAKISTAN'S MISSILE: A LONG STEP INTO DANGER
June 16, 2004

Late last month Pakistan's Prime Minister Zafarullah Khan Jamali watched a test-launch of the country's Ghauri missile, whose 1,500-kilometre range allows it to deliver nuclear warheads anywhere in India except Assam and the far south. There was the usual communiqué saying, "The prime minister made it clear that Pakistan's edge over its adversaries will be maintained at all costs." And then just a brief reference to the fact that some time this month will see the first test-flight of Pakistan's longest-range missile, the Ghauri III missile, which can strike at targets 3,500 kilometres away.

Now, what target do you suppose that new missile is

meant for? It can't be just India, because no part of India is much more than half that distance away from Pakistan. Time to get the atlas out. Okay, the Ghauri III can reach Thailand and Vietnam, but Pakistan has no quarrel with them. It can just about reach Beijing, but China is sort of an ally (at least in the sense that it also sees India as a strategic rival). So what could it be? . . . Oh, look, it can reach Israel.

Back in 1982, in Tel Aviv, I interviewed a man called Meir Pa'il. He was a left-wing member of the Knesset who had once served as a colonel on the Israeli general staff, and he told me a story. It was about Israel's nuclear weapons, which Israel never officially confirms that it has, and since he didn't want to end up in jail for eighteen years like Mordechai Vanunu later did, he told his story very carefully, without ever saying the magic words "nuclear weapons." But his meaning was absolutely clear.

The subject was hot, because just the previous year Israeli planes had flown all the way to Iraq in an unprovoked attack to destroy an experimental nuclear reactor, Osirak, which was under construction there. Basically, it was an election stunt by Menachem Begin's Likud government, which was in the midst of a hard-fought re-election campaign and needed a patriotic boost. The reactor could not produce weapons-grade material, and in any case Israeli intelligence must have known that Saddam Hussein was at least ten years away from nuclear weapons. But the subject was on people's minds.

Pa'il told me that in the late fifties the Israeli government had been deciding to build a new weapon (which must remain anonymous) that would give it total strategic superiority in the region. Like every member of the general staff, he had the right to demand a full conference to make his case to his colleagues if he thought that a serious mistake was being made. If they didn't agree with him, of course, his military career would be finished—but he demanded the meeting anyway.

Pa'il argued that Israel was already militarily secure, and could not be beaten for the foreseeable future by any combination of Arab armies. Perfectly true; in fact, it's still true today. So why, he asked, would any Israeli government take the lead in introducing a new weapon into the region which, if the Arabs eventually got it too, would negate Israel's existing military superiority and expose it to the danger of annihilation? Indeed, wouldn't Israel's possession of this weapon actually goad the Arabs into trying to match it?

They heard him out and rejected his argument, so he retired from the army and went into politics. Israel's nuclear weapons were duly built—there are now at least two hundred of them—and for over forty years Israel has got away with it. Pa'il's concern was reasonable, but he was wrong: no Arab country except Iraq ever seriously tried to get a nuclear weapon, and even Saddam Hussein gave up when United Nations arms inspectors dismantled his whole program after his defeat in the Gulf War of 1991. Israel has been very lucky—until now.

Pakistan's nuclear weapons were not built with Israel in mind, of course. They were a response to India's determined drive for nuclear weapons, partly because it felt vulnerable to China, partly just as a badge of great-power status.

It is not known if any colonel on the Indian general staff ever pointed out that India enjoyed unchallengeable military superiority over Pakistan—six times the population and almost ten times the economy—*unless* both sides acquired nuclear weapons, in which case both sides would be equally and totally vulnerable to destruction. If he did, nobody listened.

So India got nukes, and therefore Pakistan got them. Eventually, in 1998, India tested its weapons publicly, so Pakistan did, too. But long before that both sides were already building missiles to deliver the nuclear weapons. India wanted a long-range one (because it thinks in terms of a nuclear conflict with China), so Pakistan's armed forces asked for a long-range missile, too. Did the generals who asked for it know that it would put Israel within range of Pakistan's nuclear weapons? I don't know, but most generals can read maps.

Nobody's luck holds forever: Israel will soon be vulnerable to a nuclear strike at last. The present Pakistani government would never consider such a thing, but if Islamist extremists should ever seize power there — well, Pakistan is very vulnerable to an Israeli preemptive nuclear strike, and Israel never lets the other side get in the first blow if it can help it.

ISRAELI TAIL, AMERICAN DOG
October 11, 2004

In a US election campaign that is more about foreign policy than any presidential race in decades, one issue is completely off-limits: the Israeli-Palestinian conflict. George W. Bush and John Kerry both back Israel one hundred percent, and neither man will offer a single word of criticism about Israeli Prime Minister Ariel Sharon's "disengagement" plan, even though it means abandoning the notion of a peace settlement. Once again, the Israeli tail is wagging the American dog.

Last week, Sharon's chief of staff and most trusted adviser, Dov Weisglass, indulged in a carefully calculated indiscretion in an interview with the newspaper *Ha'aretz*. "The 'disengagement' is actually formaldehyde," he said. "It supplies the amount of formaldehyde that is necessary so there will not be a political process with the Palestinians." Perfectly true, of course, and yet it was a shocking thing to say out loud.

Sharon was never really going to accept a peace deal with the Palestinians that required giving up most of the illegal Jewish settlements in the occupied territories conquered by Israel in 1967. (Indeed, he was the man responsible for starting the settlements in the first place.) Yet, when he came to power in 2001 he inherited the Oslo peace accords, which imagined an Israeli–Palestinian peace based on two states living side by side—and the Palestinian state was to be created on exactly those territories.

Sharon had to pretend that he agreed with that goal because the whole international community (including the US) supported the two-state solution. Over the past few years the "Oslo process" mutated into the so-called roadmap to peace, but the goal remained the same: Israeli evacuation of the occupied territories and the creation of a Palestinian state living peacefully alongside Israel. In the past six months, however, Sharon has achieved breakout.

His escape involved two mechanisms. One was the "security fence," a barrier to stop Palestinian attackers infiltrating into Israel that runs not along the border but deep inside the occupied territories, leaving most of the illegal Jewish settlements on the Israeli side. (It was condemned by the International Court of Justice in July, not because it tries to protect Israelis but because it ignores the border and effectively annexes large parts of the occupied Palestinian territories to Israel.) The other was disengagement.

Disengagement means that Israel will evacuate its settlements in the densely populated Gaza Strip, where 8,500 Jews live surrounded by 1.3 million Palestinians, and four other tiny settlements with only a few hundred people that lie beyond the security fence in the northern West Bank. They never made any sense in terms of the cost of protecting them anyway, but by abandoning them Sharon can seem to be making a major concession for peace—while hanging on to all the other West Bank settlements (where the vast majority of the settlers live) forever.

Forever is a long time, and Sharon still maintains the pretense that at some future time, when there is a different Palestinian leadership, there might be further negotiations about a Palestinian state. But Dov Weisglass spilled the beans on October 6, pointing out that he had negotiated an agreement with the Bush administration in late August in which the United States had changed its policy of thirty-seven years and agreed that the illegal Jewish settlements in the West Bank would eventually become part of Israel. The one hundred and ninety thousand Jewish settlers there, he boasted, "will not be moved from their place."

"What I effectively agreed to with the Americans was that part of the settlements would not be dealt with at all, and the rest will not be dealt with until the Palestinians turn into Finns," said Weisglass, adding that this would stall the peace process indefinitely. "When you freeze that process, you prevent the establishment of a Palestinian state, and you prevent a discussion on the refugees, the borders and Jerusalem. Effectively, this whole package called the Palestinian state, with all that it entails, has been removed indefinitely from our agenda . . . all with a presidential blessing and the ratification of both houses of Congress."

Weisglass said what he did to win back the more fundamentalist supporters of Sharon's Likud Party, who are threatening to abandon the party on the grounds that God gave Israel the land and it must never yield an inch of it. Bush presumably did what he did in order to safeguard the votes of the extreme evangelical Protestants, estimated to account for a third of the Republican core vote, who believe that God's plan requires the expansion of Israel and a great war in the Middle East. But why does Kerry go along with it?

As for Kerry, he probably goes along with it because his advisers tell him that in a tight election it would be suicide to alienate American Jews, most of whom reflexively support any Israeli government, regardless of its policies, and most of whom are still traditionally Democratic voters. It all makes sense in terms of political tactics, but it commits America to a policy that is contrary to international law and is not supported by any other government in the world except Israel's.

Then Yasser Arafat died in November 2004, the Palestinians elected Mahmoud Abbas as his successor, and soon there was a genuine ceasefire in the intifada plus much talk about peace talks. But nothing really fundamental had changed.

FALSE DAWN
February 10, 2005

Peace is at hand! Democracy is spreading like wildfire! Free lunch for everybody! I'd like to believe it, but I'm sorry, I just can't. No Israeli–Palestinian peace settlement is in sight. Democracy is not sweeping the Arab world. And lunch costs the same as usual.

343

The mainstream Western media are sometimes pathetically easy to manipulate. President Bush gives a couple of speeches in which he declares yet again that "freedom is on the march" in the Middle East, there are elections (of a sort) in Iraq and Saudi Arabia, Israeli and Palestinian leaders shake hands—and suddenly the talk is all of "windows of opportunity" and "democratic transformation" in the region.

Mr. Bush talks like that because it pushes all the right buttons in the only audience he really cares about, the American one, but what real evidence is there for a new dawn of peace and democracy in the Middle East?

That is a misleading question, in a way, because the Middle East has already been at peace for over a decade. Apart from the US invasion of Iraq two years ago and occasional Israeli forays into Lebanon and Syria, no military forces have crossed any international frontier in the region since 1991. When the Western media talk about "peace," they really mean a permanent peace settlement between Israel and the Palestinians who have lived under Israeli military occupation for the past thirty-eight years.

It is generally accepted that that settlement must involve a "two-state solution" that turns the occupied Palestinian territories into an independent Palestinian state. The three main obstacles to that settlement have always been the same: the desire of millions of Palestinian refugees to return to their former family homes in what is now Israel; the Jewish settlements that have been illegally planted all over the occupied Palestinian territories; and the Palestinian demand that East (Arab) Jerusalem be the capital of their new state.

Few Israelis will accept the Palestinian right of return, on the grounds that the influx of so many Palestinians would fatally dilute the Jewish character of the state. A majority of Israelis would accept the abandonment of the settlements as a reasonable price for a lasting peace, but they are much more ambivalent on the question of re-dividing Jerusalem. The Israeli right has consistently been able to play on these fears and doubts to ward off any peace deal that would sacrifice the settlements.

For Palestinians, the boot is on the other foot. A majority are realistic enough to know that Israel will never yield on the "right of return," and would accept a peace that gave the refugees adequate compensation. They are less willing to let go of Jerusalem as their capital, and they simply will not accept a peace deal that leaves the majority of the Jewish settlements in place. This gives Palestinian "rejectionists" ample scope to condemn any peace settlement that meets Israeli minimum demands as a sellout.

None of this has changed for years, and it isn't changing now. Yasser Arafat is dead and his elected successor Mahmoud Abbas wears a suit and tie, but he is still answerable to the same community—and he is still dealing with the same Israeli leader, Ariel Sharon, who hasn't changed his spots either.

After thousands of deaths and years of poverty and misery, most Palestinians are so exhausted that they welcome an end to the intifada, and even the militants will go along with Abbas's ceasefire for now. They will bide their time, and wait for Palestinian frustration at the lack of real progress on a peace settlement to grow.

Sharon is perhaps even less delighted with the ceasefire, since it makes it harder to go on building his "security fence," whose unavowed purpose is to impose de facto borders on the West Bank that leave all the main areas of Jewish settlement within Israel. But the noisy and prolonged business of pulling a mere seventy-five hundred Jewish settlers out of the Gaza Strip should give Sharon sufficient cover to finish the fence. (The White House has promised not to ask any other concessions from him until the Gaza pullout is completed.)

So "peace" is not in the offing, and democracy is not spreading like wildfire through the Arab world either. It might, one of these days—there is nothing in Arab culture or Islamic values that makes it impossible—but it isn't happening now.

Municipal council elections in Saudi Arabia, with half the council members still appointed by the royal family and no women allowed to vote, may be a great step forward for Saudi garbage and sewage, but it's not a very big deal for actual Arabian people. The Palestinians voted for Mahmoud Abbas in free elections last month, but then they voted freely for Yasser Arafat years ago; nothing new there.

Iraq's election was a genuine achievement despite the inevitable Sunni Arab boycott, but the Bush administration can hardly take credit for it. The "Coalition Provisional Authority" tried hard to avoid or postpone an election until Shia pressure (and the implicit threat that Shias might also join the predominantly Sunni revolt against the US occupation) forced it to grant Grand Ayatollah Ali al-Sistani's insistent demand for free elections. And what will come of them in the end, God only knows.

In other words, things are not worse in the Middle East than they were last year. They might even be slightly better. But peace and democracy are not breaking out all over.

CHAPTER TWENTY

THE RICH AND THE POOR

It's hard to write about North–South issues without sounding either angry or whiny. But the blame-and-guilt game serves no useful purpose—in the end, it just makes everybody resentful and defensive—and there are better ways to discuss the subject. You could start by treating people like grown-ups.

THE MIDDLE THREE-FIFTHS
August 3, 2003

When the *Human Development Report* 2003 came out two weeks ago, there was obviously something wrong with it, but I couldn't put my finger on it. Today, sitting in a campsite at the southernmost point of Turkey (even journalists take vacations), I know what it was. The document virtually ignored the whole middle of the world.

The *Human Development Report*, an annual jeremiad issued by the United Nations Development Program, is always a contradictory mix of rhetoric that says the sky is falling and statistics that tell a more hopeful story. This year, the rhetoric says that the richest 1 percent of the world's population, some 60 million people, now receive more income than the whole bottom half. Western Europeans, we are told, were three times richer than Africans in 1820; now they're thirteen times richer. Life expectancy at birth in Britain is 78.2 years; in Zimbabwe, a former colony of Britain's, it has now fallen to 33.1 years.

Sitting here in Anamur, one of the poorer parts of an upper-range "developing" country, I realized what the UNDP report was missing. Most of the people around here live in ugly concrete boxes now, much less attractive than the traditional dwellings they have come to despise, but the ugly boxes do have electricity and indoor plumbing and the roofs don't leak. They drive like maniacs, but many of them have cars. They complain about their poverty, but they do have cash incomes. And their kids live to grow up, and go to school, and will have very different lives from their parents.

The only resources in this region are bananas and a bit of tourism, but compared to when I first saw it thirty years ago it has been transformed. This is not because Turkish governments have been very good over the past thirty years; they just haven't been completely terrible. Even modestly competent government, almost regardless of the resources available, will produce a reasonably healthy, fairly well-educated population in only one or two generations—and in one more generation they will probably have decent social services as well.

People everywhere have ambitions for themselves and their children, and they will work hard to make decent lives for themselves if they see any hope of success. All they need is a reasonable degree of physical security (the first job of any government), and a political environment where the wealth they create for themselves and their children will not immediately be stolen by the most powerful people in their society, and time. So the truth of the matter, largely hidden in the report, is that most of the world is now making its way up the ladder towards security, prosperity and even democracy.

Read the statistics of the report rather than the rhetoric, and it's quite clear: during the 1990s, the proportion of the world's population living in absolute poverty—less than a dollar a day, at purchasing power parity—fell from 30 percent to 23 percent. Alas, we are told, most of this change was due to improving living standards in China and India—as if that were surprising, given that these two countries alone account for over half the population of the developing world, and as though poor Indians and Chinese were somehow less deserving than poor Africans, for example.

The squeaky wheel gets the grease, and in this case the wheel that gets everybody's attention is the accelerating decline of living standards in most of Africa. Some countries in Latin America and the Middle East also went backwards economically in the 1990s, and most of the former Communist bloc in Europe experienced falls in living standards (although everybody assumes that that is merely transitional). But it is sub-Saharan Africa, with a tenth of the human race, whose plight causes near despair in the "development community" and drives the kind of crisis rhetoric that infects the report.

The crisis in Africa is real, but its major cause is truly awful governments. Even more than the AIDS epidemic, it is corruption and war that have driven Africa to the bottom of every index of human development during the past forty years. (Nobody except Africans remembers it now, but in 1960 most African countries had higher incomes and better public services than most Asian countries.) And even the AIDS plague is far less devastating in countries like Uganda that have moderately competent governments.

The extreme rhetoric about collapsing living standards and growing gaps between rich and poor is meant to galvanize people in the richer countries into action, and maybe it is needed in order to persuade them to do painful but necessary things like opening their markets to agricultural exports from Africa, but it is also deeply misleading. About one-fifth of the world is rich, and another fifth is desperately poor and getting poorer, but the middle three-fifths is actually making solid progress—not because of foreign aid or some special political or economic formula, but because it only takes security, sensible government and time for people anywhere to climb the ladder.

FARMING IS DIFFERENT
September 4, 2003

On September 9–14 the World Trade Organization brings together the trade ministers of 146 countries in Cancun, Mexico, to try for a new deal on liberalizing global trade. There has already been progress on various fronts—last week there was even a deal of sorts on making cheap generic drugs available to poor countries—but on one critical issue they remain deadlocked: agriculture. As usual.

The average cow in Europe earns more per day in subsidies (around $2) than the total daily income of the average cattle-owner in West Africa. America's twenty-five thousand cotton farmers received over $3 billion in subsidies last year, and can therefore undersell the 11 million people in West Africa who depend on cotton for their main source of income. Why is it farming, rather than mining or manufacturing, say, that makes the governments of the rich countries go into ultraprotectionist mode and spend money like crazy?

Listen, for example, to the European Union's agriculture commissioner, Fritz Fischler, defending the $2-per-day subsidy for cows in Brussels last Thursday. Criticisms of the $700-a-year cows "may be a nice PR stunt, but unfortunately this argument is not only intellectually dishonest, it is factually irrelevant. Yes, in the developed world we are spending our money on many things. Not because we are all stupid, but because our standard of living is higher."

He wasn't finished. "What next? Criticizing governments for spending public money on hospital beds, costly noise protection walls or fancy trees in parks rather than sending it all to Africa? Societies around the world must have the right to choose which public goods and services are important to them." And what's really important to Mr. Fischler is very high-maintenance cows.

Going into the Cancun summit, the rival proposals on agriculture from the rich and the poor countries are poles apart. The European Union and the United States, which together spend $370 billion a year on farm and food export subsidies while blocking food imports with tariffs as high as 350 percent, talk of modest cuts in subsidies and tariffs, but refuse to discuss actual figures at all. The developing countries demand deep cuts in rich-country subsidies and tariffs, and do not want to make equal cuts in their own tariffs against agricultural exports from the developed world.

Fritz Fischler dismisses this position with his customary tact: "If I look at the recent extreme proposal sponsored by Brazil, China, India and others, I cannot help getting the impression that they are circling in a different orbit. . . . If they choose to continue their space odyssey they will not get the stars, they will not get the moon, they will come up with empty hands." One assumes that Fischler is ranting like this on behalf of a domestic audience that wants him to defend the interests of European farmers—but given that farmers are only a tiny proportion of any Western population, why are they the tail that wags the dog?

Ending all agricultural subsidies in the US and EU would save the average Western family of four close to $1,000 a year in taxes. Ending import tariffs would let developing countries earn between $30 billion and $100 billion a year by expanding their food exports to the rich countries, while cutting consumer prices in the rich countries. When Western factories shut down and shift production to Mexico or China, Western governments generally accept their arguments about competitiveness and efficiency, so why not apply the same logic to the farming industry?

Because it's not just an industry. Farming is what has shaped the landscape that people know and love, and it's a big part of what shapes them culturally as well. No more than 2 or 3 percent of the population live on the land in any Western country these days, but it's only a century since more than half of them did. So of course people in the West feel differently when family farms go under than they do when a textile mill closes down or a telephone call centre moves its operations to India.

Farmers, naturally, play on this sympathy for all it's worth, and the subsidies grow and grow. This creates artificial opportunities for large-scale agribusiness, so soon most of the subsidies are going to big businesses, not to family farms. Meanwhile, the global trade in food gets more and more distorted: European farmers produce sugar from beets at over twice the average cost of production of sugar cane in Brazil or Zimbabwe, but dominate the European market thanks to tariffs of up to 140 percent.

What is wrong is not the wish to preserve the countryside and the rural way of life in the developed countries; it is the obsessive, doctrinaire insistence on doing it by a market model. The rich countries want to preserve the family farms because they make cultural, ecological and even aesthetic sense. But they don't make economic sense in a global market, and all the subsidies in the world will not change that. So just acknowledge that your real goal is to preserve the rural society and landscape, and change the system. Subsidize the farmer, not the food.

It's not as simple as it sounds, of course, but it couldn't be more complicated and expensive than the current system of subsidies. It certainly wouldn't be as harmful. And at one stroke it would remove the biggest obstacle to a world of freer and fairer trade.

Maybe in twenty years . . .

What actually happened at the 146-nation WTO *trade talks in Mexico in 2003 was quite encouraging: the bigger developing countries finally managed to hang together as a bloc (the "Group of 21" led by China, India and Brazil) on the question of the rich-world's agricultural subsidies and high tariffs on food imports. The usual divide-and-rule tactics of the industrialized nations didn't work, and they eventually walked out in fury at the impudence of the poor. "This is the first time we have experienced a situation where . . . we can sit at the table as equals," said South Africa's trade minister Alec Erwin. "This is a change in the quality of negotiations between developing and developed countries."*

The issue is still unresolved, but it may not take twenty years after all.

THE "BRICS": BACK TO THE FUTURE

October 15, 2003

Thirty-three years after China launched its first satellite, a high-tech boom box called Mao 1 that broadcast a tinny version of "The East Is Red" to an underwhelmed world, it has finally put a man into space. But the pace is picking up: Beijing is planning to put Chinese *yuhangyuan* (spacemen) on the Moon in just another seven years. If it stays on course, it will soon overtake Russia to become the second biggest player in space—and around 2040, according to a study released earlier this month by investment bankers Goldman Sachs, it will overtake the United States to become the world's largest economy.

Even then China won't be the richest country in per capita terms, but it certainly won't be poor anymore: in terms of GDP per head, Chinese citizens will be at about the same level as the richer European countries are now by 2050, the cut-off date of the Goldman Sachs study. Other big developing countries like India and Brazil will only have reached the same income level as present-day Portugal — but that's not so terrible either, and there will be an awful lot of Indians and Brazilians by then. The Chinese launch is telling us that the world is changing in a fundamental way.

Five centuries ago, on the eve of Europe's rise to world empire, average incomes in China and India were about the same as average incomes in western Europe — and average incomes in the Muslim Middle East were probably higher. Then the Europeans burst out of their continent and over-ran the planet. They and their overseas descendants ended up far richer than everybody else, partly because of their empires and partly because they took the scientific and industrial lead. The new status quo has been around for so long that it has come to seem natural, but it is ending now.

The Goldman Sachs paper is a sophisticated exercise in prediction that takes into account factors like population growth and changing age structures, capital accumulation and likely productivity growth, rather than just doing straight-line projections of current trends. It focuses on what it calls the "Brics": four lower-middle-income countries — Brazil, Russia, India and China — that have big populations and already have significant industrial and technological skills and resources. And it tells us where it thinks we will all be in 2050.

The world's biggest economy will be China's, of course, with the United States in second place (although America may still be China's equal in technological innovation). India is not too far behind—and then, a long way after the Big Three, come Japan, Brazil and Russia. Bringing up the rear, so far as the major players are concerned, are Britain, Germany, France, Canada and Italy. With the exception of the US, Brazil and Canada, "New World" countries that were not home to modern mass civilizations five hundred years ago, it is a return to the same list, in almost exactly the same order, that you would have drawn up in the year 1500.

That makes a kind of sense. In a globalized society and economy where the West no longer enjoys absolute political control, you would expect the distribution of global power to return gradually to what it used to be, with the big populations on the large land masses having greater wealth and power than small western European countries. But it will take a lot of getting used to, especially for the Western countries that have had their own way for so long.

What conclusions should we draw from all this, apart from the obvious one that the first human beings on Mars will probably be Chinese? One is that the real environmental crisis is coming at us even faster than the pessimists feared: 4 or 5 billion people in the Brics and other Asian and Latin American countries who will be consuming at current European levels by 2050 will put huge additional stress on the environment. The time for emergency measures is probably now—not that there is any hope of such a thing.

The second conclusion is that we desperately need to revive and refine the kind of multilateral global governance for which the existing United Nations system is a sketchy first draft. The prospect of a world that is highly competitive

economically and under acute environmental pressure—
and where there are five or six nuclear-armed major powers,
no longer contained within the old bipolar system of the
Cold War—absolutely requires an inclusive international
system that works. Rather like the one currently being
destroyed, in fact.

And the third conclusion? Westerners had better start
working on their manners.

THE GLOBAL ECONOMY: AN ENORMOUS SUCKING SOUND
November 28, 2003

"That enormous sucking sound you hear," third-party candidate Ross Perot told American voters during the 1992 presidential campaign, "is American jobs disappearing south to
Mexico." But now the enormous sucking sound comes from
the west across the Pacific: US Treasury Secretary John
Snow reckons that America has lost 2.4 million manufacturing jobs to China. If his numbers are right, Chinese competition accounts for about 90 percent of the drop in US
manufacturing jobs (from 17.3 million to 14.6 million) since
the Bush administration came into office three years ago.

They won't be coming back—not when labour costs an
average of $16 an hour in the US and only 60 cents in China.
Revaluing the Chinese currency by 40 percent, as many
American officials now demand, would merely raise the cost of
labour there to 84 cents an hour, which is hardly going to
change the picture. Desperate union officials offering concessions to US manufacturers to save jobs are told that American
workers could work for nothing and still not match the cost
structure in China, once overheads are taken into account.

357

British manufacturers have been saying the same thing for years, because Britain is much further down the road to de-industrialization. Yet Britain has prospered mightily in recent years, with a much higher growth rate than the other big countries in the European Union, because it has managed to balance its lost industrial jobs with new jobs in the service sector. Some are unskilled, low-paying jobs in call centres and the like, but many more are in high-paying fields such as financial services, computing and design, and average incomes have gone up. So far, so good, but now Britain's new service-industry jobs are starting to drain away too.

The American economy has actually been following the British model with some success in the last few years. The so-called jobless growth under the Bush administration has seen industrial jobs vanish in large numbers, to be replaced by about the same number of service-sector jobs at higher average wages. These new jobs don't necessarily appear in the same places, so "rust-belt" cities that depend on traditional manufacturing have taken big hits, but the overall US economy is growing very fast at the moment. The threat to American prosperity from China may be greatly overrated—but the US has not even begun to contend with the challenge from India.

The immense Chinese export boom—heading for a trade surplus of over $100 billion with the US this year—is based on industrial goods and largely financed by American business, which cannot resist the cost savings of outsourcing production to China. Manufacturing processes are easy to transfer to another language and culture, and manufactured goods move easily between countries in a more or less free-trading world. It used to be assumed that services are far harder to outsource, but that was before people realized the full potential of Internet-based technologies. The British have just woken up to discover that a lot of their service industry is moving to India.

It has to be India, not China, because the services must still be delivered in good English and only India has the large numbers of educated English-speaking people who can do the same job for one-tenth of the British salary. But over the past few months the announcements by British companies moving thousands of jobs from their home-based call centres to India have been falling like rain—BT, British Airways, HSBC, Lloyds Bank, National Rail Enquiries, Prudential, Reuters, Standard Chartered and half a dozen more—and that is only the tip of the iceberg.

So far the work being outsourced to India is mainly data-processing (which already accounts for several hundred thousand jobs) and now the call-centre jobs, but in a year or two it will also include accountants and corporate lawyers, managers and insurance underwriters, architects, designers and engineers. In August, London's *Evening Standard* published leaked consultancy documents that concluded that Britain would lose at least thirty thousand executive-level jobs in the finance and insurance industries to India in the next five years. In the same month, US consultants Forrester Research forecast that United States will export 3.3 million white-collar jobs between now and 2015, mostly to India. It is almost certainly an underestimate.

Not every service-industry job is equally mobile. Some 60 percent of the economic activity in any country is almost impossible to outsource beyond the borders: construction, health and education, retail sales and leisure services. Natural advantage or consumer preferences will continue to favour some countries even in manufacturing: most snow-mobiles will continue to be made in Canada, Sweden and Russia, and most espresso machines will still be made in Italy. But a very large chunk of the world's jobs is now open to the lowest international bidder.

This is not just a trend; it is an earthquake that is going to reshape the global economy. Fifty years ago, a small fraction of the world's people living in Europe, North America and a few other places like Japan and Australia had a virtual monopoly on the world's good jobs: they did all the design-ing, engineering and manufacturing, and owned most of the professional, technical and scientific jobs as well. Fifty years from now, these jobs are going to be more or less evenly dis-tributed among the countries of the world. It's only fair, and it's high time too, but there are going to be a lot of casualties.

CHAPTER TWENTY-ONE

MISCELLANY II

Some of the articles I've put into "miscellany" were written in a random impulse of delight, like the one about chicken-powered nuclear weapons. Others were begun in sheer desperation, just to hold the ads apart, on a day when not much was happening in the world, and led me to conclusions I had not foreseen. But some, like the one just below and the one about ballistic missile defence, are articles that I have been writing every couple of years, with different words and a different hook each time but always the same basic message, for over twenty years. Maybe if you say it often enough, more people will listen.

DRUG LAWS: THE THIN END OF THE WEDGE
July 11, 2002

"It's moving further towards decriminalization than any other country in the world," warned Keith Hellawell, the ex-policeman who was the British "drugs tsar" until the Labour government belatedly realized that his job was as ridiculous as his title. He was responding to British Home Secretary David Blunkett's announcement on July 10 that being caught with cannabis* will in future be treated no more seriously than illegally possessing other Class "C" controlled drugs, such as sleeping pills and steroids. He was technically wrong, but in terms of its political impact he was right.

Hellawell was technically wrong because Britain is not leading the parade of European countries that have broken away from the prohibitionist US approach. Even after Blunkett's changes, Britain will lag behind other European countries like Switzerland, the Netherlands, Belgium and Portugal in its laws on recreational drug use. But he was right because Britain is (a) still more or less a great power, and (b) speaks English.

The main engine of the "war on drugs" is the United States, which managed to enshrine its prohibitionist views in international law during the Cold War by a series of treaties that make it impossible for national legislatures to legalize the commonly used recreational drugs. All that other countries can do without Washington's agreement is to "decriminalize" the possession and use of at least some of the banned drugs.

* Marijuana, dagga, ganja—substitute the preferred local term.

Numbers of smaller European countries have already decriminalized various drugs, but what the Portuguese or the Dutch do will never have an impact in the United States. Britain is one of the very few countries whose example will ever be seen as relevant in the country that is the real home of the "drug war." Britain's decriminalization of cannabis, and even more importantly its partial return to the old policy of prescribing free heroin for addicts on the National Health Service, could finally open the door to a real debate in the United States.

The actual changes in British law are rather timid. In future, British police will generally confiscate cannabis and issue warnings to users, rather than arresting them, but "disturb public order" by blowing cannabis smoke in a policeman's face and you're in jail. Moreover, only a small fraction of Britain's two hundred thousand heroin users will get free prescriptions. Nevertheless, this is by far the biggest crack that has yet appeared in the prohibitionist dam.

Until the late nineteenth century, all kinds of recreational drugs were legal throughout the Western world. Florence Nightingale used opium, Queen Victoria used cannabis and Sir Arthur Conan Doyle writes in a matter-of-fact way about Sherlock Holmes injecting drugs with a syringe. Then came the Woman's Christian Temperance Union (WCTU), most powerful in the deeply religious United States, which succeeded in banning one drug after another (mainly on the grounds that they were associated principally with Chinese, blacks and other racially "inferior" groups) until by the early twentieth century only the mainstream Western drugs, alcohol and tobacco, were still legal in the US.

For almost two decades, in the 1920s and 1930s, the WCTU even succeeded in prohibiting alcohol in the US. Organized crime expanded tenfold to meet the opportunity created by this newly illegal demand for alcohol—Al Capone was just as much the result of alcohol prohibition as Pablo Escobar in Colombia was of America's "war on drugs"—but eventually there was a retreat to sanity in the case of alcohol. There may eventually be a return to sanity on "drugs," too, but Britain's decriminalization of cannabis is only a very tentative first step.

The war on drugs is one of the most spectacularly counterproductive activities human beings have ever engaged in. "We have turned the corner on drug addiction," said President Richard Nixon in 1973, and predictions of imminent victory continue to be issued at frequent intervals, but the quality of the drugs gets better and the street price continues to drop. As any free marketeer should understand, making drugs illegal creates enormous profit margins and huge incentives to expand the market by pyramid selling. When cocaine was still legal, annual global production was ten tonnes. Now it is seven hundred tonnes.

Drug prohibition greatly increases the number of users, fills the jails with harmless people, channels vast sums into the hands of the wicked people who work to expand the lucrative black market, and causes a huge wave of petty crimes. It is estimated that between half and two-thirds of the muggings and property crimes in both Britain and the US are committed by cocaine and heroin addicts desperate to find the inflated sums needed to satisfy their habit.

Decriminalizing cannabis only nibbles at the fringes of this problem, because cannabis users are overwhelmingly neither addicts nor criminals. The more significant part of Blunkett's initiative is his willingness to revive the old policy of prescribing heroin to addicts (now around two hundred thousand in Britain, compared to around five hundred when that policy was dropped at Washington's behest in 1963). He's only willing to let a small proportion of them have it on prescription for now, but since those will be the only heroin addicts who stay alive and for the most part stay clear of crime, the rest will also be back on prescription sooner or later.

It will be many years yet before mainstream American politicians gain the political courage to take on the prohibitionist lobby directly, but the external environment is changing.

GAY BOMBS AND CHICKEN-POWERED NUKES
20 January 2005

The old sixties slogan urged people to "Make Love, Not War," but who says you have to choose? If you drove the other side's soldiers mad with lust, then they'd be too busy with each other to cause you much trouble. Of course, there is still a severe shortage of women in most front-line formations, but that shouldn't be a problem. In fact, it could be an advantage. We could call it the "gay bomb."

It was the Sunshine Project, a group devoted to exposing research into chemical and biological weapons, that revealed the proposal for an aphrodisiac weapon, "distasteful but completely non-lethal," that figured in a 1994 funding request from the research lab at Wright-Paterson Air Force Base in Dayton, Ohio. They also had ideas for chemicals that would make enemy troops attract wasps or give them bad breath, but it was the love-gas that really caught the eye.

"Category No. 3: Chemicals that affect human behaviour so that discipline and morale in enemy units is adversely affected. One . . . example would be strong aphrodisiacs, especially if the chemical also caused homosexual behaviour." Full marks for lateral thinking, boys, but have you considered the implications of your little idea?

There they are, Iranians or Syrians or North Koreans or whoever you're fighting this week, dug in all along the front and ready to sell their lives dearly, and suddenly the love-gas shells start landing among them with soft whooshing noises. Gas masks are no protection: like nerve gas, just a droplet on exposed skin is enough. And soon there is more and more exposed skin as they tear their uniforms off and explore the charms of the sergeant, the section leader and those cute new replacements.

So far, so good, but what happens when American troops are ordered to advance and take the sex-crazed enemy troops prisoner? What if some of the aphrodisiac lingers, and US troops start to—how shall we put this?—fraternize with the enemy?

What if terrorists get their hands on this weapon and set about to subvert America's moral fibre in a really big way? Random attacks on church services, sales conventions, high school pep rallies—the imagination quails at the prospect. But mercifully, the gay bomb was never developed. In fact, the people proposing to do the research for it didn't have the faintest idea of what chemicals, if any, might produce the results they described. They were just fighting for their share of the research budget.

But there really is no limit to the scientific imagination when it comes to weapons. Take the case of the chicken-powered nuclear land mine.

Back in the mid-fifties, the British army was wrestling with the question of how to give British troops time to retreat if the Soviet hordes broke through their defences in Germany. You generally lay mines as you retreat, if you have time, in order to slow down the pursuit—and now we are living in the atomic age. Perhaps we should look into the notion of nuclear land mines?

And so they got on with it, taking the standard British free-fall nuclear bomb of the time, the fetchingly named Blue Danube, and designing a pressurized, water-tight casing for the land-mine version. When completed, the new weapon, Blue Peacock, weighed seven tonnes. It could be buried in the ground or sunk in a lake or river, and it could be detonated either by wire, from a command post up to five kilometres away (which seems a bit close to a ten-kilotonne explosion) or by an eight-day clockwork device.

It was a quite serious if fundamentally insane piece of technology—it was even designed to detonate in ten seconds if anybody tried to move it—but there was one hitch. It gets very cold in the winter in Germany, and nuclear weapons are sensitive devices that do not like the cold. Environmental tests suggested that the warhead simply would not work if Blue Peacock was left buried in the ground or immersed in water in the coldest winter months. What to do?

The boffins at the Armament Research and Development Establishment in Kent were not daunted: in a 1957 memorandum, they suggested a variety of ways to keep the buried or submerged casing warm during the hours, or even a few days, before it was detonated. The most attractive by far was a proposal that a flock of locally recruited chickens should be put into the casing before it was closed and planted somewhere. There would be enough air to keep them alive for some days, and their body heat would keep the weapon warm.

In the end, the suicide chickens were never deployed, which is probably just as well because the designers seem to have overlooked the fact that chickens produce copious amounts of, well, chickenshit, which gums up even the finest machinery. Blue Peacock was cancelled at the end of 1957 in favour of a more compact nuclear land mine based on newer technology and with a built-in heater. Military R&D projects have a very high attrition rate.

What does it all mean? Oh, not very much, except that no idea for a new weapon is so bizarre, vicious or plain silly that it won't find an advocate somewhere in the military-industrial complex. It is a very big beast, and it has to be fed constantly.

THE SECRET OF BALLISTIC MISSILE DEFENCE
February 28, 2005

This week's tempest in a teapot in Canada has been Prime Minister Paul Martin's long-delayed decision not to take part in the US project for ballistic missile defence (BMD). Canada will share radar information about any incoming missile with the United States through the North American Aerospace Defence Command (NORAD), but it will not allow antimissile interceptors on its soil (not that the US wanted to put them there anyway), nor will it have any part in decisions to launch those weapons.

That should have kept everybody happy. The US gets the information it wants, while Canada withholds its formal approval of a weapons initiative that a majority of Canadians (and of Martin's own Liberal Party caucus) think is dangerous and wrong. But US Ambassador Paul Celucci declared that Canada was forfeiting sovereignty over its own airspace by refusing to participate in BMD, Prime Minister Martin replied that "we're a sovereign nation and you don't intrude on a sovereign nation's airspace without seeking permission," and the fat was in the fire.

What Washington really wanted from Ottawa (and what Martin was being rebuked for failing to deliver) was Canadian approval of the *principle* of ballistic missile defence. The United States has been isolated on this issue since the Bush administration tore up the Anti-Ballistic Missile Treaty, and Canadian approval would have been useful diplomatically. The controversy will die down in a few days—but it did rouse former defence minister Paul Hellyer to speak the truth that no other Canadian public figure was willing to utter: "missile defence" is not really about defence.

Writing in the *Globe and Mail*, Hellyer said bluntly that "BMD . . . has about as much to do with rogue missiles as the war on Iraq had to do with weapons of mass destruction." The notion that North Korea might fire one or two ballistic missiles at the US, even if it had a few long-range missiles and nuclear warheads to put on them, is ludicrous. The entire leadership and most of the country would instantly be destroyed by a massive US retaliation. Pyongyang is a very nasty regime, but it hasn't attacked anybody in the past fifty years, it isn't suicidal, and it can be deterred by the threat of retaliation just like Russia or China. So what is BMD really about?

In practice, any system designed to destroy incoming ballistic missiles that depends on ground-based interceptors can easily be overwhelmed just by building more missiles.

The cost to the Soviet Union of building more ICBMs would always have been far less than the cost of the interceptors needed to shoot them down and their supporting systems, so the Soviet Union could always have saturated US defences in an all-out attack. But what if Moscow were the victim of a US surprise attack that destroyed most of its missiles on the ground? *Then* a good American BMD system might be able to deal with the ragged retaliation that was all the Soviets could manage.

Such a BMD system is not yet a technological reality even now, twenty years later, but that's what it was always about: giving the United States the ability to launch a first strike against the Soviet Union and to survive the inevitable retaliation with "acceptable" losses. It seemed less urgent when the Soviet Union collapsed, but it was never abandoned— and in the later '90s the neoconservatives revived it as part of a scheme for establishing permanent US military dominance over the planet—and in particular, for preserving a first-strike capability against China.

Paul Hellyer quoted a US document, published by the Project for a New American Century in late 2000: "Building an effective, robust, layered, global system of missile defences is a prerequisite for maintaining American preeminence. Unrestricted use of space has become a major strategic interest of the United States." By "layered" they meant not just ground-based interceptors, but space-based systems that can also destroy space stations and surveillance satellites belonging to any rival power. They intend to militarize space, and they still dream of gaining the ability to carry out nuclear first strikes against other countries with impunity.

The interceptors now going into their silos in Alaska are a (technologically problematic) down payment on this hyperambitious project, but they are intended to establish the principle that America has the right, despite the old ABM treaty and the still extant treaty banning the militarization of space, to go down this road. That was why Canadian agreement to participate in BMD defence, even symbolically, was desirable to Washington. And it is why Canadians refused (though they were wise not to say so officially).

CHAPTER TWENTY-TWO

WE MUST SURELY BE LEARNING

Nobody's media did well in coping with the surprises of the past four years, but the American news media did worst of all. The budget cuts of the '90s don't account for it all, nor do the psychological trauma and the chill on critical comment that followed 9/11.

The Bush team have put more effort into news management, and have been more brazen in the ways that they did it, than any previous administration. President Bush has held fewer Washington press conferences than any of his modern predecessors, while offering extraordinary access to locally based media outlets so awestruck at the honour that they accepted his spin without question and passed it on to the national media. Fake news packages have been produced on video, using actors as journalists, and distributed directly to local broadcasters with no indication that it is official propaganda. Senior journalists have been secretly paid to promote administration policies in their columns.

In one notable case, a fake journalist was employed by a Republican front organization to attend White House press conferences under the false name Matt Gannon to lob "softball" questions and change the subject when the official spokesman got in trouble with the real journalists. (Gannon was accredited under that name by White House security, who were presumably instructed to wave him past the usual checks.) When James Guckert—to give Gannon his real name—was discovered, there were no apologies, there was no investigation and nobody was punished. Indeed, the whole affair was buried and forgotten in a couple of months.

Two recent developments in the US media help to account for these failures. One is a sustained campaign by the right-wing political forces that have been in the ascendant in America for the past quarter-century to persuade the public that there is a "liberal" bias in the mainstream news media. Few people from outside the United States have ever detected this bias, but it is now an article of faith in American public discourse, and the mainstream news media have been put on the defensive to such an extent that they go out of their way to demonstrate that they are not "liberal."

Consider the Gannon/Guckert case, for example. If Bill Clinton's administration had been caught infiltrating a make-believe journalist with a false name into the White House press corps in order to get administration spokespersons off the hook in press conferences, the resulting uproar would have filled the US national media for months. Clinton might even have been impeached for such an offence. Yet when exactly that did happen in 2004, the prevailing media environment was such that the mainstream broadcast media handled the issue with kid gloves while the right-wing media like Fox simply ignored it for the most part— and got away with it.

The other change in the US media has been a migration away from the traditional model of impartiality. The tradition is not all that old, in the sense that nineteenth-century and earlier newspapers, most of which survived chiefly on the income from sales to the public, were usually fiercely parti-san and made no pretense to impartiality. It was the advent of newspapers whose main revenue came from advertising, and which therefore wanted to avoid offending potential readers of any political leaning, that led to the rise of the impartial "Voice of God" tone so familiar over the past century.

That wasn't a bad thing, as even a pose of impartiality requires greater attention to balance and fairness than most writers would otherwise bring to a story. Indeed, it eventually led to an ideal of journalistic ethics that was light-years ahead of the rough-and-tumble polemics of the early days of the trade, and to a professionalization of the trade that actually did raise the standard of analysis—from a very low level, admittedly, and almost always avoiding serious criticism of the affairs of the paper's corporate owners and their friends, but it was better than what had gone before.

When the broadcast media came along, they formally adopted that goal of impartiality almost everywhere in the democratic world, mainly because the nature and cost of broadcasting technology meant that the sources were rela-tively few and were regulated as a public service even when they were privately owned. But both the technology and the economics have changed, the number of channels has multiplied and so that model is now under challenge in the United States. Passionate ideological disputes are a central part of American public life, so it's not surprising that this is where we have seen nakedly partisan right-wing broadcasting organizations created to challenge the neutral (or "liberal," as they would put it) mainstream media: Fox Network on television, and Rush Limbaugh and his dozens of imitators on nationally syndicated talk radio.

This is not the End Of Civilization As We Know It. It is a pattern unlikely to be copied in less ideological societies — Italy is the only other developed country where something similar has occurred — and the dramatic fall in start-up costs means that there is no insuperable barrier to the creation of partisan left-wing broadcast media that could restore the balance. It's taking some time in the United States — Air America is a pretty pale start — but these things do take time. Besides, the mainstream broadcasters are not dead; they have just been temporarily outflanked.

"Broadcasters" may be a word on the way out, because the technologies are changing, so let's call them electronic media. In ten or fifteen years, with luck, American electronic media will have evolved to cover the entire political spectrum, with the bulk of the outlets (by then probably much more numerous) still concentrated in the centre where the old mainstream channels lived. This model has worked perfectly well in the newspaper business in many countries for over a century now, and it is quite viable unless journalistic ethics and respect for the truth are abandoned in the course of the political battle. In most countries, they have not been abandoned, though they take a beating from time to time, and the current behaviour of Fox is no more a measure of the future in broadcasting than the Murdoch-owned papers are of ethical standards in the newspaper world.

There will always be an audience, on both the left and the right, that simply wants its prejudices confirmed, and that audience will increasingly be served by specialized broadcasting services that pander to their prejudices—but they are a minority, in the normal course of things. Most people expect more than that from their news media, and there is now a fine new instrument for enforcing standards on sloppy or slanted journalism: the blog.

It cuts both ways: it was the left-wing website Media Matters for America that unmasked Matt Gannon last year, and it was right-wing bloggers who swiftly discredited Dan Rather's CBS report on President Bush's military service that was based on false documents. Falsehoods and fabrications are getting exposed more rapidly and reliably than ever before. The problem is not that the lies pass unnoticed or that the truth can be suppressed for very long; it is how to get the public to care enough about the difference between truth and lies.

This may sound self-serving coming from a journalist, but in general the public gets the media it deserves—or at least the media it is willing to settle for. Nobody with access to the Internet can legitimately claim that they are helpless in the face of media manipulation, only that they don't have the time or the will to sort through the evidence and reach their own conclusions on an issue.

If they did do it themselves, they would be more aware that conclusions are fragile and conditional things, because reality and truth are very slippery items. Most people would rather have journalists do the job for them, which is understandable enough; people do have to get on with the rest of their lives. But they then let themselves forget that journalists are just a different bunch of people, perhaps a bit more experienced in these matters but not profoundly wiser, who are trying to do the same job with the same slippery reality. Even with the best will in the world, they will not always get it right—and as in any other group of people, there will be some who do not approach the task with clean hands.

There is a long tradition of media criticism in the West that analyzes who sets the agendas and how the rich and powerful manipulate the media. It is a necessary enterprise that we should support and pay attention to, but there are three elements to the chronic "failure" of the media and that is only one of them. Another is the fact that most of the time the public isn't all that interested anyway, especially in foreign stuff, or anything too complex. The third element, which I have been trying to track all the way through this book, is the fact that a lot of the time we journalists don't actually know what events mean when they hit us.

The world is not a story with a single author and a coherent plot. Different groups or countries with different perspectives and strategies are in play, and none of them knows "the whole truth" or controls the outcome. Moreover, many people will try to spin you or just lie to you outright rather than tell you even the part of the truth that they know. So journalists scramble to make sense of what events mean, and most of the time we arrive at a rough consensus in a few weeks or months—and sometimes we are wrong.

We were wrong a lot after 9/11. I got the terrorists and their strategies mostly right from the start, because that's something I know about, but I was just as much in the dark about US intentions and strategy as most other people. Indeed, I strongly suspect that only a small number of people even within the Bush administration had a clear idea about the strategic uses to which a "war on terror" might be put in the first few months after the al-Qaeda attacks, and were no more forthcoming about their ultimate goals to their own colleagues within the administration than they were to their allies and to the general public.

That does not erase my embarrassment at having taken so long to figure out what the strategy is, and even now, of course, I cannot be certain that my current analysis is correct. If you want certainty, try religion. But as a working hypothesis, I'm sorry to say, it fits the facts pretty well, and I'm stuck with it until something more convincing comes along. Let me leave you, therefore, with three recent articles, written after the formal cut-off date for the material in this book, that sum up my present view of what is happening in the world.

GRAND STRATEGY FOR BEGINNERS
March 21, 2005

Assume that the people who run defence and foreign policy in the Bush administration are as ferociously intelligent as they think they are. What would their grand strategy be?

The very phrase *grand strategy* has an antiquated ring; enlightened modern opinion rejects the notion that relations between the great powers are just a zero-sum game. But this is a group of people who are steeped in traditional modes of strategic thought: Dick Cheney, Donald Rumsfeld, Paul Wolfowitz, Stephen Hadley and Condoleezza Rice would all have worked quite comfortably for Cardinal

Richelieu or Count Bismarck. (Whether they would have been hired is, of course, another question.)

They are, in addition, patriotic Americans who are firmly convinced that US power is an instrument for good in the world. And they all know that the days of the United States as the world's sole superpower are numbered.

They must know it. They cannot be unaware of the statistics the rest of us know: a Chinese economy that has been growing more than twice as fast as the US economy for almost two decades now, and an Indian economy that has been growing at around twice the US rate for almost a decade already. And they surely understand the magic of compound interest.

China's economy will overtake that of the United States in one long generation if current trends continue. India, starting later and growing slightly slower, will not reach the same milestone for a further decade or more, but both Asian giants will be nipping at America's heels long before that. And economic power is the source of most other kinds of power.

Per capita income in China and India will still be much lower than that of the United States, but it will not be that low. Combine this wealth with populations that will be three or four times bigger than that of the United States in the 2040s, accept that there is unlikely to be any remaining innovation gap, and Washington will be facing a formidable pair of strategic rivals.

Most people are not panicked by this future because they assume that there will no longer be a Communist regime in China thirty-five years from now, and they know that India is a democracy already. There is nothing in either country's history or current behaviour to suggest that they would behave less responsibly than the existing great powers have done (though admittedly the bar has not been set very high). But seeing the United States reduced to only one great power among others cannot be a prospect that appeals to American strategic thinkers of a traditional bent—so what is their grand strategy for averting it?

They must have one. Paramount powers facing relegation always have one, although it rarely stays the same for long and it never, ever works. In the past four centuries we have observed three other "sole superpowers" of the age slide down the slope of (relative) decline—Spain, France and then Britain—and none of them even came close to solving the problem: economics trumps everything else in the long run.

People who search for a long-term strategy in neoconservative policies invariably end up thinking there is none, but that's because they are looking for coherence. They expect too much. When strategists are confronted with an insoluble problem, they generally try to solve it anyway, and they are not above using irrational assumptions to stick the bits of rational analysis together.

Great powers on the brink of decline typically have incoherent and foredoomed strategies to ward off their fate, simply because no better strategies are available. "I have not become His Majesty's first minister to preside over the dissolution of the British empire," Winston Churchill harrumphed in 1940—but from the Spanish armada of 1588 to the Anglo-French invasion of Egypt in 1956, the flailing efforts of paramount powers to ward off impending demotion from "superpower" status have generally just hastened the process.

How might this apply to the senior people inside the Bush administration? Some of them clearly believe exactly what they say, no matter how simplistic and delusional it may appear to outsiders, but others genuinely are strategic thinkers. These people will not speak in traditional power-political terms in public — instead they will use the "terrorist threat" or any other excuse that comes to hand to justify their strategies — but they know about the coming erosion of American power and they will be desperately seeking ways to avoid it.

Is the invasion of Iraq, and the whole project of resurrecting *Pax Americana* that lies behind it, just such an attempt to head off impending relative decline by putting the US back in the global driving seat, as much the "leader of the free world" as it was in the halcyon days of the Cold War? Very likely. Will it work? Don't be silly. It never works: economics rules, and there is no way of stopping China and India from catching up with the current Lone Superpower short of nuking their entire economies.

And no: I don't think the neocons would do that. But their little adventure will almost certainly have the long-term effect of hastening America's relative decline. That sort of strategy usually does.

The real danger of this strategy is that it will operate as a self-fulfilling prophecy that today's world has really not changed in any fundamental way since the dog-eat-dog lawlessness of the traditional international order. When the world's greatest power puts its faith almost solely in its own military strength and abandons its commitment to international law, there is a real risk that it will force the other great powers to follow suit. They clearly don't want to go down that road, but they are not led by saints either.

GWYNNE DYER

NO MORE POOTIE-POOT
February 20, 2005

President George W. Bush leaves the flourishing metropolis
of Mainz on the evening of February 23, after meeting with
German Chancellor Gerhard Schroeder, and flies to
Bratislava for a dinner with Russia's President Vladimir
Putin. (Mainz? Bratislava? Not Berlin and Moscow? Is
Mr. Bush avoiding European crowds?) The Russian and
American presidents will doubtless maintain a polite façade,
but it's unlikely that Bush will emerge from this meeting to
declare once again that "Pootie-Poot" is his soulmate.

The Russian–American relationship is not thriving, and
the proof of it is the fact that the United States granted political asylum a month ago to Alyona Morozova, a Russian
citizen who claims that her life is in danger because of her
role in investigating a series of "terrorist" bombing attacks
that killed 246 Russians in September 1999. The chief suspect in the bombings, according to her, is Vladimir Putin.

Three apartment blocks in Russian cities were destroyed
by huge bombs that month, including one that left Alyona
Morozova's mother and boyfriend dead under the rubble.
There had been peace between Russia and the breakaway
republic of Chechnya since 1996, and no Chechen claimed
responsibility for the bombings, but then-prime minister
Vladimir Putin immediately blamed the atrocities on the
Chechens and launched a second war against them that
continues to this day.

Boris Yeltsin was in the last year of his presidency then,
and he was seeking a way to retire without facing prosecu-
tion for the fortunes he and his cronies had amassed in their
years of power. Vladimir Putin, former head of the FSB (the

Soviet Union's secret police), had recently been appointed prime minister by Yeltsin but was still largely unknown to the Russian public.

The deal was that Yeltsin would pass the presidency to Putin at the end of the year, and Putin would then grant Yeltsin an amnesty for all crimes committed while he was in office. But there was still the tedious business of an election to get through, and Russians who scarcely knew Putin's name had to be persuaded to vote for him on short notice. How to boost his profile as Saviour of the Nation? Well, a war, obviously.

Alyona Morozova (and many others) claim that Putin's old friends at the FSB carried out the apartment bombings themselves, in order to give their man a pretext to declare war on Chechnya and make himself a national hero in time for the presidential elections. It would be just one more unfounded conspiracy theory—except that only days after the big Moscow bomb, a resident at a similar apartment building in the city of Ryazan spotted three people acting suspiciously and called the local police.

The police found sacks in the cellar that they initially said contained hexogen, the explosive used in the other bombings, together with a timer set for 5:30 a.m. They also discovered that the three people who had planted the explosives were actually FSB agents. Nikolai Patrushev, the head of the FSB, insisted that the sacks contained only sugar and that the whole thing was a training exercise, and the local police fell silent, but there was no proper investigation.

Alyona Morozova fears the Russian government's wrath because a number of other people who have tried to investigate the incident have been murdered or jailed on trumped-up charges of "espionage." So she asked for political asylum in the United States: nothing surprising in that. It's much more surprising that the US government actually granted her asylum, because it is implicitly acknowledging the possibility that President Vladimir Putin, in addition to being a mass murderer of Chechens, may also be a mass murderer of Russians.

You do not do this to countries you expect to be friends with. It may be the right thing to do, in moral terms, but that has not been a significant constraint on US policy towards trusted allies like Algeria, Egypt and Turkmenistan. Something else is going on here.

Just straws in the wind, but count them. Russia has refused to cut its support for Iran's nuclear power projects despite all of Washington's blandishments. Moscow is on the brink of a surface-to-air missile deal with Syria that would give that country the ability to challenge Israeli and even American overflights. The European Union is about to end its embargo on arms sales to China. The EU will go ahead with its Galileo satellite geopositioning system, which can greatly improve missile accuracy, despite US protests that the existing American system (with fuzzed data for non-US military customers) is good enough for everybody. And the Europeans will sell the Galileo data to the Chinese.

There is a realignment going on, and it isn't about ideology. If Russia were a fully democratic country, its foreign ministry would still be worried by US adventurism in the Middle East. If China were a democracy, it would probably be *more* active in opposing the American military presence in East Asia. And France and Germany, which are genuine democracies, increasingly see the US as a threat—not to them directly, but to global stability.

This shift in attitudes is not yet an accomplished fact, and a change of course in Washington could still abort the trend. But most of the world's other major powers are starting to see the United States as a rogue state, and gradually they are responding to that perception. Nothing George W. Bush will say or do on this European trip is likely to change their minds.

INDIA AND CHINA: AVOIDING THE PAST
April 11, 2005

It wasn't the sort of statement that sets the blood racing: "We have more or less reached agreement with regard to the political parameters and the guiding principles for the settlement of the boundary dispute." But Indian national security adviser M.K. Narayanan's announcement on April 10, during Chinese Premier Wen Jiabao's four-day visit to India, is good news for those who hope that their children or grandchildren will not die in the Third World War.

There will have to be further talks before India and China actually start demarcating their long Himalayan frontier, where the existing uncertainties led to a brief border war between the two Asian giants in 1962. More things also need to happen if China and India are to avoid confrontation as both countries take their place in the front rank of the great powers over the next generation—a free trade area would help, and a mutual security pact wouldn't hurt, either—but this is definitely a step in the right direction. And not a moment too soon.

It has become urgent because the Bush administration is trying to lure India into an alliance with the United States that would implicitly define China as the enemy. When US Secretary of State Condoleezza Rice visited New Delhi last month, she told Prime Minister Manmohan Singh that it is now America's policy to "help India become a major world power in the twenty-first century," and the State Department briefer emphasized that Washington "understands fully the implications, including the military implications, of that statement."

The biggest American bribe on the table is the recent announcement that India would be allowed to buy the next generation of advanced combat aircraft from the US, which would give it definitive air superiority over China (and Pakistan) in a single bound. Other inducements will be deployed in coming months, and the White House hopes that by the time President Bush visits India later this year, the two countries can reach an understanding—it won't actually be called an alliance—on military cooperation in Asia.

The neoconservatives in the Bush administration have a high opinion of their own strategic abilities, and they imagine that they are replaying the Nixon–Kissinger strategy of thirty years ago. Then America's great strategic adversary was the Soviet Union, and Nixon's rapprochement with China gave the Russians something else to worry about by completing their encirclement. Now, the neoconservatives see China as the emerging strategic rival, and want to draw India into a military alliance against it.

Except that the US strategy of encircling China is more likely to convince Beijing that it must build up its military power in order to protect itself. The right analogy for what is happening now is not Nixon's China policy of the early 1970s. It is the period before 1914, when the traditional great powers who were facing a future of relative decline, Britain and France, sought to contain the rapid growth of German industrial strength by making an alliance with the other rising power, Russia. And that led to the First World War.

Nobody was actually to blame for the First World War. Germany's rapid industrial growth after unification in 1870 triggered the old balance-of-power reflex in the existing top dogs, Britain and France, who got together to "contain" it. That persuaded the Germans that they were encircled—as indeed they were, once Russia, the other rising industrial power, had been drawn into an alliance with the Western great powers.

No analogy is perfect, but this one feels pretty convincing. America is playing the role of Britain and France, China is being cast in the role of Germany, and India gets to play Russia. We have seen this movie before, and it did not even end well last time, when we were only playing with machine-guns and trenches. This time around, we are playing with nuclear weapons. If China were hell-bent on conquering the planet, other countries might have to accept the risk that a "containment" policy entails, but it isn't.

Even under the current Communist regime, China has not been expansionist. The various border quarrels that led to brief outbreaks of shooting thirty or forty years ago, with the Soviet Union, India and Vietnam, were driven by genuine boundary disputes and prickly Chinese nationalism, but the territories at issue were not large or important, and China forces never pushed past the specific territories they claimed. In most cases, indeed, they were withdrawn again after making their point.

China's occupation of Tibet and its claim to Taiwan are both contentious issues, but they are seen in Beijing essentially as domestic issues having to do with the country's historic territorial integrity. They do not constitute proof of a more general Chinese expansionism—which would be, in any case, pretty pointless in the current era of the global economy.

The master strategists in Washington are trapped in an old paradigm that no longer served the true interests of the great powers even a hundred years ago, and certainly will not make America or anybody else safer now. If India falls for their blandishments, they will drive China into a needless military confrontation with its neighbours and destroy the fragile hope of reconciliation between India and Pakistan.

The good news out of New Delhi this week is that the Indian government seems not to be falling for them. There is a lot of work still to be done on Sino–Indian relations, but at least the trend is away from confrontation, not towards it.

So don't despair. Common sense and goodwill may yet prevail.

INDEX

Gwynne Dyer was born in Newfoundland and entered the Canadian navy at 17. He has served in the Canadian, British and American navies. He holds a Ph.D. in war studies from the University of London, has taught at Sandhurst and serves on the Board of Governors of Canada's Royal Military College. In addition to teaching and lecturing, Dyer writes a syndicated column that appears in more than 150 newspapers around the world. He lives in England with his wife and children.